Globe and Hemisphere

Latin America's Place
in the
Postwar Foreign Relations of the
United States

by
J. Fred Rippy *Professor of American History*
University of Chicago

Published in cooperation with
FOUNDATION FOR FOREIGN AFFAIRS, INC.

GREENWOOD PRESS, PUBLISHERS
WESTPORT, CONNECTICUT

The Library of Congress has catalogued this publication as follows:

Library of Congress Cataloging in Publication Data

Rippy, James Fred, 1892-
   Globe and hemisphere.

   Original ed. issued as no. 1 of the Foundation for Foreign Affairs series.
   Includes bibliographical references.
   1. United States—Relations (general) with Latin America. 2. Latin America—Relations (general) with the United States. I. Title. II. Series: Foundation for Foreign Affairs series, no. 1.
[F1418.R54 1972]   327.73'08   72-606
ISBN 0-8371-5718-8

© *Henry Regnery Company, Chicago, 1958*

Originally published in 1958
by the Henry Regnery Company, Chicago

Reprinted with the permission
of the Henry Regnery Company, Publishers

Reprinted from an original copy in the collections
of the University of Illinois Library

First Greenwood Reprinting 1972

Library of Congress Catalogue Card Number 72-606

ISBN 0-8371-5718-8

Printed in the United States of America

To my

GRADUATE STUDENTS

Past and Present

Contents

		Preface . . . . *Page* ix	
CHAPTER	1	The Western-Hemisphere Concept: Permanent or Fleeting?	1
CHAPTER	2	Investments of United States Citizens in Foreign Countries: The First Fifteen Billions	30
CHAPTER	3	The Bond-Selling Extravaganza of the 1920's and Its Aftermath	53
CHAPTER	4	A Postwar Decade of Private Direct Investment Abroad	71
CHAPTER	5	A Decade of Assistance by the Government of the United States to Underdeveloped Countries	81
CHAPTER	6	The Inter-American Highway	96
CHAPTER	7	The Leverage of the Canal Zones . . .	109
CHAPTER	8	Rubber-planting Fiascos in Tropical America	126
CHAPTER	9	Sugar and Other Commercial Problems in Inter-American Relations	148
CHAPTER	10	Fishery Troubles	166
CHAPTER	11	Bolivia: An Exhibit of the Problems of Economic Development in Retarded Countries	175
CHAPTER	12	Cultural Relations, Hemispheric and Global: "The Voice of America" . . .	189
CHAPTER	13	Foreign Aid and the Problem of Nonintervention	203
CHAPTER	14	Myopic Drifting?	226
		Notes	243
		Index	269

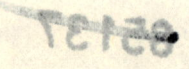

List of Tables

1. Investments of United States Capital in Latin America, End of 1897 . . . . *Page* 32
2. Distribution of the Major Investments of United States Citizens in Latin America, End of 1897 33
3. Investments of United States Capital in Latin America, End of 1914 34
4. Investments of United States Citizens in Latin America, End of 1914 (Distribution) 38
5. Investments of United States Capital in Latin America, End of 1930 39
6. Direct Investments of United States Citizens in Latin America, End of 1929 41
7. Investments of United States Capital in Latin America, End of December, 1930, and End of May, 1943 43
8. Number of Enterprises Controlled by United States Citizens Operating in Latin America, 1929, 1940, and 1943 . . 45
9. Yields of Some Profitable Enterprises Owned by United States Citizens in Latin America 50
10. Income Received by United States Citizens from Direct Investments in Latin America, 1943 52
11. Long-Term Dollar Issues of Latin-American Government Bonds Marketed by Investment Bankers of the United States, 1920-1930 54
12. Gross Profits of American Bankers on Latin-American Dollar Government Bonds, 1920-1930 56
13. Latin-American Dollar Government Issues in Default, End of 1934 62
14. Latin-American Government Dollar Issues in Default, End of 1945 64
15. Ownership of Latin-American Dollar Bonds, End of 1945   66

16. Latin-American Dollar Issues in Default, End of 1948 . . 68
17. Market and Par Values of Latin-American Bonds Owned by Citizens of the United States, End of 1948 69
18. Expansion of the Long-Term Private Investment of U. S. Citizens in Foreign Countries, 1946-1955 72
19. Long-Term Private Direct Investments of Citizens of the U.S. in Certain Foreign Countries, 1950-1955 80
20. Aid to Latin America by the U. S. Government, Fiscal Years 1946-1955 82
21. Contributions by the U. S. Government to the Inter-American and Related Highways, Fiscal Years 1946-1955 . 84
22. Contributions of the Latin-American Countries to the OAS Program of Technical Cooperation, Calendar Years, 1951-1955 85
23. Scale of Assessments, Inter-American Organizations, for the Year 1956 86
24. Allocations to Latin America by UNCF and the UN Technical Assistance Board from the Beginning Through 1955 87
25. The UN and Affiliated Special Agencies: Assessments, U. S. A. and Latin America, Calendar Year 1956 88
26. U. S. Government Aid to Several Countries of Asia and Africa, Fiscal Years 1946-1955 91
27. Allocations to Several Countries of Asia and Africa by UNCF and the UN Technical Assistance Board from the Outset Through 1955 92
28. The UN and Affiliated Special Agencies, Scale of Assessments, Countries of Asia and Africa, Calendar Year 1956 . 93
29. Grants and Credits by the U. S. Government to Latin America, Fiscal Years 1956-1957 231
30. Grants and Credits by the U. S. Government to 20 Underdeveloped Countries in Asia and Africa, Fiscal Years 1956-1957 232

Preface

THIS SMALL VOLUME seeks to present in a global setting the main aspects of inter-American relations during the first decade following World War II. Because I felt that I had nothing of importance to add to what journalists, commentators, and compilers have said on purely political, diplomatic, and military subjects, I have given very little attention to these. The polarization of the globe by Soviet aggressive tendencies and efforts of the United States to combat them; the verbal encounters that characterized international conferences and the proceedings of the United Nations; the Rio de Janeiro Security Pact and its political and military implementation; NATO, SEATO, and the Baghdad Pact; the revolt against colonialism; the troubles and tragedies of Iran, Indonesia, Korea, and Indochina; the baffling political problems arising from the establishment of a Jewish state in Palestine and the dispute regarding the control of Suez; the sadistic Soviet repression of the Russian satellites—familiarity with all these and the involvement of the United States in connection with them I have taken for granted. They are much-discussed topics concerning which I have nothing of significance to contribute. If any mysteries still cluster about them, they have not been revealed to me, nor are they likely to be disclosed before the present generation is replaced by another.

The emphasis that I have given to economic relations also arises from the fact that economic relations actually received major stress during the period. If the subject has been overindulged, the governments of the Americas and the world are to blame rather than this writer, who does not ignore the significance of intellectual association and emotional communion but merely follows what seems to be the trend of the times. Probably nowhere in the Americas or elsewhere this side of the

ix

PREFACE

Iron and the Bamboo curtains were the Marxists and other economic determinists in the majority. Yet the officials of the "Free World" often acted as though the economic determinists were predominant everywhere and as if they themselves had been converted to their views—and indeed it may well be a correct assumption that improvement of economic conditions in most of the world is fundamental in the attainment of the ultimate values so highly esteemed by the idealists of our times. Cultural relations, though decidedly stressed during these troubled ten years, appear to have been considered as the handmaiden of economic development. The United States Information Agency, acting under this and other names, concerned itself primarily with combatting Communist propaganda and extolling the merits of both government spending and private enterprise as means of achieving material prosperity—or so the published accounts of its operations appear to suggest.

Even in respect to Latin America itself, the subject of major emphasis, I have omitted many specific details. The reader will notice, for example, that I have said little about Guatemala and the Communist episode there. I have not written more because the fundamental facts regarding the relationship of the United States to the overthrow of the Communist-infiltrated Guatemalan government have not been disclosed. But I have devoted a short chapter to Bolivia in order to illustrate the problems often confronted in the development of economically retarded countries such as Guatemala, Haiti, Ecuador, and Paraguay, all of which I might have discussed if adequate information had been available and it had seemed worth while.

A few more comments regarding the nature of this monograph seem necessary before I place it in the lap of the gods and expose it to the mercy of reviewers. Some of my chapters are loaded with statistics that may repel readers afflicted with an allergy to figures, but I am convinced that figures must be tolerated if the character of the hemispheric and global relations of the United States during this decade is to be understood and appraised. The first three chapters are mainly introductory and may seem rather long, but I believe they are justified for purposes of perspective and clarification. The last of the three, which deals with the bond-selling extravaganza of 1919-1930, is not meant to be a belated missile hurled at the bankers. The story has been told in considerable detail in order to explain the aftermath of lack of confidence in government bonds, a distrust which seems to have made government-to-government loans and grants at the expense of taxpayers a required supplement to direct private investment in foreign countries. I have no disposition to dwell upon irrelevant misdemeanors and scandals. Nor should any of my occasional remarks of a critical or skeptical character be interpreted as uncompromising isolationism. I have merely tried to suggest that too much too soon might sometimes be almost as imprudent as too little too late. I am neither a pure idealist nor a hard-boiled realist. My preference is for a mixture of the two in these days of strain and anxiety.

Parts of several chapters included in this volume have been published during the past decade in professional journals, especially *Inter-American Economic Affairs*, whose editors have kindly granted permission to make use of these materials in revised and expanded form. For such permission I gladly take this opportunity to express my sincere gratitude.

J. FRED RIPPY

*For centuries the face of Europe had been turned toward the east.
... The Atlantic lay at the world's back door.... Then, suddenly,
... Columbus ... found an [almost] empty continent.... Never can
that moment of unique opportunity fail to excite the emotion of all
who consider its strangeness and richness; a thousand fanciful histories of the earth might be contrived without the imagination daring to conceive such a romance as the hiding away of half the globe
until the fulness of time had come for a new start in civilization....
What was [the purpose] of the men who founded America ... ? [It
was] to serve the cause of humanity, to bring liberty to mankind, ...
to set up standards here in America ... as a beacon ... to all the
nations of the world.—*WOODROW WILSON, 1912.

*Until the fifteenth century of our era Western Europe was at a dead
end.... [Its] inhabitants had their backs to an ocean they could not
cross. [Then a new sailing ship was invented which] gave the peoples
of the Atlantic seaboard of Europe the mastery not only of the
previously untraversable Atlantic but of all the other oceans as well.
... By linking together all the coasts of all the habitable parts of the
earth the Western European conquerors of the ocean ... created the
framework for a literally world-wide society—the first society in history, so far, that [seems destined to] embrace the whole of mankind.*
—ARNOLD TOYNBEE, 1956.

*The United States cannot live either happily or safely as an oasis of
prosperity in a desert of misery.... Always the wealthy and economically developed have in fact helped the less-developed countries
to develop.... That is a law of social life, and we cannot violate it
except at our peril.—*JOHN FOSTER DULLES, 1956.

CHAPTER 1   THE WESTERN-HEMISPHERE CONCEPT: PERMANENT OR FLEETING?

NATIONAL security and prosperity are two fundamental objectives of the foreign relations of the United States, and the Western Hemisphere was long assumed to be of greatest importance in the attainment of both. But this assumption is now said to be outmoded. The champions of the new One-World idea have buffeted and berated this Western-Hemisphere concept until it may never recover its lost prestige. Since the late 1930's they have vigorously attacked it with three main arguments: (1) the "shrinkage of the earth" by inventions in transportation and weapons of war and resulting magnification of the external threat to Hemispheric security; (2) inadequacy of the Hemisphere as a self-sufficient economic unit; (3) geopolitical pronouncements that reduce the Hemisphere's two continents to a mere island surrounded by the immense land masses of Eurasia and Africa—a mere island with an area of only sixteen million square miles!

The Western-Hemisphere concept, with all that it implies, may not survive. It may not deserve to survive without prudent modification. It could be consigned to the rubbish-heap of discarded presiding ideas if public officials of the United States and those who elect them aspire—or continue to aspire—to lead the entire world into an era of global peace and plenty and expend more energy and larger resources in shaping the destiny of the peoples of the Old World than in improving the fortunes of the New.

Only the future can reveal whether this aspiration exceeds

the capabilities of the United States and, if so, how soon voters and politicians will be convinced of it. In any event, a good portion of the occupants of the Americas, probably including nearly all of the most articulate Latins in particular, will not suffer neglect without complaint and will be likely to cling to this Hemispheric concept in order to advance their best interests as they see them or because of nostalgia for the recent past.

Predicting the demise of the Western-Hemisphere idea a short time ago, a prominent historian devoted to Latin America added a word of solace. Its death, he said, would not be sudden or swift. Few would realize that it was actually dying or know the exact hour of its passing. It was not going out like the ebbing tide; the tide always comes back. The concept of the Unique Western Hemisphere, where a portion of the race had supposed it had a chance to make a new start unfettered by Old-World involvement and unhampered by European oppression and "contamination," this grand idea was going out never to return, and therefore its ebbing could not be compared with the movement of the tides.

Its disappearance should rather be thought of in terms of the recession of the glaciers. The snows that fall on the mountain peaks do not melt at the glacier's end until a good many years later. Most of the earth's glaciers are now in full retreat, but some of the longest of them are still advancing in spite of diminishing snows.

Pan-Americanism is in similar condition, this historian contends. Founded and periodically developed with the conviction that "the peoples of the Hemisphere stand in special relationship to one another which sets them apart from the rest of the world"—a conviction based upon geography (as viewed until a few years ago); upon a feeling of superiority in respect to political, economic, and social arrangements (or a cheerful optimism in reference to such important matters); upon a sense of fear and incapacity in regard to the efficacy of efforts to improve the habits of perverse Europe (if not those of other and less familiar parts of the world); upon a creed which held that the inhabitants of the New World are bound together by a common history and a community of ideals—Pan-Americanism so defined, based, and created should be likened to one of these long glaciers, its advances during recent years, if any, mainly the result of snows that had fallen in the past. The climate had changed, was still changing, and the almost unreplenished glacier would soon be in steady retreat, never to thrust itself forward again. Or dropping this frigid simile and reverting to the warmer though sadder human analogy, this historian announced that the Western-Hemisphere concept was dying, but dying so gradually and placidly that neither the victim nor its friends and observers were fully aware of its plight. The few who had begun to wail were grieved not because they had assumed that the disease was deadly but because they did not know its nature. Physicians have a word for this kind of death—they call it *euthanasia*—but it is death just the same.[1]

Measured by global historians to whom a bundle of centuries is a mere bagatelle, the Western-Hemisphere concept is young. The date of its birth is uncertain. Perhaps it was born with the arrival of the first European settlers in America, or with the landings at Jamestown and Plymouth Rock. Its growth has been intermittent. Its whimsical curves and configurations befuddle. It grew to maturity only yesterday. But old or young, the time for its funeral is said to be near. The proponents of a United World have concluded that it has become useless—even dangerous because it is injecting poison into the global atmosphere—and therefore it must be buried, like all the anachronous ideas that have outlived their day.

It is possible, however, that its final passing may give rise to more hand-wringing and commotion than anticipated. It has a noble ancestry. It is true that noble progeny sometimes become degenerate and perverted and that the descendants of the nobility must also die. But mourners usually surround the moribund; every corpse claims its funeral; and some deathbeds and funerals are more agitated and noisy than others, depending upon the prestige of the dying and the deceased. It may even be possible that the disease will not prove fatal.

That the Western-Hemisphere concept has a distinguished ancestry, immortalized by the founding and development of a score of nations, not even the enthusiasts of the new global aspiration can deny without stultifying themselves. Among its progenitors are George Washington, Alexander Hamilton, Thomas Jefferson, James Monroe, Henry Clay, James G. Blaine, Simón Bolívar, Juan Egaña, Antonio Muñoz Tebar, José Cecilio del Valle, and Domingo F. Sarmiento. Let some of them speak.

George Washington, 1796: "Europe has a set of primary interests which to us have none [no] or a very remote relation. Hence she must be engaged in frequent controversies, the causes of which are essentially foreign to our concerns."[2]

Thomas Jefferson, 1811: "What, in short, is the whole system of Europe towards America . . .? One hemisphere of the earth, separated from the other by wide seas on both sides, having a different system of interests flowing from different climates, different soils, different productions, different modes of existence, and its own local relations and duties, is made subservient to all the petty interests of the other, to their laws, their regulations, their passions and wars."

Thomas Jefferson again, 1813: "America has a hemisphere to itself. It must have a separate system of interests which must not be subordinated to those of Europe. The insulated state in which nature has placed the American continent should so far avail it that no spark of war kindled in the other quarters of the globe should be wafted across the wide oceans which separate us from them."[3]

Henry Clay, 1820: "It is within our power to create a system of which we shall be the center and in which all South

[Latin] America will act with us. . . . Let us break these [European] political and commercial fetters; . . . let us become real and true Americans and place ourselves at the head of the American system."[4]

James Monroe, 1823: "Our policy in regard to Europe . . . remains the same, which is not to interfere in the internal concerns of any of its powers. . . . But in regard to these continents [of the Western Hemisphere] circumstances are eminently and conspicuously different. It is impossible that the allied powers should extend their [despotic and power-balance] political system to any portion of either continent without endangering our peace and happiness; nor can anyone believe that our southern brethren, if left to themselves, would adopt it of their own accord."[5]

James G. Blaine, 1889: "Common fate has made us inhabitants of two continents. . . . Like situations beget like sympathies and impose like duties. . . . We believe that hearty co-operation . . . will save all American states from the burdens and evils which have long and cruelly afflicted the older nations of the world. We believe that a spirit of justice . . . will leave no room for an artificial balance of power like unto which has led to wars abroad and drenched Europe in blood. We believe that friendship, avowed with candor and maintained with good faith, will remove from American states the necessity of guarding boundary lines . . . with fortifications and military force."[6]

Juan Egaña of Chile, 1811: "Peoples of America, each one retaining its own particular domestic . . . policy, need to unite for their security against the plans of Europe and to avoid wars among themselves. . . . The day when America assembled in Congress . . . speaks to the rest of the world, its voice will command respect. . . ."[7]

Simón Bolívar, 1815 and 1824: "How beautiful it would be if the Isthmus of Panama were for us what Corinth was for the Greeks! God grant that some day we may have the fortune there to install an august congress . . . to deal with . . . nations of the other three parts of the world. . . . An immortal epoch in American . . . history will be established on the day our plenipotentiaries exchange their credentials. When, a hundred centuries later, posterity . . . remembers the pacts that consolidated its destiny, they will examine . . . [the proceedings] of the Isthmus with respect. . . ."[8]

Antonio Muñoz Tebar of Venezuela, 1813: "The lessons of experience should not be lost. . . . The spectacle which Europe offers us, drenched in blood [seeking] to reestablish an ever-perturbed equilibrium, should correct our policy and protect us from those bloody reefs. . . . It is necessary . . . to resist the aggressions which European ambition might attempt. And this colossus of Power which must oppose that other colossus cannot be formed except by . . . union . . . so that [it] . . . may apply all its enormous resources to . . . resisting . . . foreign aggression and, by multiplying mutual cooperation, elevate us to the peak of Power and prosperity."[9]

José C. del Valle of Central America, 1822: Let us "create: (1) the great federation that must unite all the American States; (2) the economic plan that must make . . . [America] rich . . . a general trade agreement . . . for all the American States . . . and . . . the merchant fleet needed. . . . It is impossible to enumerate [all] the benefits that should be produced. . . . Relations among the Americans, united by the great bond of common interest, would become closer; they would learn to identify their interests; they would form . . . one large family."[10]

Still other progenitors could be associated with similar statements, but further quotations might strain the reader's patience. Their ideas and sentiments are sometimes a little vague, unrestrained, and impatient of evils such as power-balances to which statesmen have had to resort because they were unable to contrive anything better. In modernistic terminology, their concept might be summed up in the phrase "American Community."

The four principles of action that have served as the community's cohesive substance are these: (1) detachment from European domination and European politics (if not from the political affairs of the rest of the planet); (2) freedom of the seas and equality of treatment in commercial relations, a principle later advocated also for investment relations; (3) devotion to democracy and civil liberty; (4) inter-American collaboration for the attainment of security, peace, and progress. Since the early 1940's economic progress has been generally proclaimed as the solid basis for other objectives; but Latin Americans have not been content with the emphasis this has received. Aware of the economic assistance extended by the United States to other regions—perhaps exaggerating its magnitude in some cases and less vividly conscious of the peril it is designed to combat—they have felt neglected. Motivated mainly by eagerness to have their own economic welfare promoted in the same manner and even in larger measure, they have become the foremost advocates of the Western-Hemisphere concept. The first of its four principles of action, detachment from foreign control and avoidance of reinvolvement, has been half discarded. The third, democracy and civil liberty, is still an ideal imperfectly realized, especially in most of the Latin-American republics, but an ideal that has not been renounced even by the dictators and despots that have oppressed them. The other two are still alive, but not in good health, it is said.

2.

The United States, the first of the American nations to win its independence, became the original champion of the democratic republic, the independence of the Western Hemisphere, and the freedom of its peoples from further involvement in European politics. Still very young and comparatively weak when the inhabitants of Latin America began their struggle for self-government, the United States failed for this and other reasons to give them military support. At first the oldest of the American nations was absorbed in bitter disputes with Great Britain and France; later it was consumed by eagerness to acquire the Floridas from Spain or held in check by fear of provoking European intervention and by doubts regarding the capacity of the Latin-American insurgents to maintain their independence and establish personal freedom.

North American statesmen of the early national period made interesting comments on the capacity of the Spanish Americans for free government (so astute that it seems appropriate to repeat some of them here). The two Adamses were wholly pessimistic; Henry Clay took the opposite view; Thomas Jefferson's reflections followed a middle course.

Early in 1818 John Adams wrote his son, who was then secretary of state: "General ignorance can never be free, and the Roman Catholic Religion is incompatible with free government. South [Spanish] America . . . independent of Spain, will be governed by a dozen Royalists . . . each of them seeking alliances in Europe. . . ."[11]

Three years later John Quincy Adams bluntly told Henry Clay: "I have seen and yet see no prospect that they will establish free or liberal institutions of government. . . . They have not the first elements of good or free government. Arbitrary power, military and ecclesiastical, is stamped upon their education, upon their habits, and upon all their institutions. Nor is there any appearance of a disposition to take any political lessons from us."[12]

Clay's far more generous appraisal in 1818 won for him eternal renown in Spanish America. "I am inclined," he said, "to believe they will establish free governments. We are their great example. Of us they constantly speak as brothers. . . . They adopt our principles, copy our institutions, and, in many instances, employ the very language and sentiments of our revolutionary papers. But it is sometimes said that they are too ignorant and superstitious to admit of the existence of free government. . . . It is the doctrine of thrones that man is too ignorant to govern himself. . . . Self-government is the natural government of men. . . . With regard to their superstitions, they worship the same god with us. . . . Nor is there anything in the Catholic religion unfavorable to freedom. All religions, united with government, are more or less inimical to liberty. All, separated from government, are compatible with liberty."[13]

The great philosopher in retirement at Monticello frequently expressed misgivings regarding the political capacity of the Spanish Americans of his day but was always hopeful about their future. "I join you sincerely in wishes for the emancipation of South America," he wrote Lafayette late in 1813. "But the result of my enquiries does not authorize me to hope they are capable of maintaining a free government. Their people are immersed in the darkest ignorance and brutalized by bigotry and superstition. Their efforts, I fear, . . . will end in establishing military despotisms. . . . But their future wars and quarrels among themselves will oblige them to bring the people into action, and into the exertion of their understandings. Light will at length beam in on their minds, and the standing example we shall hold up, serving as an excitement as well as a model for their direction, may in the long run qualify them for self-government."[14] At the same time Jefferson remarked to Humboldt: "The different castes of their inhabitants, their mutual hatreds and jealousies, their profound ignorance and bigotry, will be played off by cunning leaders, and each be made an instrument of enslaving others. . . . But in whatever governments they end they will be American governments, no longer to be involved in the never-ceasing broils of Europe."[15] Five years later Jefferson wrote John Adams: "Ignorance and Superstition will chain their minds and bodies under religious and military despotism. I do believe it would be better for them to obtain freedom by degrees only. . . . But these are speculations, my friend, which we may as well deliver over to those who are to see their development. We shall only be lookers on, from the clouds above. . . . Perhaps, in that supermundane region, we may be amused with seeing the fallacy of our . . . guesses." [16] And two years before (1816), Jefferson already had written his old New England rival and friend: "We are destined to be the barrier against the returns of ignorance and barbarism. . . . What a colossus we shall be when the southern continent comes up to our mark! What a stand will it secure as aralliance for reason and freedom of the globe! I like the dreams of the future better than the history of the past."[17]

Few indeed were the North American leaders of that early day who did not long to see the Latin Americans win their independence. Sympathies were held in restraint by caution or immediate national interest, but the government of the United States did not fail to take its stand as a referee strongly resolved that Spain should receive no European assistance in her effort to subdue her revolting colonies. The policy of the United States with respect to the conflict was soon announced in the Monroe Doctrine; and this pronouncement, supported by the parallel policy of Great Britain, probably contributed to the final success of Latin-American revolutions against European control. It certainly became an important factor in the preservation of Latin-American independence after the region's independence was won. This is a fact too well known to require any supporting evidence here. Non-American governments have been warned of the contents of Monroe's manifesto a hundred times.

3.

The desire to throw off the commercial shackles of Europe was one of the strongest motives for the independence movement in the Americas, and the United States, after gaining its independence, promptly formulated a policy regarding international trade and the use of the seven seas for commercial purposes. Among its maxims were the conditional most-favored-nation principle (namely, equality of treatment for equality of concessions), the right of each nation to determine by its own laws what constituted a national vessel, and the maxim that whatever could be exported to or imported from one American nation in its own ships could also be exported or imported in the vessels of any other American nation. The United States also insisted that in time of war enemy's goods on neutral vessels and the goods of neutrals on the vessels of the enemy, excepting contraband, should be free from capture; that contraband lists should be short; and that blockades, in order to be binding, must be enforced by warships in the vicinity of the ports subjected to blockade. On several occasions during the course of the first century of its independence the United States actually urged the total abolition of warfare against private property on the high seas (even including enemy's goods on enemy's ships and payment for captured contraband). In short, the commercial policy of the United States, framed and announced before the Latin Americans won their independence, was equality of treatment among the trading nations and freedom of the seas in times of war as well as in times of peace, and officials of this country sought to make its policy a part of the American System. Although intended primarily to promote the trade and maritime interests of the United States, this policy also favored Latin America, both before and after its emancipation, even as it favored all weaker nations, but especially those which could manage to avoid participation in European wars.

Great Britain was long the most formidable opponent of these principles and contentions. A strong sea power determined to maintain her dominance because her security and prosperity depended upon the control of the high seas, she insisted upon British maritime rules and regulations and tried to prevent the growth of rival maritime powers. The struggle between the two Anglo-Saxon nations over these issues continued intermittently for nearly a century and a half; and the United States repeatedly attempted, not without considerable success, to commit the Latin-American countries to its maritime maxims. The story is too long and technical to compress here; but a quotation from John Quincy Adams may be introduced at this point in order to illustrate the intense emotions which the subject aroused in this Massachusetts diplomat. Writing of the Panama congress scheduled to meet in 1826, Adams declared: "It may be that in the lapse of many centuries no other opportunity so favorable will be presented to the Government of the United States to subserve the benevolent purposes of Divine Providence." Adams had in mind the promotion of the commercial and maritime maxims of the United States: "First, equal reciprocity and the mutual stipulation of the most favored nation in the commercial exchanges of peace; secondly, the abolition of private warfare upon the ocean; and thirdly, restrictions favorable to neutral commerce upon belligerent practices with regard to contraband of war and blockades." Marshaling all the eloquence of an ex-professor of oratory at Harvard, Adams declared in the grandiloquent language then in vogue: "If it be true that the noblest treaty of peace ever mentioned in history is that by which the Carthagenians were bound to abolish the practice of sacrificing their children . . . I can not exaggerate to myself the unfading glory with which these United States will go forth in the memory of future ages if by their friendly counsel, by their moral influence, by the power of argument and persuasion alone they can prevail upon the American nations at Panama to stipulate by general agreement among themselves, and so far as any of them may be concerned, the perpetual abolition of private warfare [namely, warfare against private property] upon the ocean."[18]

Freedom of the seas was long a cardinal principle of the American Community. Since 1914, however, all the noble maritime principles for which the Americas have stood have been violated and rejected by the great powers. Private property is no longer safe in wartime on either sea or land. The submarine and the bombing plane have changed the character of war.

4.

The desire to isolate a large segment of the earth for the development of a democratic way of life unhampered by the interference and "contamination" of repugnant political systems was an important motive for detaching the New World from the Old. This was especially true of the early leaders of the United States, who sought to set the course for the Western Hemisphere and foster democratic republics in the Americas. The sentiments and anxieties of the great statesmen of the early national period have already been illustrated. The first diplomats sent by the United States to Latin America were instructed to explain in an unobtrusive way the operation and superior virtues of this new political system. Abraham Lincoln's agents sent out to the region thirty years later during the crisis of the Civil War received similar instructions, and some of the high officials of later times, notably Woodrow Wilson, sought to promote democracy in countries south of the Río Grande. To most political thinkers and leaders of the two Americas the goal of the Hemisphere is not merely the preservation of political independence but the attainment of genuine democracy and personal liberty as well.

The domestic politics of the majority of the Latin-American countries have keenly disappointed many outstanding individuals both in the United States and in other parts of the New World. Statesmen and diplomats of the United States have often sounded the pessimistic note since the days of the

Adamses and Jefferson, whose less hopeful predictions have been more accurate so far than the optimistic forecasts of Henry Clay. This disappointment finds illustration, for instance, in the following quotation from the State Department's instructions to the chargé sent out to Bolivia in 1848:[19]

"The enemies of free government . . . point with satisfaction to the perpetual revolutions and changes in the Spanish American Republics. They hence argue that man is not fit for self-government; and it is greatly to be deplored that the instability of these Republics and . . . their disregard for private rights have afforded a pretext for such an unfounded presumption. Liberty cannot be preserved without order; and this can only spring from a sacred observance of the law. So long as it shall be in the power of successive military chieftains to subvert the governments of these Republics by the sword, their people cannot expect to enjoy the blessings of liberty. . . . In your intercourse with the Bolivian authorities you will omit no opportunity of pressing these truths upon them."

As late as 1952, when Germán Arciniegas published a book entitled *The State of Latin America,* written at the invitation of Alfred Knopf, that distinguished Colombian filled his volume with lamentations and included this passage from a prominent Mexican regarding conditions in 1950:[20]

"There is not a decent man or woman who can contemplate the panorama Latin America presents today without . . . physical revulsion. Of the twenty countries . . . seven are indisputable tyrannies; nine . . . stand on such precarious political footing that any crisis . . . can plunge them into open dictatorship; and no one would put his hand in the fire on the faith that the remaining four . . . are immune to tyranny. . . ."

During the first sixty or seventy years of the nineteenth century the abandonment of the republic for monarchy was feared; totalitarian inroads caused uneasiness in later decades. But were conditions during the latter period any better in this respect in the overseas world than in Latin America?

Enthusiasm for an American political system different from that of Europe sometimes impelled the United States to pursue rather energetic policies, one of which was intervention, mild or even drastic, in Latin America's domestic politics in the hope, among others, of promoting democracy. For many years, however, a firm adherence to the policy of non-intervention usually held democratic enthusiasts in check. Only Joel Roberts Poinsett in Mexico and William Henry Harrison in Colombia were accused of improper interference in the internal political affairs of the Latin-American countries during the early national period, and both were recalled in response to these accusations. Jefferson's maxim that "they have the right, and we have none, to choose for themselves"[21] was carefully observed for almost a century. The main departures occurred after 1898 and were motivated by humanitarian as well as political and economic objectives. The policy of intervention to quell political turbulence in Latin America was inaugurated by Theodore Roosevelt; Woodrow Wilson was the most outstanding champion of the policy of fostering democracy in the region.

This interventionist policy aroused deep resentment among its hypothetical beneficiaries and was soon discontinued. Promotion of democracy by intervention in the domestic politics of the American countries is not a practice that is generally approved by the American Community. And yet, if the democratic republic should be widely denounced and ridiculed in the Americas, if the democratic state should be displaced by the dictatorial and despotic state, one of the historic pillars of the American System would be demolished. Moreover, if the ideal state in the concept of the American Community is a free association of individuals who exercise their freedom under laws of their own, enforced by officials of their own choice, then one of the major problems of this community is that of finding a way to promote this ideal without arousing national resentment. It may be doubted that democracy can be imposed by force. This seems to be borne out by the experience of the United States in dealing with the five protectorates it established between 1900 and 1915 and eventually released. Nor can democracy be achieved by mere decree or legislative enactment, or exhorted from a hat. By ridding themselves of dictators the Latin-American nations merely gain the opportunity, which they may not be capable of utilizing, to work in favor of democracy. The overthrow of dictators may result in the chaos that breeds new dictatorships. Democracy seems to require tireless cultivation from generation to generation, with deep faith like that of the magnanimous Jefferson in the potentialities of human nature.

Perhaps the best approach to the problem is a tactful and persistent effort to remove the obstacles to the survival and growth of democracy. In Latin America, and to some extent in the United States as well, these obstacles are: (1) poverty, which limits political freedom and imposes a bondage of its own by causing social insecurity and despair, and rivets attention upon immediate practical objectives rather than democracy; (2) illiteracy, which not only accompanies poverty but perpetuates it; (3) social immobility that frustrates the more ambitious intellectuals; and (4) political behavior marked by selfishness, dread of innovation, intolerance, extreme emotionalism, and demagoguery. Success in the removal of such obstacles requires avoidance of the patronizing spirit and agents with motives free from every taint of suspicion.

5.

Inter-American collaboration for *security*, *peace*, and *progress* was the last of the four fundamental principles of the American Community to be clearly formulated. So far as the

United States was concerned, the security of Latin America—or parts of it—was long merely incidental to its own security. It did not adopt security measures in consultation with its American neighbors. The Monroe Doctrine was not "Pan-Americanized" until the late 1930's, and in the opinion of some Latin Americans was not completely Pan-Americanized even then. It was until a few years ago a United States security policy applied by the United States with a lone hand.

Nor were efforts by this country to preserve peace in the Americas made in collaboration prior to the presidency of Woodrow Wilson, and they were made in consultation with Latin Americans only occasionally thereafter until Franklin D. Roosevelt entered the White House. Latin Americans themselves tried to work together in the promotion of their own peace and security from the outset of their struggle for independence, but without much effect. Six major Latin-American wars and several minor ones were fought between 1825 and 1935, some of them implicating more than two countries at a time.

Collaboration in behalf of Pan-American progress was seldom seriously considered until the twentieth century. There were of course considerable exchange of goods, particularly between the United States and its American neighbors, and some exchange of ideas, along with a small migration of individuals and a larger migration of capital and technology—the capital and technology flowing mostly from the United States southward. But these exchanges occurred without any general plan and almost devoid of any motive save the motive of immediate national interest or individual profit (always excepting some missionaries and teachers and a few others like them). No fructifying ideal of co-operation was brought forward as a mainspring of action until the collaborative ideal began to be adopted in connection with World War II. Inadequate and expensive transportation made business and cultural relations among most of the Latin-American nations difficult as late as the 1950's; but such relations could become increasingly important with economic and cultural advance. For the immediate future, as in the past, the currents flowing south and north are likely to be more numerous and much larger than those moving in other directions.

Viewing the subject of Pan-American collaboration with long perspective, it seems unfortunate—even from the standpoint of those with global aspirations—that the United States failed to give it more attention from the outset. Henry Clay may have been imprudent when he demanded recognition of the insurgents of Spanish America four or five years before recognition was finally granted; but in urging deeper sympathy for the Latins and deeper devotion to the American System, he probably exhibited both wisdom and foresight. "What would I give," Clay exclaimed in 1820, "could we appreciate the advantages which may be realized by pursuing the course which I propose!" He then made the confident declaration previously quoted: "It is within our power to create a system of which we shall be the center and in which all South [Latin] America will act with us.... Let us break these [European] political and economic fetters;... let us become real and true Americans and place ourselves at the head of the American system."[22]

Clay's final exhortation was a bit extreme and in some respects impossible to attain. But how much further advanced in education, in public health, in economic development, and even in politics might the Latin Americans have been by the 1950's if the ideal of collaboration for peace, security, and progress had been adopted a century earlier! How much better off would the United States have been, and now be, with more flourishing and stronger neighbors in the New World and with supplemental supplies of plantation rubber, numerous hard fibers, and many other strategic and critical materials near at hand instead of largely in more distant regions where they might not be accessible in times of grave crisis!

But lack of intelligent planning has permitted the development of a far different state of affairs. Aggressive territorial and economic expansion by the United States and the exploitation of a vast continental domain interfered during earlier years; and later too much attention was probably diverted from Latin America to the Orient and other regions. The Latin Americans were somewhat neglected or dealt with too often as peoples to be used rather than developed. Those who drew their millions from Latin-American banana and sugar plantations or mines and oil wells made little or no returns in the form of benevolent activities designed to promote the general welfare of the region. The concept of a more liberal distribution of the benefits of economic enterprise too seldom entered the heads of shrewd and vigorous men determined to accumulate fortunes to be utilized at home in conspicuous consumption or to increase their power. Their profits either remained in the United States or were spent and invested in other parts of the world than Latin America. No positive ideal of benevolence toward Latin America ever infused the spirit of the people of the United States as a whole or inspired its businessmen or political leaders until this ideal began to be adopted a decade or so ago.

But it does no good to lament lost opportunities. What has passed has vanished. The American Community—nearly half of it more in need of help than able to provide it for others—can act only in the present and the future, neither of which seems very promising at the moment. But the people of the Americas must somehow find the wisdom to make the best of an unsatisfactory state of affairs. Money and technical assistance bestowed by the United States upon the teeming millions of Europe, Asia, and Africa—no matter how necessary or commendable—cannot be spent or invested in Latin America. Commodities purchased elsewhere reduce purchases from Latin America. Hardly anything is now produced, or can be produced, in Latin America that cannot be produced somewhere else. The United States probably should seek a more judicious balance of gifts, cheap loans, technical aid, and procurement, perhaps allotting to Latin America a larger share.

The instruments and agencies of the American Community are fairly well established: an Organization of the American States with a permanent secretariat; consultations of cabinet officials; arrangements for mutual defense and for the preservation of peace in the hemisphere; agencies for many and various kinds of technical aid and development. A major problem seems to be the problem of finance. It is doubtful that the United States can support a tremendous armament race and continue to make cheap loans or send large gifts to all the world that remains free from Communist domination. The scope of assistance will have to be kept within limits that can be afforded. Few people are now so heavily taxed as the people of this country. Politicians who are so highly paid that they can ignore the falling value of the dollar after the subtraction of taxes may continue to boast of prosperity along with those who profit most from the whirring of export industries and the buzzing of foreign trade; but poverty will soon be stalking our land, victimizing particularly the groups engaged in cultural pursuits and all those who neither produce nor sell material goods and must depend upon relatively fixed incomes constantly reduced by devaluation of the dollar—inverting our pattern of values, turning the pyramid of culture upside down, forcing the spiritual apex steadily toward the bottom. Many of the irreplaceable resources of the nation, including its minerals and metals and some of its richest top-soils, are approaching the point of exhaustion. Somebody, somewhere, may have to get along with less of this bounty.

6.

Will Latin Americans be the first to be deprived despite their hitherto comparatively meager share? Not if they can prevent it by their pleas. As stated earlier in this discussion, they have become the most ardent supporters of this Western-Hemisphere concept. Article 51 of the United Nations Charter, permitting the continuance, or establishment and operation, of regional systems within the world organization, was mainly their handiwork. The late Carlos Dávila of Chile, who helped to accomplish that feat, probably expressed the prevailing sentiment of the region when he declared in a recent book[23] that he favored a World Federation "organized on a regional basis" and a New World "economically, politically, and militarily integrated, self-sufficient, and self-protected from pole to pole," and when he complained that the people of the Western Hemisphere had been compelled to "adapt" themselves to "events on other continents," having done "nothing to shape them." "Pan-Americanism," he declares, "has been tail-endism or has not existed at all."

"In world affairs," Dávila adds, "Pan-Americanism has never wielded any influence other than that of the United States. Latin America has had little more than a vicarious sense of weight in world affairs through the power of the United States, on whose global policies the other American republics were never consulted until that country was already committed, and carried along by the stormy winds blowing and directed from beyond the oceans."

Voicing the postwar opinion of many Latin-American leaders, Dávila lamented that the Western Hemisphere had "missed its destiny when it failed to organize itself as one entity, powerful and independent enough to move world affairs instead of being swallowed up by them." "A massive barrage of propaganda," much to his regret, had "led the public to believe that to follow European policies is internationalism, while to follow hemispheric policies is isolationism."[24]

But these were only Dávila's political views. Like most articulate Latin Americans of the postwar era, he placed major stress on economic collaboration. He pointed out that the United States had urged the countries of Western Europe "to put some order in their continental economics, set up some form of coordination or customs union," and yet seemed unconcerned about "this Western Hemisphere," which remained "totally unorganized, in a state of very dangerous economic anarchy," making very limited use of virtually "unlimited resources." Although short of money—or at least the will and wisdom to invest it in the most productive way—Latin Americans had more urgent needs for "machinery, tools, and know-how" and a fuller share of the United States market, already too largely supplied and likely soon to be more completely occupied by Africa and Asia.[25]

Regarding the need for markets, Dávila was most emphatic: "The solution lies in markets," he said, "markets in the United States to safeguard Latin-American production; markets in Latin America to keep open an outlet for North American production." Differing from many of his compatriots, especially those in national administrative posts, he disclosed no enthusiasm for official loans from Washington. "The era of political government loans to Latin America should be ended," he wrote, "no matter what dollar-hungry governments may say." Such loans had not "benefited the republics to the south" or promoted the interests of the United States. He pleaded instead for market "integration," which would not be difficult in any but the Río de la Plata countries, and good management might include even these without serious sacrifice.[26]

A noted Mexican diplomat and publicist, Ezequiel Padilla, stressed Latin America's dire need for both capital and markets. Writing in 1943, he contended: "Within the limits of the American continent, we must not permit the competition of merchandise which comes tainted with starvation wages . . . not merely to guarantee the well-being of American man, but also to . . . hold up to shame the exploitation of peoples of the rest of the world."[27] A decade later he complained:[28]

"Just as quinine and rubber were transplanted to the jungles of Malaya, Burma, and Indonesia, so hard . . . fibers, copra, cocoa, sugar, peanuts, coffee, cotton, and about 20 other less important agricultural products are now being intensively cultivated in Africa.... Production ... of minerals such as tin and copper is usurping the share of similar Latin-American enterprises in world markets. Moreover, modern technology is conspiring against New World products by substituting synthetics for fibers.... Copper ... is being successfully replaced by aluminum alloys. Even petroleum may be replaced as fuel by atomic energy ... in the near or distant future."

The remedy Padilla advocated was economic unification of the Western Hemisphere. "The essence of Pan-Americanism," he contended, "is economic solidarity. Numerous institutions for economic cooperation have ... been established," he complained, "but when the question of actually constructing a unified continental system comes to the fore, the Pan-American spirit seems to fade away. An assured market and the stimulation of a fair price are the legitimate ideals for economic security of Latin America.... The Coffee Convention ... was a model of what can be done. It brought a sharp rise in prices and still exerts a beneficial effect.... The various committees engaged in adjusting agricultural production throughout the United States can serve as examples of how an assured consumption of Latin-American products might be organized. Likewise minimum prices can be established by contracts for given periods. The objective would be to treat the whole hemisphere as one economic unit and thus rescue Latin-America from the grip of blind economic forces.... Latin-American producers are unorganized. Nothing and no one defends them. They are at the mercy of foreign markets over which they have no shadow of control."

Padilla completely ignored the American consumer, now the Hemisphere's almost forgotten man. His sole concern was for the Latin-American producer. He suggested, however, that an assured market and higher prices for Latin-American commodities would increase the purchasing power of Latin America and thereby enrich United States exporters. He also declared that private investment by citizens of this country in Latin America would result in mutual benefits. Their capital would find a "secure outlet, and its employment would solve the struggle for funds which ... frustrates the best and most legitimate aspirations of Latin Americans."[29] More than ten years earlier Padilla had written:

"The United States hopes to maintain the extraordinary standard of living it has created. Latin America is trying to establish a standard of living it has not yet known. The pooling of our ... resources will achieve this common end. ... From this fruitful combination will come a united, fraternal continent."

In this manner the United States could avoid another catastrophic depression. "The advance toward the West will become the advance toward the South," he declared, "a healthy expansion which will establish the reciprocal prosperity of our nations."[38]

Latin Americans, Mexicans in particular, often dwell upon the theme of international investment as a hedge against this recurring threat of economic depression. Though familiar with Karl Marx, they prefer to quote the utterances of United States citizens or the works of economists more orthodox than Marx. One Mexican writer included in his book the following statement made by Milo Perkins in 1942:[31]

"This is a long, long fight to make a mass-production economy work. ... The battle will be won when we have built up mass consumption to a point where markets can absorb the output of our mass-production industries running at top speed. ... Complete victory will not be won until there is full and increasing use of the world's resources to lift living standards from one end of this planet to the other."

It was such pronouncements as this and others like the following, probably penned by Henry Wallace—later to be ridiculed for his alleged determination to provide a daily "bottle of milk for every Hottentot"—that inflated the hopes of these other Americans. The statement was made in 1934 when advocating the Inter-American Highway:[32]

"With road connections established, the resultant benefits in exchange of goods, in development of natural resources, in growth of tourist traffic, in higher standards of living in areas hitherto barred from economic progress by lack of communication, and in interchange of ideas and international amity, seem manifest. ... But the possibilities do not end here. Throughout a very long period ... we have been dependent upon the Far East and the Antipodes for many commodities. ... Among them may be mentioned hard rice, tea, cinnamon, and other spices and condiments, camphor, quinine, and other medicinals and drugs, rubber, copra, many vegetable and essential oils, ... copal ... abaca hemp, and insecticide plants. ... What could be more prescient than to encourage, induce, and expand these commodities ... in the Central American countries, engender versatility in agriculture, and [help them to] abandon the one-crop system? The consummation of such a program would ... raise their standards of living to a salutary level."

A Mexican banker-bureaucrat, flushed with fond expectations, arrived at the following extravagant conclusion in 1941 after assembling the views of Malthus, Ricardo, John Stuart Mill, Marx, and Lord Keynes on the subject of "diminishing returns" from investment in maturing homelands:[33]

"As a natural and inevitable result of economic laws, whose workings are beyond her control, the United States is bound to export capital. ... The United States must export capital to Latin America. ... The United States must act thus if she does not wish to risk the stagnation of her economy and ... a depression similar to that of 1929. The United States must... devote herself... to creating purchasing power... by means of investments in Latin America. You may have to give your capital away, lest you become a modern Midas and witness the decline and fall of the United States in the golden age of plenty.... I say then: get rid of your treasure—lend it, give it, throw it away —if you do not wish to perish in the midst of plenty."

Such is one of the strong motivations of Latin America's devotion to the Western-Hemisphere concept. If these fond anticipations could be realized there would be no lack of snow to push this Pan-American glacier forward. The Latins of America have been disappointed so far; but unless certain high officials of the United States are engaging in what the Latins have called "Blah-Blah" Pan-Americanism, the climate is becoming more propitious. A few excerpts from the record are now offered.

The President's Cabinet meeting (July 3, 1953):[34]

"The Cabinet discussed Latin America briefly. The President observed that because of preoccupation with Europe and Asia in recent years, United States policy toward Latin America was generally unsatisfactory.... Eisenhower proposed... that consideration should be given to the possibility of developing cooperation among the Latin-American countries and greater consolidation of their various economic... resources, such as was being carried forward in Western Europe."

Stanley Andrews, Technical Cooperation Administration (July 1953):[35]

"As you know, there is terrific pressure on the part of the Latin-American people. They feel we have largely passed them by in our aid programs.... Some of our superiors in our government feel we ought to take a greater interest in Latin America. Latin America is the area of... greatest investment of American capital; it is the area where the greatest trade goes on, and it is our neighbor."

M. N. Hardesty, regional director for Latin America, Foreign Operations Administration (April 1954):[36]

"By helping build greater economic strength and stability in Latin America, we gain stronger allies for mutual defense and more effective partners in trade. These pragmatic considerations are, of course, only a part of our reasons for giving assistance.... It is at the heart of our national spirit and tradition to share our special gifts with those less fortunate to assist them in their struggle to better their lives. Certainly, this response is especially strong where we are called upon to help people who are closely linked to us by geography and history, and whose march toward freedom has so closely paralleled our own."

Henry F. Holland, assistant secretary of state for Inter-American Affairs (April 1956):[37]

"The security and well-being of . . . the United States require that we be surrounded in this hemisphere by strong, prosperous partners. . . . Justification of this contribution by the United States does not have to depend on humanitarian considerations, although they are certainly present. Our contribution can be fully justified on the basis of our own self-interest."

United States International Development Advisory Board (Sept. 1954):[38]

"Latin America is our largest customer, supplier, and field of foreign investment, an area of phenomenal growth, and an indispensable and irreplaceable ally. Latin America lies within our inner fortress; no error of omission or commission is permitted to us."

Larger appropriations than usual were voted for Latin America in fiscal years 1956, 1957, and 1958. The recession of the long glacier, if this frigid analogy may be permitted again, seems likely to be postponed. The climatic change, as subsequent chapters of this volume will indicate, has not been as drastic as many have supposed, and may have been merely temporary. The Western-Hemisphere concept may survive in spite of the injuries inflicted by its antagonists. The unique American Community which it helped to create still exists, although it is less detached from other regions than during the first century following the emancipation epoch. The trumpets of Armageddon have summoned it from its continental base, the smaller along with the larger nations, which have pressed the smaller countries into cooperation or combat. Involvement in power-politics and world organizations, inventions in the fields of transport, communications, and weapons of war, and the rise and decline of nations have tended to undermine—perhaps have completely demolished—a part of the main bulwarks of the Hemisphere's isolation and destroyed its sense of security. But the Western Hemisphere still serves as the "inner fortress." Though more exposed and less impregnable than it used to be, it is still the inner fortress. And it seems likely that neither the vital interest of more accessible markets and resources nor the ideals of democracy and civil liberty, of mutual aid for security, peace, and progress, with a little heavier emphasis on this Hemisphere than on other segments of the globe, have become entirely outmoded.

It is possible, however, that the Latin Americans, now the most vociferous champions of this Western-Hemisphere concept, need to be gently reminded of the mutuality of this closer association: tactfully advised that consumers in the United States should not be exploited; that high prices for Latin-American products stimulate efforts to find substitutes in laboratories or sources of supply in other regions; that they should not deal too drastically with United States business enterprises in their midst; that they should not expect to be pampered by their big neighbor, or ignore the heavy tax-burden that oppresses their friends in the North, or succumb to debilitating self-pity.

Injurious conflict between the Western-Hemisphere concept

and the United-World aspiration can be avoided if both are carefully defined and cautiously modified to fit changed circumstances. The isolationist sentiment embodied in the Unique-Hemisphere idea has always had its limitations. Isolationism has never applied to travel, trade, and capital investment, although the New World has at times received, and probably ought to receive, preference in these respects. The Monroe Doctrine is a creed intended to achieve the objective of security. If it proves, or has proved, inadequate for that purpose, it can be expanded so as to embrace a larger portion of the earth. It is not inelastic, nor should it be renounced. The original doctrine contains a pledge not to intervene in the politics of Europe if the European governments will abstain from intervention in the political affairs of America. But that pledge does not have to be kept by the United States if its national security demands otherwise and if friendly nations beyond the oceans not only refuse to invoke it but even urge that it be ignored. If the One-World concept can be made to serve the security and prosperity of the New World, then let it be adopted to the extent that it promotes the New World's interests, but not to the extent of depleting the energies and resources of the inner fortress. And if the Western Hemisphere can be molded into a model of peace, prosperity, democracy, and individual liberty, let this be done for the benefit of both the Hemisphere and the rest of the globe. The advocates of the two concepts, interpreted in this manner and modified in this fashion, should support each other and not engage in hostile competition. A Western Hemisphere developed in harmony with its highest ideals can better serve other regions than a Western Hemisphere divided and weakened by attempting too much too soon. The maxim of "the Americas first" will not injure the peoples overseas in the long run by carefully appraising the capabilities of this Hemisphere and prudently safeguarding this base of operations.

CHAPTER 2 INVESTMENTS OF UNITED STATES CITIZENS IN FOREIGN COUNTRIES: THE FIRST FIFTEEN BILLIONS

THE common assumption that investment of United States private capital abroad did not begin until after 1900 is not entirely correct. Foreign investments began within a few decades after the nation was founded, and the holdings of citizens of the United States in foreign countries reached a total of more than $700 million by the end of 1897, some $190 million in Canada and Newfoundland, $151 million in Europe, and the rest mainly in Latin America and the Hawaiian Islands.[1]

The assumption is especially inaccurate in the case of Latin America. Even without taking account of Louisiana, Texas, and the various borderlands annexed by the United States between 1803 and 1854, the history of this investment began before 1830 in the countries to the south, particularly Mexico, Cuba, and Chile. Considerable capital migrated to this region in the 1850's and 1860's, some of it Southern capital, so that by 1870 there was hardly a Latin-American country in which American money and skills had not been invested at one time or another. It is true that many of the early investments—in mining, farming, extraction of forest products, mercantile establishments, transportation ventures, and public utilities—were unprofitable and ephemeral; there were too many political and administrative disorders in Latin America and too much hostility in some countries toward the United States and its citizens. But they were investments none the less. Among the more permanent enterprises of this early period were the Panama Railroad; steamboat lines on the rivers of Colombia, Venezuela, and Ecuador; gas plants in Havana, Guayaquil, and Mexico City; and shipping lines connecting the United States with Cuba, Venezuela, Panama, and other parts of Central America.[2]

The stream of dollars flowing from the United States into Latin America expanded fairly rapidly between 1870 and 1890. Capital accumulated faster in the United States, and some of the Latin-American countries became more stable and receptive. It is likely that the total investment was not far less than $250 million by the end of 1890, over half of it in Mexico and most of the rest in Cuba and Central America. The investment in the South American countries would have been larger if French capitalists had not secured control of the Panama Railroad in 1881 (Panama was, of course, a part of Colombia at that time) and if British investors had not acquired major interests in several telephone exchanges originally installed in the early 1880's by United States citizens. The decade following 1880 was a period of rather brisk investment, not only in widely scattered public utilities, especially telephones and submarine cables, but also in mines, railways, and forest exploitation in Mexico and Central America, in farm and ranch lands in Mexico, in sugar and banana lands in several of the Caribbean countries, in Venezuelan asphalt, public utilities, and river transport, and even in Peruvian and Mexican petroleum.[3]

The 1890's witnessed a further acceleration of the capital movement, so that the investment, including the properties of United States citizens residing in Latin America, probably exceeded $320 million by the end of 1897, around two-thirds of the total in Mexico and a good part of the remainder in Cuba, the Dominican Republic, and Central America. Table 1 presents estimates of the distribution of this capital among the principal recipients at this time.[4]

The major part of this capital was in railways, mining, and agriculture (including extraction of forest products). Next in

TABLE 1

Investments of United States Capital in Latin America, End of 1897

(In Millions of Dollars)

Country or Region	Total
Mexico	$205.0
Cuba	50.0
Dominican Republic	6.0
Haiti	1.0
Central America	16.0
Northern Latin America	278.0
Colombia	8.2
Peru	6.0
Venezuela	3.8
Chile	2.0
Other South America Countries	8.0
South America	28.0
Cables and Shipping	14.0
Grand Total	$320.0

size of investment probably were trading firms, some of them subsidiaries of companies with their main offices in the United States; but since many of these—such as Grace and Company; Beeche, Duval and Company; Flint, Eddy and Company; Boulton, Bliss and Dallett; and several small fruit companies that were soon to be taken over by United Fruit—were engaged in other activities besides buying and selling, it has not been possible to arrive at a satisfactory estimate of the capital in trading organizations.

In anticipation of immediate future trends it is appropriate to call attention to two other types of investment. Around $6 million were already invested in petroleum: refining in Mexico and Cuba, extraction in Peru, and distribution in many countries; and holdings in public utilities, besides some $4 million in submarine cables in the Gulf-Caribbean region and extending down the Pacific Coast from southern Mexico to Chile, probably aggregated around $13 million, nearly half of the total in Mexico and the remainder in Peru, Cuba, Colombia, Venezuela, Chile, Argentina, and two or three other nations.

Except for the processing of sugar and the refining of petroleum, manufacturing enterprises were insignificant; and although citizens of the United States had purchased Mexican bonds in the 1860's and had made one or two loans to Colombia in the 1880's, they probably held no Latin-American government securities in 1897, with the exception of bonds of the Dominican Republic, where investment in Latin-American banking had been initiated by New York capitalists a few years before. Table 2 contains estimates of the distribution of United States capital in railways, mining, and agriculture.[5]

TABLE 2

DISTRIBUTION OF THE MAJOR INVESTMENTS OF UNITED STATES CITIZENS IN LATIN AMERICA, END OF 1897

(In Millions of Dollars)

Country or Region	Railways	Mining	Agriculture and Forestals
Mexico	$110.6	$68.0	$12.0
Cuba		3.0	31.5
Dominican Republic	1.0		2.0
Central America	6.0	2.5	7.0
South America	5.9	7.0	6.5
Total	$123.5	$80.5	$59.0

The railway and mining capital was invested mainly in Mexico. The railroad investment in Central America was in Guatemala and the mining investment was largely in Honduras. Agricultural capital was distributed through all the Central American countries, but the largest holdings were in Costa Rica and the smallest in El Salvador.

Railway capital in South America was confined to two nations, Colombia and Ecuador, and to a single railroad in each; the total for Colombia, nearly $5 million, includes some capital in shipping (the railway company owned a wharf at Cartagena and steamboats operating on the Magdalena River). The mining investment in South America was concentrated mainly in Colombia, Ecuador, and Peru; the investment in agriculture and the extraction of forest products was mostly in Colombia (including Panama), Venezuela, Peru, and Brazil.

So much in reference to the assumption that export of capital from the United States did not begin until after the Spanish-American War. The assumption ignores some significant history, especially in the field of technology which the United States symbolizes, and fairly large investments, not merely in Cuba, of which historians are generally aware, but likewise in Mexico and in the Caribbean countries, to say nothing of Canada and the Hawaiian Islands. It is but fair, however, to make two concessions. In the first place, this early capital was not very significant in terms of the balance of payments, in which economists are primarily interested, because much of it was held by citizens of the United States who were residing more or less permanently in Latin America; and secondly, the aggregate in 1897 was small in comparison with the total for any subsequent decade. Compared with the outflow during the sixteen years following 1898 or 1914, for example, the investment for any previous period of equal length was hardly more than a trickle. Citizens of the United States did not begin to send their money abroad in huge sums until after the end of the nineteenth century.

Nevertheless, it is not extravagant to contend that these beginnings are entitled to more serious consideration than they have received. They were pioneer investments which encountered the usual hardships and disappointments of pioneering and yet laid broad foundations for the diversified investments of the future; and notwithstanding the customary assumption that the disappearance of the free-land frontier and the maturing of industry were the motivating forces for the beginning of capital exportation, these early investors in foreign countries were not influenced entirely, or even mainly, by these forces. Excepting those who engaged in ocean shipping, trading, and the extraction of forest products—and even these were responding to the market demands of farmers and other groups as well as manufacturers—citizens of the United States who made investments in Latin America before 1898 were not primarily the emissaries of manufacturers in pursuit of industrial raw materials or food for factory workers. In the main, they were searching (1) for precious metals, for which a strong demand may exist in agrarian as well as in industrial societies, or (2) for profits they hoped to gain from farming, ranching, and the operation of transport and communication services, or (3) for escape from troubles at home and the satisfactions to be derived from pioneering in strange and distant lands. There was no urgent demand in the United States for foreign raw materials for industry or for the bananas, sugar, cocoa, and coffee these early investors produced. Such commodities were mainly luxuries which investors expected to *persuade* consumers—not merely industrial workers but farmers, merchants, clerks, and many others—to buy.

This does not mean, however, that the absence of the frontier and the mandates of a rapidly expanding industry were not to be factors of increasing importance during the decades that followed. Already American capitalists were beginning to search in foreign countries for copper, petroleum, dyewoods, tanning materials, rubber, and medicinal plants. The search would soon become more vigorous and comprehensive and include not only a great variety of minerals and metals but also a number of foods which were urgently needed in other industrial nations or had been transformed from luxuries into necessities by habitual use in the United States.

2.

Capital began to flow more swiftly from the United States into foreign countries around the turn of the century. The aggregate by the end of 1914 exceeded $3.5 billion, nearly five times the total at the close of 1897, some $867 million in Canada and Newfoundland, $692 million in Europe, well above $1.6 billion in Latin America, approximately $263 million in Asia and Oceania, and a little over $13 million in Africa. Mexico, Cuba, Chile, and Peru were the largest Latin-American recipients, and the greatest expansions in Latin America occurred in mining, petroleum, agriculture, and public utilities. Government securities were conspicuous among new types of holdings, however, and the investment in mining was also becoming prominent. Estimates of the capital invested in Latin America at the end of the year 1914 are presented in Table 3.[6]

TABLE 3

INVESTMENTS OF UNITED STATES CAPITAL IN LATIN AMERICA, END OF 1914
(In Millions of Dollars)

Country	Total
Mexico	$853.5
Cuba	265.0
Dominican Republic	16.0
Haiti	11.5
Costa Rica	24.0
Guatemala	36.5
Honduras	10.0
Nicaragua	4.5
El Salvador	7.0
Panama	13.5
Northern Latin America	1,241.5
Argentina	36.0
Bolivia	11.0
Brazil	28.0
Chile	180.5
Colombia	21.5
Ecuador	9.0
Paraguay	5.5
Peru	62.5
Uruguay	5.5
Venezuela	8.0
South America	367.5
Latin America (excluding ocean shipping and submarine cables)	$1,609.0

Of this total of well above $1,600 million invested in Latin America at the end of 1914, portfolio holdings accounted for $352.6 million[7]—mostly in government and government-guaranteed bonds, but small sums in the securities of corporations controlled by nationals of other countries—and direct investments for $1,256.4 million. The mining capital, a total of around $450 million, was now not only much larger than the investment in agricultural enterprises but also considerably in excess of the total capital in railways and public utilities combined. Next in order of value after these three was the investment in the production and distribution of petroleum, which amounted to around $130 million. Excluding the sums invested in the distribution of petroleum products, the capital in trading firms, about $32 million, was somewhat less than the investment in manufacturing, which amounted to approximately $37 million, nearly all of it engaged in Cuba, Mexico, and Argentina.

The portfolio holding of United States citizens at the end of 1914 included government securities of eleven Latin-American nations and securities of corporations operating in two of them (Mexico and Argentina). The major portfolio investment, however, was in Mexican, Cuban, and Argentine government bonds.

While the major direct investments, namely, the investments in economic enterprises controlled by United States citizens living in the United States, were in mining, agriculture, and railways, investments in the production of petroleum and in public utilities had attained importance. Capital invested in the oil wells and refineries of the principal producing countries amounted to some $107 million: Mexico, $85 million; Peru, $15 million; Cuba, $1 million; Venezuela, including asphalt, around $5 million; and the rest scattered through eight or nine countries, two or three in Central America and the others in South America. Banking capital was confined mainly to Cuba, Mexico, Panama, and Haiti. Table 4 gives the distribution of the investment in government bonds, mining, agriculture, and railways.[8]

Finally, two further items which must be mentioned in order

to complete the analysis: the investment in ocean shipping and submarine cables. Although this capital cannot be accurately apportioned between the United States and Latin America or among the several Latin-American countries, it should not be ignored. It would probably raise the total given in Table 3 from $1,609 to around $1,630 million.[9]

TABLE 4

INVESTMENTS OF UNITED STATES CITIZENS IN LATIN AMERICA, END OF 1914: GOVERNMENT AND GOVERNMENT-GUARANTEED SECURITIES, MINING, AGRICULTURE, AND RAILROADS

(In Millions of Dollars)

Country or Region	Government Bonds and Other Portfolio	Mining	Agriculture	Railroads
Mexico	$266.4	$202.0	$ 37.0	$110.4
Cuba	35.0	15.0	129.0	13.4
Dominican Republic	4.6	(?)	11.0	
Haiti	.4	(?)		10.4
Central America	3.6	11.2	36.5	37.9
Argentina	25.7			
Bolivia	8.2	2.0		
Brazil	6.1	2.0	(?)	(?)
Chile	.6	169.8		
Colombia		3.0	16.0	
Ecuador	(?)	5.0	(?)	3.6
Paraguay			5.0	
Peru	2.0	39.0	3.0	
Venezuela		(?)	1.0	
Latin America	$352.6	$449.0	$238.5	$175.7

(Interrogation marks indicate a strong conviction that investments existed but information is too scanty for an intelligent estimate.)

3.

The sixteen years beginning with 1915, and particularly the decade starting with 1919, were a "boom" period in the foreign investment of citizens of the United States. Their investment in Latin America increased to well above $5 billion by the end of 1930. Every country in this region, excepting Mexico, Nicaragua, Ecuador, and Paraguay, was a recipient of considerable sums of this expanding capital. Nevertheless, the expansion in other regions was greater than in Latin America, for its share of the total capital of United States citizens invested abroad dropped from some 46 per cent in 1914 to some 33 per cent in 1930. The most startling expansion in Latin America, as in Canada, Australia, and several of the European countries, occurred in the imprudent investment in government securities, which will be dealt with in a separate chapter, but large increases occurred also in the capital invested in the production and marketing of petroleum and petroleum products, in mining and smelting, in public utilities, in agriculture, in banking, and in manufacturing. Table 5, which omits shipping lines and sub-

TABLE 5

INVESTMENTS OF UNITED STATES CAPITAL IN LATIN AMERICA, END OF 1930

(In Millions of Dollars)

Country	Government Obligations	Other Portfolio	Direct Investment	Total
Mexico	$ 15.0		$ 694.8	$ 709.8
Cuba	126.3	$ 4.6	935.7	1,066.6
Dominican Republic	17.4		69.8	87.2
Haiti	13.3		15.2	28.5
Costa Rica	10.2		22.4	32.6
Guatemala	4.4		70.7	75.1
Honduras			71.7	71.7
Nicaragua			13.0	13.0
Panama	17.8		28.7	46.5
El Salvador	5.3		29.4	34.7
Northern Latin America	$ 209.7	$ 4.6	$1,951.4	$2,165.7
Argentina	$ 449.3		$ 358.5	$ 807.8
Bolivia	54.4		61.6	116.0
Brazil	343.9	$ 2.9	210.2	557.0
Chile	260.1		440.8	700.9
Colombia	144.0	27.7	130.0	301.7
Ecuador			11.8	11.8
Paraguay			12.6	12.6
Peru	75.3		124.8	200.1
Uruguay	53.2		27.9	81.1
Venezuela			247.2	247.2
South America	$1,380.2	$30.5	$1,625.4	$3,036.2
Latin America	$1,589.9	$35.2	$3,576.8	$5,201.9

marine cables connecting the United States with the Latin-American nations and a few other general enterprises whose capital could not be accurately distributed, gives estimates of the total investment in each of the twenty Latin-American nations.[10]

The years 1915-1930, as previously stated, were also a period of brisk investment by citizens of the United States in other regions. Their long-term investment in foreign countries amounted to approximately $15,684.3 million at the end of 1930, so that Latin America's share was a bit less than a third of the total. Canada's share was $3,941.7 million; Europe's, $4,929.3 million; and that of the rest of the world, $1,611.4 million.

Data on the distribution of the direct investment in Latin America among the major economic activities at the end of 1930 have not been found, but fairly reliable information is available for the close of the previous year.[11] The aggregate direct investment at the end of 1929 was approximately $3,462 million and the distribution among the major economic groups was roughly as follows (in millions):

Public Services ($313.7 of the total in railroads)	$ 887.1
Agriculture ($643.2 in sugar production)	807.9
Mining and Smelting	732.1
Petroleum ($79.4 in distribution)	616.8
Manufacturing	231.0
Trading Firms	119.2
Total Capital in Six Major Groups	$3,394.1

Some $35 or $40 million should be subtracted from this total, however, for investments in the Guianas and the non-Latin West Indies. The remainder of the direct investment at this time was in banking, engineering and construction organizations, motion pictures, and a few other miscellaneous enterprises.

The distribution among the principal recipient nations of the investment in the first three of these major groups is set forth in

Table 6. Nearly all of the capital engaged in producing and refining petroleum was operating in six countries; namely, Venezuela, Mexico, Colombia, Peru, Cuba, and Bolivia, listed in descending order of the size of the investment, the total for Venezuela being around $226 million, the total for Mexico nearly $202 million, and that for Colombia about $56 million, with much smaller sums in the other three. Most of the investment in manufacturing, again in descending order of size, was located in Argentina, Brazil, Cuba, Uruguay, Chile, Mexico, Colombia, and Peru; some $82 million, or more than a third of the total, mainly in the processing of meat, was in Argentina alone. And a good part of the capital in trading organizations was likewise in these eight countries.[12]

A marked decline in the value of this investment occurred in the 1930's and early 1940's. The causes of the contraction were numerous; prominent among them were not only the general economic crisis, which depressed all economic values, and general disturbances in international politics, but also the expropriation of oil properties in Bolivia and Mexico, rising economic nationalism, and the redemption or shrinkage in market values

TABLE 6

DIRECT INVESTMENTS OF UNITED STATES CITIZENS IN LATIN AMERICA, END OF 1929: DISTRIBUTION AMONG THE PRINCIPAL RECIPIENTS OF THE CAPITAL IN THREE MAJOR ECONOMIC GROUPS

(In Millions of Dollars)

County or Region	Public Services	Agriculture	Mining and Smelting	Total
Mexico	$ 164.2	$ 58.9	$ 230.4	$ 453.5
Cuba	214.9	575.0	9.0	798.9
Dominican Republic	(?)	61.3	(?)	61.3
Central America	133.8	70.8	11.6	216.2
Argentina	147.8		(?)	147.8
Bolivia	(?)			40.7
Brazil	96.9	2.0 (?)	(?)	98.9
Chile	66.7		331.5	398.2
Colombia	24.9	15.8	10.6	51.3
Peru	11.3	4.0	79.5	94.8
Total (approx.)	$ 860.5	$ 787.8	$ 713.3	$2,361.6

of large blocks of Latin-American securities. Available statistics, for the end of May, 1943,[13] disclose a decline in values in fourteen of the twenty nations and no marked increase in any of them save Panama, Venezuela, and Guatemala. The total investment at this time was around $3,424 million as compared with $5,202 million at the end of 1930, a shrinkage of some $1,778 million. The total in Canada, Europe, and the rest of the world was $10,028 million, representing a contraction since 1930 of some $454 million. The most conspicuous contraction in Latin America was in government bonds, which shrank from an aggregate of almost $1,590 million in 1930 to a total of hardly more than $214 million in 1943. Other portfolio investments in Latin America, although still of minor importance in value, expanded by almost $70 million; namely, from $35.2 million to $104.7 million. The shrinkage in direct investments in this region was more pronounced than available statistics indicate. They declined from $3,576.8 million in 1930 to considerably less than $3,105.3 million in 1943 (arrived at by subtracting $319 million, the portfolio investment in 1943, from the total investment of $3,424.3 million), since this $3,105.3 million included both short-term investments and investments of United States nationals domiciled in Latin America which the estimate for 1930 omits. Table 7 gives a comparative view of the investments in each country at these two periods.

These figures disclose a slight increase in the investment in trading firms and a considerable increase in the capital engaged in manufacturing, but expansions in these two were far more than offset by shrinkages in the investments in mining and smelting, agriculture, and public services. Investment in the production and marketing of petroleum was well sustained in spite of reverses (expropriation) in Mexico and Bolivia. The aggregate capital invested in the six major groups registered a decline of $822.5 million, but the total for the year 1929, as already observed, included $35 or $40 million for the Guianas and the non-Latin West Indies, so that the difference is less than the figures indicate. The remainder of the direct investment in 1943,

TABLE 7
Investments of United States Capital in Latin America, End of December, 1930, and End of May, 1943
(In Millions of Dollars)

Country	Total 1930	1943
Mexico	$ 709.8	$ 422.2
Cuba	1,066.6	590.5
Dominican Republic	87.2	80.5
Haiti	28.5	17.7
Costa Rica	32.6	36.7
Guatemala	75.1	93.0
Honduras	71.7	42.2
Nicaragua	13.0	13.5
Panama	46.5	154.4
El Salvador	34.7	20.4
Northern Latin America	$2,165.7	$1,471.1
Argentina	807.8	497.5
Bolivia	116.0	24.0
Brazil	557.0	334.7
Chile	700.9	388.1
Colombia	301.7	178.9
Ecuador	11.8	13.3
Paraguay	12.6	10.0
Peru	200.1	88.8
Uruguay	81.1	19.3
Venezuela	247.2	398.6
South America	$3,036.2	$1,953.2
Latin America	$5,201.9	$3,424.3

The following tabulation indicates roughly the trend in direct investments in Latin America in the major economic groups (in millions):

	1929	1943
Public Services	$ 887.1	$ 869.9
Agriculture	807.9	275.3
Mining and Smelting	732.1	396.0
Petroleum: production and distribution	616.8	559.7
Manufacturing	231.0	332.3
Trading Firms	119.2	138.4
Total in Six Major Groups	$3,394.1	$2,571.6

nearly $644 million, consisted of real estate (presumably urban) valued at approximately $71 million, considerable banking capital (which appears not to have been very prosperous in Cuba and Uruguay), investments in trust funds and estates, shortterm loans and advances, bank deposits, stocks of bullion and other commodities, and small miscellaneous items.

Elaborate comment on the distribution of the investment among the various countries in 1943 seems unnecessary in view of the analysis presented for 1914 and 1930. The largest investments in government bonds, in terms of market value, were in the bonds of Argentina, Brazil, Chile, Colombia, Cuba, Uruguay, and Panama; those of Peru, Bolivia, and Mexico were quoted at far below par. The portfolio corporate investment was mainly in Argentina, Chile, Mexico, Cuba, and Panama. The major mining capital was still in Mexico, Chile, and Peru, although considerable sums were active in Bolivia, Argentina, Cuba, Honduras, and Nicaragua. More than 60 per cent of the petroleum investment was now in Venezuela; other major recipients were not Mexico and Bolivia, but Colombia, Argentina, Brazil, Peru, Panama, and Cuba. (Petroleum and banking capital, together with a considerable sum in public utilities, accounted for the pronounced increase in United States investments in Panama.) By far the largest public utility investment, approximately $272 million and nearly a third of the total in Latin America, was in Cuba. Next in order was Argentina, with almost $182 million; Mexico, with about $105 million; Brazil, slightly less than $88 million; Chile, $66 million; Guatemala, almost $63 million; Panama, $22 million; and Colombia, nearly $18 million. The major investments in manufacturing (in millions) were concentrated in six nations: Argentina, $101; Brazil, $66.4; Cuba, $65.4; Chile, $27.5; Mexico, $22.3; and Uruguay, $16.8.

4.

The number of economic enterprises controlled by United States citizens in Latin America was probably more significant than their aggregate value. For the years 1929, 1940,[14] and 1943 the statistics, although not complete for the first two dates, are impressive. They are presented in Table 8.

TABLE 8

NUMBER OF ENTERPRISES CONTROLLED BY UNITED STATES CITIZENS
OPERATING IN LATIN AMERICA, 1929, 1940, AND 1943

Country	Number of Enterprises		
	1929	1940	1943
Mexico	285	200	359
Cuba	219	208	338
Dominican Republic	21	23	39
Haiti	23	15	24
Costa Rica	16	14	26
Guatemala	26	22	32
Honduras	27	24	25
Nicaragua	14	20	22
Panama	22	42	79
El Salvador	6	9	17
Northern Latin America	659	577	961
Argentina	99	125	249
Bolivia	14	14	21
Brazil	90	112	265
Chile	51	56	96
Colombia	63	64	140
Ecuador	16	10	34
Paraguay	9	5	6
Peru	36	39	89
Uruguay	32	28	51
Venezuela	52	49	86
South America	462	502	1037
Latin America	1121	1079	1998

The figures for 1943 indicate a striking increase in numbers over the preceding years, an almost incredible expansion in view of the fact that those for 1943 include only enterprises controlled by corporations while the statistics for 1929 and 1940 include all enterprises controlled by nationals residing in the

United States. The remarkable increase in numbers may be explained in part by war investment, but a far more complete coverage is probably the most significant factor.

Since a large majority of the business organizations listed for 1929 and 1940 and all of those tabulated for 1943 were controlled by corporations domiciled in the United States, the paramount significance of corporate capital in inter-American relations seems quite obvious. It is likely that less than 300 United States corporations owned practically all of the numerous enterprises operating in Latin America in the 1930's and 1940's. Some corporations had several affiliates concentrated in three or four countries; others, such as W. R. Grace and Company and Electric Bond and Share, or the International Telegraph and Telephone Company and some of the major oil and motion-picture corporations, or the National City Bank, had subsidiaries and affiliates in the majority of them. The extent of concentration is further illustrated by the following statistics for 1943: 225 corporations in the United States controlled the 359 business enterprises operating in Mexico, 207 corporations controlled the 338 operating in Cuba, 157 controlled the 265 in Brazil, and 171 controlled the 249 in Argentina. (Excepting sugar companies in Cuba, practically the same corporations controlled the enterprises in each country.) The influence of American business organizations, especially corporate enterprises, was significant in nearly all the countries except Haiti, Paraguay, and possibly Bolivia and Ecuador; and they practically dominated the economics of the Dominican Republic, Cuba, the Central American nations, and Venezuela.

The operation of these numerous business enterprises requires many intimate associations and a multitude of contacts between managerial and investment groups of the United States and Latin Americans of every class. This is emphatically true of banks, transport, telephone, and electric utility systems, sugar and banana plantations, mines, and various types of manufacturing.

Thousands of business men and technicians from the United States were brought into close touch with millions of Latin Americans almost every day in the year. It therefore seems quite evident that Pan-American harmony depends in large measure upon harmony in business relations.[15]

5.

It is not an easy task to ascertain the profits of specific enterprises owned by citizens of the United States in Latin America at any time, and especially after the arrival of the era of holding companies, of huge corporations with branches and affiliates operating at the same time in several countries, and of securities having no par value assigned to them. But diligent research has disclosed the yields of a few business organizations that richly rewarded their owners.[16]

Railways and public utilities were not among them. American-owned railroads in Latin America seldom paid steady dividends on their common stock, and the most profitable public utility controlled by citizens of the United States, the Mexican Telegraph Company, returned a nominal average of no more than 10 per cent during the period for which statistics are available (1887-1920), although stock dividends aggregating at least 114 per cent were mainly responsible for expanding its capitalization from $2 million to nearly $5 million.

Most agricultural enterprises owned by United States citizens in Latin America had only a few profitable years. There were, however, at least two exceptions: the Cuban American Sugar Company, founded in 1906, and the United Fruit Company, organized in 1899. On common stock amounting to between $9 and $10 million, figured at par, Cuban American paid an average annual nominal dividend of 9.7 per cent for the 35 years beginning in 1916 and a stock bonus of 40 per cent besides. In addition to stock bonuses amounting to 145 per cent, United Fruit returned to the holders of its common stock—$12,369,500 in 1900 and $118,500,000 in 1950—a nominal average of 10.4 per cent annually during the first 51 years of its existence, without passing a single dividend.

Some big profits were made in mining and petroleum. The dividends paid by two small mining companies operating in northern Mexico are almost incredible. Lucky Tiger-Combination Gold Mining Company, organized in Arizona in 1903 to work gold and silver mines in Sonora, returned an annual average of 124.5 per cent on a nominal paid-up capital of $650,000 for a period of 19 years (1908-1926). El Potosí Mining Company, incorporated in New Jersey in 1901 to exploit silver, lead, and zinc ores in Chihuahua, yielded an annual average of 945.8 per cent on an original nominal investment of $60,000 for the 24 years beginning in 1903!

Citizens of the United States probably owned no other mining enterprises in Latin America that could be classed with these two, but several more brought them ample rewards. The Fresnillo Company, mining silver, lead, and zinc in Zacatecas, with some English investment, returned an average of 61 per cent per annum on a nominal capital of slightly more than a million dollars for over two decades (1929-1950). The Howe Sound Company, a Maine corporation organized in 1903 to engage in mining in Canada and Mexico, harvested its profits mainly from Mexican ores and paid its common stockholders an annual average of 49.7 per cent for a period of 33 years (1918-1950) on a nominal investment ranging from $2 to $3 million. With an investment of from $1.5 to $2 million, figured at par, the New York and Honduras Rosario Mining Company, in addition to stock dividends, returned an annual nominal average of 17.7 per cent for a period of 64 years (1887-1950), failing to reward its stockholders in only one single year. South American Gold and Platinum Company, organized in 1916, extracted from the placers of Colombia and the purses of consumers an annual nominal average of 22 per cent on its some $2 million of common stock for the 18 years beginning with 1933. Working gold and silver mines in the Mexican state of Jalisco, Amparo Mining Company, incorporated in New Jersey in 1902, paid an annual average of 12.2 per cent on $2 to $3 million dollars for more than a quarter of a century (1903-1929). Chile Copper Company, organized in 1913, returned an annual nominal dividend of only 9.3 per cent for the 28 years beginning in 1923, but its common-stock capital, around $110 million, was many times larger than that of any of the other mining companies mentioned here.

Readers familiar with the mining world will note the absence of some well-known companies in the list examined: American Smelting and Refining, American Metals, Anaconda Copper, Cerro de Pasco, Greene-Cananea, Kennecott Copper, the Vanadium Corporation, and perhaps others. All of these probably made rather large profits on their Latin-American investments, but exact rates of return are almost impossible to determine. And this is also true of most of the oil companies, for they are either the subsidiaries of giant corporations active in many parts of the world or they have "no-par" common stock that creates serious mathematical problems.

The Latin-American subsidiaries of Standard Oil, Gulf Oil, and the Texas Corporation will illustrate this point. The investment manuals fail to reveal the dividend records of most of these subsidiaries, and it is likewise impossible, or almost impossible, to ascertain the profits of the Doheny companies. Operating mainly in Mexico, Edward L. Doheny put in some $5 million and took out at least $75 million in less than 25 years, thus surpassing Hernando Cortés, Count Regla, and Lord Cowdray. When Doheny sold his petroleum properties to the Standard Oil group in 1925, his two major companies—Mexican Petroleum, founded in 1907, and Pan American Petroleum and Transport, organized in 1916—were capitalized at a total of around $200 million, half of this sum, however, representing stock bonuses, and they had not only paid the Doheny group an aggregate of some 90 per cent on their common stock but had regularly serviced 6, 7, and 8 per cent bonds amounting to approximately $34 million.[17]

Regarding the yields of two other profitable petroleum companies, both subsidiaries of Standard Oil of New Jersey, a more precise statement is possible. Creole Petroleum Corporation, operating in Venezuela, paid an annual average dividend of 31.8 per cent on its common stock—a nominal of $34,876,915 in 1936 and a nominal of $129,326,550 in 1950—for the 15 years beginning with 1936. International Petroleum, organized in 1920 and garnering its profits mainly from Peruvian and Colombian oil, returned an average dividend of 40.1 per cent per annum for three decades (1921-1950) on a nominal capital of some $35.8 million in ordinary shares and paid the same average annual rate on a nominal of $500,000 in participating preferred.

Such were the yields of 14 of the most profitable enterprises owned by citizens of the United States in Latin America. Rates of return of 10 of these during the most profitable five years of their existence prior to 1951 are set forth in Table 9 (dividends paid in stock excluded). There may have been several other very remunerative enterprises whose profits have not been revealed to the author of this work. It is well to remember, however, that citizens of the United States controlled at one time or another during this period more than two thousand business organiza-

TABLE 9

YIELDS OF SOME PROFITABLE ENTERPRISES OWNED BY UNITED STATES CITIZENS IN LATIN AMERICA

Company	Nominal Capital (common stock)	Highest Five Years	Annual Average
Amparo Mining	$ 2,000,000	1916-1920	17.5%
Chile Copper	110,387,575	1945-1949	12.8
Fresnillo	1,050,000	1946-1950	114.4
Howe Sound	2,500,000	1936-1940	88.4
N. Y. and Honduras Rosario	2,000,000	1935-1939	42.9
So. Am. Gold and Platinum	1,760,000	1933-1937	24.0
Creole Petroleum (approx.)	130,000,000	1946-1950	58.4
International Petroleum	35,810,220	1934-1938	98.0
Cuban American Sugar	10,000,000	1916-1920	20.0
United Fruit	118,500,000	1946-1950	25.5

tions in this part of the world, and that many of them yielded only moderate profits and many more—especially those engaged in efforts to grow plantation rubber in Mexico and Central America (1890-1910), as will be pointed out later—suffered heavy losses.

Average annual returns on the total capital invested in Latin America for most of the time since the investments began are unknown to this writer. Statistics based on the book value of capitalization published by the United States Department of Commerce indicate good yields on the direct investment in Latin America during the early 1940's.[18] Net earnings from economic enterprises controlled by citizens of the United States rose from an average of 9.4 per cent on $2,643 million in 1941 to 11.2 per cent on $2,784 million in 1945. Income actually distributed averaged 6.8 per cent in 1941 and 8.4 per cent in 1945. Net earnings for the five years beginning with 1941 averaged 9.9 per cent annually and income averaged 7.4 per cent.

Net earnings and income varied of course with types of investment and from country to country. Income paid to investors in 1943, for instance, averaged 9 per cent on the book value of their capital in petroleum and 11.9 per cent on their investment in mining and smelting, but only 4.9 per cent on their capital in agriculture and 2.8 per cent on their investment in public utilities; and net earnings in 1945 averaged 20.4 per cent from petroleum, 12.9 per cent from manufacturing enterprises, 8.7 per cent from mining and smelting, a rather unusual 15.2 per cent from agriculture, and only 3.8 per cent from public utilities. Table 10 indicates the amount of capital invested (book value at the end of May, 1943) by United States citizens in controlled economic enterprises in the leading countries of Latin America and the rates of income for 1943.

Data for income from each of the various republics are not available for earlier years. It seems likely, however, that the average rates of return were about the same for the 1920's as for 1943 and that, excepting Mexico and a few other turbulent countries,

TABLE 10

Income Received by United States Citizens from Direct Investments in Latin America, 1943

(In Millions of Dollars)

Country	Capital	Yield
Peru	$ 70.8	11.3%
Uruguay	5.5	10.9
Venezuela	370.5	10.3
Chile	336.2	10.3
Brazil	232.0	10.1
Dominican Republic	70.5	8.1
Mexico	286.2	5.9
Panama	112.9	5.3
Guatemala	86.9	5.1
Honduras	37.0	4.9
Argentina	393.3	4.0
Cuba	527.8	3.8
Other Countries	198.7	2.8
Latin America	$2,728.3	6.6%

they may have been approximately the same also for the first two decades of the century, if not for some earlier years. For the 1930's they were no doubt much lower. The returns were certainly much smaller during the 1930's from the investment in Latin-American government securities, a subject which will now be discussed.

CHAPTER 3 THE BOND-SELLING
EXTRAVAGANZA OF THE
1920'S AND ITS AFTERMATH

INVESTMENT bankers of the United States sold, mainly in the domestic market, huge quantities of government and government-guaranteed bonds of foreign countries during the twelve years following 1918. The total par value of the long-term issues of this type marketed by American investment houses during this period was approximately $6.2 billion. Latin America's share of these issues was nearly $1,894 million, more than 30 per cent of the total, and the gross profits of the bankers from the sale of these bonds amounted to some $95 million, or an average of 5 per cent of the face value of the Latin-American long-term issues which they floated. The large flotations of the government bonds of Canada, Europe, and the rest of the world yielded approximately equal profits. But citizens of the United States who purchased these securities soon discovered that in most instances they must suffer for their imprudence.

The vast majority of American investors who bought Latin-American government bonds were unaware of the debt records of these governments. They had little or no knowledge of the long history of Latin-American defaults or of the scandals in which British investment houses were involved in the 1820's and again in the 1860's and 1870's. Their experience with such bonds was limited. Except for Mexican bonds, it included nothing that recommended caution. Aside from Mexican government and government-guaranteed securities, purchases of United States citizens before 1919 had been confined mainly to the bonds of the Caribbean protectorates, issues for which their government had assumed a measure of responsibility; and favorable experience with respect to these, together with the knowledge that the Washington authorities were aware of the loan contracts of 1919-1930 and kept copies of them in their files, seems to have been an important influence in facilitating sales during the extravaganza. Market conditions were propitious, and the bankers utilized them to their immense advantage. Tables 11 and 12 summarize the results. The figures they contain may not be absolutely accurate in every case, but they are essentially correct.[1]

TABLE 11

Long-Term Dollar Issues of Latin-American Government Bonds Marketed by Investment Bankers of the United States, 1920-1930

(000 Omitted)

Country or Region	Par Value
Cuba	$ 99,000
Panama	24,800
Dominican Republic	20,000
El Salvador	16,500
Haiti	16,000
Guatemala	9,965
Costa Rica	9,800
Northern Latin America	$ 196,065
Argentina	$ 486,353
Brazil	424,530
Chile	340,112
Colombia	182,035
Peru	129,500
Bolivia	68,000
Uruguay	66,252
South America	$1,696,782
Latin America	$1,892,847

The gross profits of the bankers on some of these issues were so large that they cast an unfavorable reflection upon the reputations of both the bankers and the governments involved. Senate investigating committees disclosed scandals in loan negotiations and sales methods alike. Eagerness for profits warped the judgments of bankers or seared their consciences, and dishonesty or lack of experience in high finance on the part of Latin-American financial agents resulted in the acceptance of contracts that should have been rejected. The loan agreements contained no recapture clauses placing limitations upon excess bankers' profits. The investment bankers were left free to take all above the original purchase prices that clever salesmen could extract from investors. By no means all of the participants in the extravaganza had their reputations tarnished (except possibly by association), but more than a few of them did.

Table 12 sets forth the gross profits of the most important banking firms involved, to the extent that this writer has been able to discover such profits. It is impossible, of course, to determine what would have been a just charge in these transactions. This would depend upon market conditions, credit ratings, and the size of issues. But it would not be unreasonable to contend that where the cost of floating bonds bearing interest at nominal rates of 5.5 to 8 per cent (as practically all of these issues did) was higher than 3 or 4 per cent of the face value of the securities to be marketed, it might have been better for the Latin Americans to have struggled along without the loans (provided they really intended to fulfill their contractual obligations).

Inspection of Table 12 reveals that only four of the banking firms listed obtained an average gross spread of less than $4 on each $100, and even these four require comment. (1) J. P. Morgan and Company, outstanding among the group for their moderation, since their average gross spread was only 3.35 points, collected a gross profit of 5 points on a Chilean issue of $24 million in 1921 and a gross profit of 4 points on an issue of $45 million for the Argentine National Government in 1925. (2) Chase Securities Corporation, which took an average gross spread of 3.68, had some unsavory dealings with a Cuban tyrant named Gerardo Machado and grossed 9 points on a Province of Buenos Aires loan of $4,200,000 in 1926. (3) Kuhn, Loeb and Company, with an average gross spread of 3.87 and no gross profits exceeding 4.5 points, paid Dreyfus and Company a "finder's fee" of $450,000 and Norman H. Davis a handsome $35,000 for a mere introduction to a financial agent of the Mortgage Bank of Chile who had lost his way in New York.[2] (4) W. A. Harriman and Company, with the same average spread as Kuhn, Loeb and Company, took a gross profit of 4.5 points on a Panama issue of $4,500,000 in 1923.

The other fifteen banking houses listed in Table 12 were more

TABLE 12

Gross Profits of American Bankers on Latin-American Dollar Government Bonds, 1920-1930

Firm	Par Value of Total Issued	Gross Profits	Average Gross Spread
Hallgarten and Co.	$253,495,500	$10,668,840	$ 4.21
J. P. Morgan and Co.	242,800,000	8,145,730	3.35
Dillon, Read and Co.	190,500,000	11,570,000	6.07
National City Co.	167,912,000	6,898,830	4.11
Kuhn, Loeb and Co.	130,000,000	5,025,000	3.87
Blair and Co.*	127,072,000	8,808,360	6.93
J. and W. Seligman and Co.	115,500,000	6,730,000	5.83
Chase Securities Corp.	109,060,000	3,906,700	3.68
Speyer and Co.	82,500,000	5,289,000	6.41
Lee, Higginson and Co.	49,750,000	2,705,750	5.43
Blythe, Witter and Co.†	45,000,000	3,771,250	8.38
Stifel-Nicholaus Inv. Co.	29,000,000	2,435,000	8.40
First National Corp.**	24,121,000	1,869,377	7.75
F. J. Lisman and Co.	16,500,000	1,875,000	11.36
W. A. Harriman and Co.	14,500,000	567,500	3.87
Harris, Forbes and Co.	5,943,000	475,440	8.00
Central Trust Co. of Ill.	3,000,000	240,000	12.60
Equitable Trust Co.	2,885,000	234,850	8.00
Marshall Field, Glore and Ward	2,500,000	315,000	8.14
Total	$1,612,038,500	$81,531,627	$ 5.06

* Blair and Co. marketed an aggregate of $196,194,500; the gross profits on $69,122,500 have not been ascertained.
† Blythe, Witter and Co. floated another $6,792,000 for which the gross profits were not revealed.
** First National Corp. marketed an additional $11,675,000, but the gross profits on these are not known to this writer.

incontinent in their operations. They will be considered briefly in descending order of their gross gains. (1) Central Trust Company of Illinois took its spread of 12.6 on bonds marketed for the City of Barranquilla (Colombia) for the purpose of improving its waterworks. (2) F. J. Lisman and Company siphoned their $11.36 on each $100 from El Salvador loans; the little republic was under the dictatorship of the Meléndez family, and a beggar named Minor C. Keith, well known in that part of the world, shared $120,000 of the profits. After this lucky break and after bribing Juan Leguía, son of Peru's incumbent dictator, Frederick J. Lisman retired from the banking business.[3] (3) The Stifel-Nicholaus Investment Company, a St. Louis firm, extracted its average gross spread of 8.4 points from two Bolivian issues. (4) Blythe, Witter and Company obtained their major profits from Peruvian bonds and bonds of the Colombian Department of Caldas, piling up a gross spread of 6.09 on the former and 12.6 on the latter. (5) Marshall Field, Glore, and Ward took their average gross of 8.14 from three issues floated for the Colombian City of Cali; on one of the three their gross spread was 11 points. (6) The Equitable Trust Company, perhaps not entirely equitably, raked in its 8 points on an issue marketed for the Colombian City of Medellín. (7) The 8 points harvested by Harris, Forbes and Company were taken from bonds issued by the Argentine Province of Córdoba. (8) The gross of 7.75 retained by the First National Corporation came from three issues floated for the Province of Buenos Aires. (9) Blair and Company, with an average gross of 6.93, made their biggest profits on bonds of the Province of Buenos Aires and of the Federal Government of Brazil, retaining a spread of more than 9.21 on the first and 8 on the second. (10) Speyer and Company made their average gross of $6.41 on each $100 by concentrating on São Paulo, the Brazilian coffee state that was just recovering from a revolution.

(11) Dillon, Read and Company and (12) J. and W. Seligman and Company, although their gross profits of 6.07 and 5.83

respectively were somewhat less than the haul of the ten banking firms mentioned in the preceding paragraph, were close competitors for the worst record written during the period in the marketing of Latin-American government and government-guaranteed bonds. The words "shear," "fleece," and "bribe" can be used in describing most of their operations without doing them injustice.

Dillon and Read siphoned off $9 on each hundred for the issues they marketed for the Agricultural Mortgage Bank of Colombia and for the City of Bogotá, slightly more than $7.88 on each $100 from Bolivian bonds, $7.75 on each $100 for floating the securities of the City of Rio de Janeiro, and $5.69 from each $100 sold for the Federal Government of Brazil. In connection with the Bolivian flotations there were suspicions of bribery. The Bolivian minister of finance was accused of accepting a bribe of $40,000, but apparently the evidence was not convincing. Some aspects of Dillon, Read and Company's operations seem decidedly reprehensible. They had a large interest, for example, in an engineering firm headed by Leonard Kennedy, and not only was Kennedy paid $70,000 for going down to Bolivia to investigate prospects for railway construction but he was actually granted a construction contract for building some fifty miles of railway through the Bolivian mountains, not to mention an unnamed engineer who was given a present of $10,000 for introducing a Bolivian financial agent to Dillon and Read. And the story of the Rio de Janeiro security flotation was essentially the same. First, the banking firm paid Imbrie and Company $120,000 for the privilege of managing the loan, which had a face value of $12 million and was to be utilized in large part for the removal of a hill, called Castle Hill, that was hampering the growth of Brazil's capital city. Afterwards, Leonard Kennedy's engineering organization, in which the banking firm had a large interest, was awarded the contract for removing the hill. The net profits of Leonard Kennedy and Company, profits shared by Dillon, Read and Company, were $350,000.[4]

J. and W. Seligman and Company attract special attention because they paid out bribes, which they called "finder's fees," in connection with almost every Latin-American loan they marketed. In securing the Department of Cauca Valley (Colombia) issues, which aggregated $4 million, Phanor J. Eder, member of an influential family with some of its components living in that part of Colombia, was paid a finder's fee of $42,000 in cash and bonds, and the average gross spread was 11.4 points. On a Department of Cundinamarca (Colombia) flotation of $12 million Antonio Borda received a fee of $33,981.64, but the gross spread was only 5 points. For finding the opportunity to float a Costa Rican issue of $8 million, Felipe J. Alvarado was rewarded with a fee of $38,677.46; the spread on this issue was 7.5 points. For the same service in respect to a City of Callao loan, G. A. Helfert received $7,500. The grand total for bribery, influence, advice, and blackmail in connection with Seligman's flotations for the Peruvian national government was $533,000, distributed as follows by Frederick J. Lisman: Juan Leguía, $416,000; Bolster and Company, $67,000; Samuel A. Maginnis, recently minister of the United States in Bolivia, $40,000; T. V. Salt, $10,000! By the terms of the loan contracts, the Peruvian government itself agreed to assume these heavy outlays, which were described as "expenses and disbursements of council." Seligman and Company managed the flotation of a total of $90 million of Peruvian government bonds and retained a gross spread of 5.53 points. The evidence indicates that the bankers sold these bonds in spite of repeated reports from their own agents to the effect that Peru was a bad credit risk.[5]

The profits of the three remaining firms listed in Table 12 require no more than brief comment. (1) Lee, Higginson and Company's average gross spread, 5.43, was sharply reduced by an average gross of only 2.71 points on three issues aggregating $20 million floated for the Dominican Republic. On the remainder of this firm's flotations—two issues for the state of Rio Grande do Sul and three for the City of Porto Alegre—the average gross spread was 7.27. (2) Hallgarten and Company's average was brought down to 4.21 by two issues of the Colombian National Government, amounting to a total of $60 million, on which the gross spread was only 2.71 and by an issue of $17,581,-000 for the Uruguayan National Government on which the gross spread was only 2.98. Gross profits were much higher on this firm's other flotations; on a City of Medellín (Colombia) loan of $3 million, for instance, the gross spread was 8.25 and on a Province of Buenos Aires issue of $10,613,500 it was 6.5. (3) Although the average gross profits of the National City Company were only $4.11 on each $100, its gross ran as high as 5.5 on a $7,500,000 issue marketed for the Uruguayan National Government in 1925, and the National City Company is said to have made a profit of $2 million by dealing as "insiders" in the securities of a Haitian railroad.[6] It should be noted further that this banking firm was closely associated with Gerardo Machado, the Cuban dictator, and that it sold two bond issues which it knew to be unsound for the state of Minas Geraes.[7]

Were these profits from bond flotations abnormal? Data for a positive answer to this question are lacking. Until the 1930's, no facts were more carefully concealed from the public than the profits of investment houses on the marketing of securities. Their profits, as a rule, had been disclosed only when investors who felt that they had been defrauded demanded and obtained investigations. The record of 1919-1930 was certainly a variation from the norm in two respects. Never in their history had the Latin-American governments sold abroad such huge quantities of bonds in so short a period and seldom had they received such high prices for their securities. Their sales to foreign investors within a decade probably exceeded their sales abroad during the entire previous century, and the investment bankers rarely paid them less than 85 per cent of par for an issue; in fact, the Latin-American governments usually received 90 or more. The profits of the bankers, although immense because the aggregate issues were immense, were probably smaller in proportion to the size of their transactions than the profits taken by the European bankers on many flotations during the previous half-century and certainly smaller than those they retained during the 1820's and on several issues of the 1860's and 1870's.

Profits made by European bankers on Latin-American flotations of the period between 1881 and 1910 may be suggested by a few illustrations. On a flotation for the Argentine national government in 1881 amounting to £4,085,000 the gross spread was 11 points. On an Argentine issue of £40 million in 1886 the gross spread was only 5, but on a £4,290,100 issue floated the next year it rose to 7.75.[8] On two issues sold for the Mexican national government shortly before the overthrow of Porfirio Díaz gross bankers' profits were as follows: Loan of 1904, £40 million, 5 points; Loan of 1910, £11,100,000, spread of 2.875.[9] These two governments had the best credit ratings in Latin America at the time these bonds were marketed.

A comparison of the profits taken by certain American bankers before 1920 with the profits they made during the following decade indicates no important variations in practice. In the case of Cuba, for illustration, Speyer and Company retained large gross spreads on the loans of 1904 and 1909: on the first, with a face value of $35 million, the gross spread was 6.5, and on the second, $16,500,000, it was 9.4. J. P. Morgan and Company, as usual, were more moderate; their gross spread on a $10 million issue of 1914 was only 4.5, and this seems to have been the widest spread the Morgan firm ever took on a long-term Cuban issue.[10]

2.

The unpleasant story of defaults must now be recalled. Defaults on these Latin-American dollar government or government-guaranteed bonds began in 1931, and by the end of the year 1934 nearly all of the fourteen republics that had marketed dollar issues between 1919 and 1930 had defaulted on sinking-fund payments or interest, or both. Omitting defaults on amortization, Table 13 sets forth the sad situation. (Mexico is not included because its dollar bonds were marketed earlier.)

TABLE 13*

LATIN-AMERICAN DOLLAR GOVERNMENT ISSUES IN DEFAULT, END OF 1934

(Par Values)

Country or Region	Total Outstanding	Total in Default as to Interest
Cuba	$ 91,878,100	$ 40,000,000
Panama	18,728,500	14,453,500
Dominican Republic	16,292,000	none
El Salvador	12,619,300	12,619,300
Haiti	10,511,360	none
Costa Rica	8,781,000	8,781,000
Guatemala	2,214,000	2,214,000
Northern Latin America	$161,024,260	$ 78,067,800
Argentina	$361,289,400	$ 92,055,400
Brazil	354,175,300	330,913,300
Chile	264,608,500	264,608,500
Colombia	143,655,400	143,655,400
Peru	91,286,000	91,286,000
Uruguay	63,367,500	63,367,500
Bolivia	59,422,000	58,422,000
South America	$1,337,804,100	$1,043,308,100
Latin America	$1,498,828,360	$1,121,375,900

* Based upon Foreign Bondholders Protective Council (New York), *Annual Report, 1934*, pp. 223-24.

Table 13 reveals that interest was being paid at the close of 1934 on only a small segment of the bonds sold during the extravagant bond-selling period under consideration; namely, on the majority of the Cuban and Argentine issues, on all those of Haiti and the Dominican Republic, and on an insignificant fraction of those of Panama and Brazil. The total was only $377,452,-460, a little more than a fourth; an aggregate of $1,121,375,900, almost three-fourths of the bonds, was in default as to interest.

Failure of the Latin-American governments to service their bonds may be attributed to lack of capacity or lack of disposition, or to a combination of both. On the relative significance of these two factors, bondholders and governments are likely to disagree. In some cases it had been difficult and probably even impossible to service the securities because the proceeds had been unwisely used and because world conditions following 1929 had made apparently prudent investments unproductive. On the other hand, indifference or indisposition may have been in some measure responsible for the continuation of defaults in the case of several issues, and this may be accounted for in part by exasperation arising from revelations of dishonesty in connection with a number of flotations and from the disclosure of the large gross profits taken by the bankers. Moreover, a universal decline in interest rates tended to create a disposition on the part of the governments involved to effect reductions in interest as a condition of resuming service on their outstanding bonds.

The large defaults and the demand for adjustments in interest rates led to the organization in the United States of a Foreign Bondholders Protective Council in 1933, and vigorous negotiations followed, sometimes supported by the Washington government and sometimes steered by it so as to favor the Latin Americans. Settlements more or less satisfactory to both the creditors and the debtors were reached within a decade in most cases. The status of the bonds in respect to interest payments at the end of 1945, under either the new agreements or the original loan contracts, is presented in Table 14. Again the defaults on sinking funds are omitted. (As in 1934, these sinking-fund defaults covered only slightly larger sums than defaults on interest.)

A comparison of Tables 13 and 14 will indicate that the income of the bondholders had decidedly improved during the twelve-year period. Bonds in default on interest in 1945 aggregated only $483,340,708, although this sum was still nearly 47

TABLE 14

LATIN-AMERICAN GOVERNMENT DOLLAR ISSUES IN DEFAULT, END OF 1945
(Par Values)

Country or Region	Total Outstanding	Total in Default as to Interest
Cuba*	$ 95,853,900	$ 307,000
Panama	15,640,519	1,198,074
Dominican Republic	12,086,000	none
El Salvador	8,846,425	8,846,425
Haiti	6,684,315	none
Costa Rica	8,093,976	8,093,976
Guatemala	878,000	none
Northern Latin America	$148,083,135	$ 18,445,475
Argentina	$183,804,180	$ 886,090
Brazil	217,297,385	69,724,945
Chile	150,554,500	150,554,500
Colombia	138,716,602	95,820,500
Peru	85,656,500	85,656,500
Uruguay	48,543,001	1,677,000
Bolivia*	60,575,698	60,575,698
South America	$ 885,147,866	$464,895,233
Latin America	$1,033,231,001	$483,340,708

* The totals outstanding for Cuba and Bolivia were larger in 1945 than in 1934 because the figures for 1945 apparently include some dollar bonds not publicly offered and those for 1934 do not. The statistics presented in this table have been taken from the *Annual Report, 1945*, of the Foreign Bondholders Protective Council (New York, 1946), pp. 108-9.

per cent of the total outstanding and the percentage was higher for the issues of the South American governments. In Northern Latin America only El Salvador and Costa Rica were in default on all of their bonds; but in South America three countries—Chile, Peru, and Bolivia—with much larger sums outstanding were in total default. Moreover, many of the governments that were paying interest on their securities had obtained reductions in interest rates; seven of the nine countries that were remitting interest on the whole or an important part of their bonds had in fact permanently defaulted on several of their original contracts respecting interest. Regarding the five governments still in default on the total of their dollar issues in 1945, it should be noted that in every case there were either irregularities in the loan negotiations or unusually large bankers' profits, and that there may be a relationship between these two facts. Moreover, whether for these reasons or others, some of the Latin-American governments had marred their reputations by "buying in" bonds at prices depressed by their failure to service them.

By no means all of the dollar securities outstanding at the end of 1945 were the property of citizens of the United States. A good part of the bonds were now owned by other investors. According to the Department of Commerce, the face value of the dollar issues of the fourteen countries under inspection held by citizens of the United States at this time was only some $436.5 million, and this total probably included a few corporate bonds issued without any government guaranty. Unless there are important discrepancies between these figures and those given by the Foreign Bondholders Protective Council, almost 58 per cent of these bonds were in the portfolios of other foreign investors or the Latin Americans themselves, whereas only a very small fraction of the securities had originally been purchased outside of the United States. This means, of course, even allowing for discrepancies, that American investors had sold a large portion of their holdings and taken their losses. Table 15 deals with the ownership of these bonds at the end of 1945 and compares the market and the par values of those in the hands of citizens of the United States at this time.

Table 15 (assuming that the statistics it presents are essentially accurate) discloses several interesting facts. Citizens of the United States owned at the end of 1945 less than a fourth of the outstanding dollar government bonds of the seven republics of Northern Latin America and less than half of those of the seven South American countries. They held only a little more than a tenth of the Cuban bonds, less than a third of those of the Dominican Republic and El Salvador, a little more than a third of Haiti's, slightly more than half of Panama's and Costa Rica's,

65

TABLE 15

Ownership of Latin-American Dollar Bonds, End of 1945

(In Millions of Dollars)

Country or Region	Total Outstanding Par Value	Total Held by U. S. Citizens Par Value	Market Value
Cuba	$ 95.9	$ 10.4	$ 9.7
Panama	15.6	9.7	9.7
Dominican Republic	12.0	3.2	3.3
El Salvador	8.8	2.9	1.0
Haiti	6.7	2.3	2.2
Costa Rica	8.0	4.6	2.1
Guatemala	.9	.8	.4
Northern Latin America*	$147.9	$ 33.9	$ 28.4
Argentina	$183.8	$ 51.4	$ 50.3
Brazil	217.3	111.6	65.1
Chile	150.6	86.2	24.8
Colombia	138.7	63.1	31.1
Peru	85.7	38.4	10.9
Uruguay	48.6	13.7	12.0
Bolivia	60.6	38.4	5.7
South America*	$ 885.3	$402.8	$199.9
Latin America*	$1,033.6	$436.7	$228.3

* Figures are rounded to the nearest tenth and therefore do not exactly correspond with the totals given in Table 14. Those in the first column are taken from Foreign Bondholders Protective Council, *Annual Report, 1945*, pp. 108-9; those in the second and third columns are from U. S. Department of Commerce, *International Transactions of the United States during the War* (Washington, D. C., 1948), p. 215.

but nearly all of Guatemala's; while in South America their holdings included less than a third of those of Argentina and Uruguay, less than half of Colombia's and Peru's, and slightly more than half of the dollar bonds of Brazil, Chile, and Uruguay. A comparison of the figures in the second and third columns of the table will disclose that the holdings of citizens of the United States at the end of the year 1945 had a market value of only a little more than half of their par value; considerably less than half for those of the South American republics, but more than four-fifths for the bonds of the republics of Northern Latin

America. Only the bonds of five of the fourteen countries—Cuba, the Dominican Republic, Panama, Argentina, and Uruguay—had market values not far from their par values. All the dollar issues of El Salvador, Costa Rica, Bolivia, Peru, and Chile had been in default for some twelve to fourteen years!

Between 1945 and 1948 the defaults were reduced. Only two of the countries, Costa Rica and Bolivia, were in default as to interest on all of their issues in 1948. Chile, Colombia, and Peru, however, were still failing to pay interest on the major part of their outstanding bonds. Table 16 indicates the status of the securities at the end of 1948. Haiti, the Dominican Republic, and Argentina had redeemed their dollar issues. A small part of the total listed for Chile and Colombia may be corporate issues lacking a government guaranty. Table 16 reveals that more than half of the issues of the South American governments and almost half of those of all Latin America were still in default on interest payments in 1948. Although the situation had vastly improved in Northern Latin America, it should be pointed out that most of the Mexican issues (excluded from this analysis because they were marketed before 1920) were not being serviced. Of Mexico's total outstanding issues of $273,582,029 at the end of 1948—by no means all of them held in the United States—$232,843,429 were in default on interest.

Excepting the issues of Cuba, El Salvador, Panama, and Uruguay, the market value of these bonds of the extravaganza epoch was still very low. Table 17 compares the par and market values at the end of 1948 of those still in the hands of citizens of the United States.

American holdings of Latin-American dollar bonds had an average market value at the end of the year 1948 of less than 42 per cent of par. Sale of the bonds at that time, assuming that they were still held by the original purchasers, as a good part of them may have been, would have occasioned a loss of between $150 and $175 million, and dividends on the investment had been very scanty for a decade and a half. Average annual yields during the period are not precisely known, but the average nominal rate paid each year probably ranged from around 1 per cent in the mid-thirties to a little more than 2 per cent in the mid-forties. It is easy to imagine a much more profitable investment. The Latin-American countries, American exporters and shippers, and the investment bankers who promoted the bond-selling extravaganza, especially the bankers, were the main beneficiaries. Except for the first few years after the securities were purchased, most investors not only received no returns, or almost none, but in many instances eventually lost a large part of their capital. In short, they discovered that they had bought a collection of souvenirs of misplaced confidence.

TABLE 16*

LATIN-AMERICAN DOLLAR ISSUES IN DEFAULT, END OF 1948

Country or Region	Total Outstanding (Par Values)	Total in Default as to Interest
Cuba	$ 72,875,600	$ 107,000
Panama	15,083,060	688,500
Dominican Republic	....	....
El Salvador	7,920,305	1,006,200
Haiti	....	....
Costa Rica	8,102,469	8,102,469
Guatemala	800,000 (?)	....
Northern Latin America	$104,781,434	$ 9,904,169
Argentina	....	....
Brazil	182,245,775	21,372,045
Chile	135,401,773	112,616,000
Colombia	138,488,457	97,280,500
Peru	80,444,300	60,621,500
Uruguay	46,032,500	1,356,500
Bolivia	59,422,000	59,422,000
South America	$642,034,805	$352,668,545

* Compiled from Institute of International Finance, *Statistical Analysis of Publicly Offered Foreign Dollar Bonds*, Bulletin No. 161, New York, 1949, pp. 24-25. The figure for Guatemala is perhaps too high.

Although Argentina, the Dominican Republic, and Haiti had redeemed their dollar bonds long before the end of 1954 and

TABLE 17*

MARKET AND PAR VALUES OF LATIN-AMERICAN BONDS OWNED BY CITIZENS OF THE UNITED STATES, END OF 1948

(In Millions of Dollars)

Country or Region	Par	Total Market
Cuba	$ 14.6	$ 14.2
Panama	9.5	8.1
El Salvador	3.7	2.0
Costa Rica	2.9	0.4
Guatemala	0.6	0.3
Northern Latin America	$ 31.3	$ 25.0
Brazil	$ 90.3	$ 44.4
Chile	71.4	24.2
Colombia	70.1	33.9
Peru	35.4	4.7
Uruguay	13.5	10.8
Bolivia	38.4	3.7
South America	$319.1	$121.7
Latin America	$350.4	$146.7

* Compiled from U. S. Department of Commerce, *The Balance of Payments of the United States, 1946-1948* (Washington, D. C., 1950), p. 268.

only two countries—Guatemala, $600,000, and Bolivia, $38,400,000, both in par values—were still defaulting, not merely interest but principal as well had been reduced in many cases and current market values disclosed lack of enthusiasm for such securities. Including Mexican bonds—around $22 million at par but only some $3 million at market—the holdings of United States citizens at the end of 1954 aggregated a face value of $279 million and a market value of only $143 million, or nearly 49 per cent less than par. Investors who had bought the bonds at close to par had been receiving interest since 1948 at an average annual rate of less than 2.5 per cent; returns for speculators rarely exceeded an average of 5 per cent annually. The records of some of the countries—Cuba, the Dominican Republic, Haiti, Panama, Argentina, Uruguay—were almost unblemished; but the defaulters had apparently spoiled the prospects, if not the reputations, of the entire group. During the six years following 1948 the par value of the investment had contracted from $283 million to $279 million (including the Mexican securities) and the market value had dropped from $151 million to $143 million. In striking contrast, the par value of the capital of citizens of the United States invested in the dollar bonds of Western Europe had shrunk very little during this period—from $231 million to $218 million—and the market value had actually risen from $52 million to $160 million; and both the par and the market values of their investment in Canadian bonds and those of other countries outside of the Iron and Bamboo Curtains had experienced a marked expansion: Canada's from a par of $1,053 million in 1948 to a par of $1,573 million in 1954 and from a market value of $1,096 million to $1,604 million; other countries from a par of $203 million in 1948 to a par of $347 million in 1954 and from a market value of $127 million to $309 million.[11]

A similar trend was also revealed in other portfolio investments of United States citizens. It is true that these had expanded in Latin America, but only to the extent of $33 million, rising from a market value of $315 million at the end of 1948 to a market value of $348 million at the close of 1954. Meantime this type of portfolio capital had increased in Canada from $1,769 million to $2,030 million, in Western Europe from $1,169 million to $1,388 million, and in other foreign countries from $191 to $294 million.[12] And portfolio private investments of all kinds were the types of foreign private investment that Latin Americans preferred!

CHAPTER 4 A POSTWAR DECADE OF PRIVATE DIRECT INVESTMENT ABROAD

CAPITAL owned by citizens of the United States in foreign countries almost doubled in value during the first ten years following World War II. The total increased from $13,659 million at the beginning of 1946 to $26,129 million at the end of 1955. But for reasons already stated, expansion of the portfolio investment was far less striking than expansion of the direct investment. Portfolio holdings increased from $5,289 million to $6,944 million, hardly more than 31 per cent; direct investment increased from $8,370 million to $19,185 million, over 117 per cent. Most of the expansion in portfolio capital occurred in Canada and countries other than European and Latin American. Portfolio holdings in Europe actually shrank to the extent of $2 million during the decade and the portfolio expansion in Latin America amounted to only $65 million, while the expansion elsewhere—mainly in Canada, Australia, and the Philippines—increased by $1,592 million. Table 18 exhibits the growth of the long-term private investment of United States citizens abroad by countries and regions during this decade.

The analysis that follows is concerned *solely* with the direct investment, its expansion, its distribution, and the rates of return therefrom, with particular reference to Latin America and other underdeveloped regions. Canada and Europe will be considered only for purposes of comparison and contrast.

A little more than 30 per cent of the total private direct investment was in Canada at the beginning of 1946 and slightly more than 25 per cent in Europe. Latin America had nearly 36 per

TABLE 18*

EXPANSION OF THE LONG-TERM PRIVATE INVESTMENT OF U. S. CITIZENS IN FOREIGN COUNTRIES, 1946-1955

(In Millions of Dollars)

Country or Region	Capital Beginning of 1946	End of 1955
All Countries: Total	$13,659	$26,129
Direct Investment	8,370	19,185
Portfolio Investment	5,289	6,944
Canada: Total	5,235	10,344
Direct	2,527	6,464
Portfolio	2,708	3,880
Europe: Total	3,670	4,636
Direct	2,018	2,986
Portfolio	1,652	1,650
Latin America: Total	3,672	7,293
Direct	3,000	6,556
Portfolio	672	737
Other Regions: Total	1,082	3,856
Direct	825	3,179
Portfolio	257	677

* Compiled from *Survey of Current Business,* Nov. 1949, p. 21, Jan. 1954, pp. 6-7, and Aug. 1956, pp. 18-23.

cent and the rest of the world less than 10 per cent. By the end of 1955 Canada's share had expanded to almost 34 per cent of the aggregate and Europe's share had contracted to less than 17 per cent. Latin America's relative portion had also contracted by this time, but only slightly from 36 to 34.2 per cent. The share of the rest of the world had risen from less than 10 per cent to nearly 17 per cent of the total. The distribution of the capital increment which took place during the decade was approximately as follows: Europe, 9 per cent of the aggregate expansion; Canada, 36 per cent; Latin America, 33 per cent; all other countries, 22 per cent.

Three types of direct investment accounted for the major part of this expansion: (1) extraction, refining, and distribution of petroleum and its products, 39.3 per cent; (2) mining and smelting, 10.5 per cent; (3) manufacturing 33.8 per cent. Approximately 63 per cent of the total capital was in these three categories in 1946 and more than 74 per cent of it in 1955.

Net earnings and income were higher from Latin America and other underdeveloped regions—especially the latter—than from either Canada or Europe.[1] Average annual net earnings for the decade were as follows: Canada, 10.8 per cent; Europe, 13; Latin America, 14.6; all other regions, 29.8. Income distributed to investors was smaller, however; decidedly smaller in the cases of Canada and Europe. From Canada the annual average was 5.1 per cent and from Europe it was 6.1 per cent; but from Latin America it was 11.2 per cent and from other regions it was 23.9.

The highest returns among the various types of investment came from petroleum, commercial agriculture (mainly sugar in Latin America and plantation rubber in Africa and the Orient), manufacturing, trading, and mining and smelting. The lowest returns were yielded by public utilities, with the capital operating mainly in Latin America and the Philippine Republic. Average annual net earnings and income in these six categories were as follows:

	Net Earnings	Income
Petroleum	21.9 per cent and	14.5
Manufacturing	15.1 and	7.5
Mining, Smelting	12.1 and	9.5
Agriculture	17.3 and	13.3
Trading	14.4 and	8.5
Public Utilities	2.5 and	3.2

The averages for agriculture, trade, and public utilities run for only eight years (1946-1953); the rest are for the full decade. Note that the rate of income distributed exceeded the rate of net earnings in the case of the utilities; reserves were being depleted. Comparatively little capital expansion occurred in public utilities during the period under inspection. The investment was $1,357 million at the beginning of 1946 and only $1,508 at the end of 1953.

Petroleum from the producing areas, as one would expect,

recorded the largest profits. But Canada, where exploitation was just beginning, was an exception, net earnings from this country averaging hardly 4 per cent and income less than 0.5 per cent. From Europe the rates were 12.1 and 6; from Latin America, 24.4 and 20.4; from the rest of the world, largely the oil-rich Near East, 33.8 and 29.

Mining and smelting enterprises were least profitable in Europe and Canada and only a little more remunerative in Latin America than in Canada. The big profits in this type of activity came from other regions. Average annual net earnings and income from Europe were 4 per cent and 1.4 per cent; from Canada, 9.9 and 5.9; from Latin America, 11.5 and 10.8; but from other regions (mainly Africa) net earnings averaged 27.3 per cent per annum and income 21.5 per cent.

Agriculture in Latin America yielded smaller profits than in Africa and the Orient, plantation rubber probably accounting for the difference. Net earnings from agricultural enterprises in Latin America were at the annual rate of 16.8; from other underdeveloped regions they were at the rate of 24.4. Income from Latin America amounted to 13.6 per cent; from the other underdeveloped regions it averaged 15.3.

Manufacturing enterprises were less remunerative in Europe and Latin America than elsewhere. Net earnings in manufacturing in Europe averaged 15.8 per cent annually and income 6.5 per cent. In Latin America the averages were 14.4 and 7; in Canada, 14.1 and 8.4; in the rest of the world, 22.8 and 11.2.

Trading profits averaged higher in Latin America and other underdeveloped regions than in Europe or Canada. Net earnings from this category in Canada during the eight years beginning with 1946 were at the average annual rate of 14.2 per cent and income was at the rate of 5.9; from Europe the average rates were 11.6 and 8.3. But from Latin America net earnings for the same period averaged 17.3 per cent per annum and income 9.1 per cent, while from the rest of the world the rates were 23 and 14.7.

2.

At the risk of becoming tedious, profits from direct investment for the six years starting with 1950 and ending with 1955 will be examined in greater detail. The six-year average rates of return on American capital in all foreign countries were 16.5 per cent for net earnings and 10.8 per cent for income. For Canada the average rates were 10.8 per cent for net earnings and 5.9 for income; for Europe, 16.6 and 7.6; for Latin America, 14.6 and 11.6; for other countries—mainly the underdeveloped countries of Africa and the Orient—32.6 per cent and 26 per cent. Net earnings from the independent nations of Africa averaged 24.1 per cent during the period and income averaged 13.6 per cent. From the dependent territories of Africa they were 24.2 and 14.3. From the independent non-Communist countries of Asia and Oceania—including Japan, Australia, and New Zealand, where profits were comparatively moderate—net earnings were at the average annual rate of 33.6 per cent and income at the annual average of 27.6. From the dependent territories of Asia and Oceania they were 45.3 and 41.5! Underdeveloped Latin America, with net earnings averaging only 14.6 per cent and income averaging 11.6 per cent, evidently had strong competitors for American private direct investment in the tropics of the Old World.

Inspection of still smaller units in which this capital was operating will further emphasize this competition. The largest average profits from Latin America during this six-year period were from the following countries:[2]

Country	Net Earnings	Income
Venezuela	29.0%	26.3%
Honduras	18.4	16.6
Dominican Republic	12.9	9.9
Panama	16.9	7.5
Costa Rica	20.2	20.0

Country	Net Earnings	Income
Peru	14.6	11.7
Chile	8.8	8.2
Brazil	13.9	7.5

Contrast these with ten countries and groups of countries in Africa, non-Communist Asia, and Oceania (the abbreviation DOTS indicates dependent overseas territories):

Country	Net Earnings	Income
Egypt	11.9%	7.9%
Union South Africa	22.7	14.3
DOTS, Africa	24.2	14.1
Indonesia	48.9	39.2
Other Independent, Asia	43.5	39.7
Liberia	28.1	16.8
Other Independent, Africa	64.7	43.2
India	29.7	22.5
Philippine Republic	20.8	15.5
DOTS, Asia and Oceania	45.3	41.4

Then include Europe's dependent territories in the Western Hemisphere and some of the more highly industrialized countries in order to complete the panorama:

Country	Net Earnings	Income
Switzerland	22.2%	17.0%
United Kingdom	19.7	9.7
Italy	14.4	6.5
Netherlands	12.2	5.5
Japan	19.1	11.2
Portugal	20.7	12.9
Belgium	17.5	8.7
Sweden	11.5	6.2
Australia	16.5	5.6
DOTS, Western Hemisphere	13.9	9.5

It should now be quite obvious that the Latin-American countries, at least from the viewpoint of profits, had many strong competitors for the dollars of American private investors.

3.

But Latin Americans worry about foreign investments in spite of the fact that the profits of the investors are smaller from their republics than from many other countries. They complain of the influence of foreign businesses in their countries, of the rapid exhaustion of their non-renewable resources, of the prices for products taken out to foreign markets, of shortages of capital, and of other related subjects. Only two of the causes of their worries will be discussed at the moment, however: the closely associated topics of "siphoning out" of profits and meager inflow of new capital.

What is meant by siphoning out of profits? Do such profits come from a single source? If it is certain that profits could not be garnered from Latin America by investors of the United States in most instances without the Latin-American commodities which these investors produce and distribute, it is also certain that profits would rarely be made by such investors in the absence of foreign markets for these commodities. Both external consumers and Latin-American resources are prime essentials in this production and traffic, and the profits are derived as much from foreigners as from Latin Americans and the products of Latin America. No doubt a siphoning process occurred, but the siphons were sunk in many wells, in the wells of Latin-American resources but likewise in the wells of numerous external markets. Otherwise why did Latin Americans complain of comparatively low prices for their foods and raw materials that were sold in the United States and elsewhere and why did they protest about sugar quotas and quotas or excise taxes on petroleum, metals, and many other commodities produced by foreign enterprise in their countries? They may think that they alone were "exploited"—to use a term frequently employed by them and others—but if exploitation occurred in this connection, consumers in the world outside were also among the victims. Latin Americans might have been the lone victims if foreign investors had bought and sold, or produced and marketed, exclusively in Latin America. Foreign-owned manufacturing plants operating in Latin America, utilizing only Latin-American materials, and selling the whole of their output in Latin America might buttress their argument, since Latin America would then be the sole well from which the profits would be drawn. Yet Latin Americans are said to prefer this type of direct investment! (Profits derived from foreign-owned public utilities in Latin America are another example of this sort.)

Latin-American worry over the lethargic inflow of new capital arises also from comparisons of net earnings and income with expansion of the capital invested. Sometimes they consider only income in this connection, but occasionally both net earnings and income are brought into the discussion. Investors from the United States, they contend, are not putting any new capital into Latin America; they merely reinvest their net earnings and often only a part of these. Already the falsity of this theory has been disclosed. In cases where the income withdrawn over a period of years exceeded the expansion of the investment there is a sounder basis for their complaints, for the money thus withdrawn into the coffers of foreign investors is not permitted to operate in Latin America; but even in these instances it would be incorrect to assume that it had been siphoned from the region, since in most cases this income had not been derived solely from Latin America but partly from the purses of foreign consumers who had purchased Latin-American commodities such as sugar, bananas, petroleum, copper, vanadium, manganese, iron ore, and other foods, minerals, and metals. Only in respect to their public services and their much-favored manufacturing establishments would their contention be sound, and in the case of the latter, as already suggested, provisos would have to be added regarding the source of the raw materials utilized and the limitation of the market. It could be that Latin Americans should have a larger share of the profits extracted by foreign enterprises from Latin-American resources and foreign consumers; but this is a somewhat different problem the solution of which would have to depend on many circumstances both in Latin America and in other parts of the world: comparative treatment of investors, comparative risks, comparative returns on investments, market demands for Latin-American products, and general competitive conditions and trade barriers.[3]

Even if all the contentions of Latin Americans in respect to the "siphoning out" of profits and the lethargic flow of new capital were granted, Latin Americans would still have no foundation for exclusive self-pity. The profits "siphoned" from Latin America during the postwar period and particularly during the years 1950-1955 were smaller than those "siphoned" from many other regions in similar circumstances. It is not easy to find countries where, during the latter period, the expansion of the investment exceeded either net earnings or income withdrawn. In the case of the long-term private direct investments of citizens of the United States there were only four instances (excepting a few European nations) where increases of capital were greater than total net earnings—namely, Egypt, Japan, Australia, and Canada—and only ten instances (again excluding the European countries) in which expansion of investment was in excess of income withdrawn: Argentina, Brazil, Mexico, Peru, India, the Union of South Africa, and, of course, Egypt, Japan, Australia and Canada; and Canada is usually represented as a model of the mutual benefits derived from international investment. That any of the Latin-American countries could be thus exhibited as a model is doubtful, although recent investment relations of United States citizens with Venezuela, Peru, the Dominican Republic, and possibly a few others have been satisfactory. Table 19 presents a comparative view of profits and expansion of investment during 1950-1955, with emphasis on the major underdeveloped countries and groups of countries.

TABLE 19*

Long-Term Private Direct Investments of Citizens of the U. S. in Certain Foreign Countries: Profits and Expansion of Investment 1950-1955

(In Millions of Dollars)

Country or Region	Net Earnings	Income	Expansion of Investment
Latin America	$4,781	$3,667	$1,966
Other Underdeveloped Areas	3,929	3,151	1,611
Argentina	154	60	117
Brazil	659	357	519
Chile	311	289	118
Colombia	103	88	88
Costa Rica	72	73	4
Cuba	286	233	104
Dominican Republic	95	67	32
Honduras	80	72	41
Mexico	328	206	225
Panama	379	170	142
Peru	179	141	153
Uruguay	44	24	23
Venezuela	1,990	1,809	388
Egypt	31	21	34
Liberia	182	82	214
Union of South Africa	232	147	152
DOTS,† Africa	145	83	48
Australia	271	92	333
Japan	57	34	114
India	88	64	69
Indonesia	198	163	24
Philippine Republic	207	154	94
Other Independent Asia	1,806	1,667	365
DOTS,† Asia and Oceania	656	598	107
Canada	2,811	1,495	3,318

* These statistics have been compiled from the sources cited in note 1 above, especially *Survey of Current Business,* Jan. 1954, pp. 6-7, and Aug. 1956, pp. 18-23.
† Indicates dependent overseas territories.

CHAPTER 5 A DECADE OF ASSISTANCE BY THE GOVERNMENT OF THE UNITED STATES TO UNDER-DEVELOPED COUNTRIES

A FEELING of neglect seems to have permeated Latin America, or at least its official circles, since the middle of 1945; and Latin Americans have expressed this feeling on so many occasions that they have succeeded in communicating it to a number of diplomatic agents and lawmakers of the United States. But it is not the purpose of this chapter to present Latin-American complaints or illustrate the views of United States officials whose sympathies have been aroused by them. It will be limited to a summary of the aid extended by the United States government to this region during the first decade following World War II (July 1, 1945-June 30, 1955, unless otherwise stated). Some readers may be surprised at the variety of channels through which this assistance has flowed, but it is hoped that none will conclude that the survey here offered is a sort of attorney's brief for the United States. Its primary objective is to direct attention to the facts and the figures.

The Office of Business Economics of the Department of Commerce has been assigned the task of keeping abreast of the grants and credits extended to foreign countries by the United States government since it assumed major responsibility for the "peace and prosperity" of the world. But while that office has exhibited commendable industry in assembling and publishing data, its figures are incomplete. Statistics included in Table 20 have been compiled from one of its recent publications—omitting, however, approximately $277,704,000 granted in the form of military supplies and services (because the distribution among the various countries is a state secret).[1]

TABLE 20

AID TO LATIN AMERICA BY THE U. S. GOVERNMENT, FISCAL YEARS 1946-1955

(In Thousands of Dollars)

Country	Grants	Credits Utilized	Total
Argentina	$ 198	$ 101,675	$ 101,873
Bolivia	30,833	37,605	68,438
Brazil	21,047	575,176	596,223
Chile	9,499	121,546	131,045
Colombia	6,116	60,992	67,108
Costa Rica	5,953	702	6,655
Cuba	1,249	26,490	27,739
Dominican Republic	1,678	......	1,678
Ecuador	7,547	23,705	31,252
El Salvador	3,708	576	4,284
Guatemala	8,711	132	8,843
Haiti	9,367	15,091	24,458
Honduras	4,569	223	4,792
Mexico	104,658	226,669	331,327
Nicaragua	2,896	600	3,496
Panama	5,216	4,000	9,216
Paraguay	7,245	795	8,040
Peru	13,394	21,596	34,990
Uruguay	1,892	11,554	13,446
Venezuela	2,069	13,301	15,370
Unspecified	11,088	5,952	17,040
Total, Latin America	$ 258,933	$1,248,380	$1,507,313

The following items account for most of the $258,993,000 in grants: Technical assistance and economic development, $227,146,000; famine and urgent relief, $19,844,000; agricultural commodities donated through private agencies, $6,119,000. Over 60 per cent of this total of nearly $259 million went to three countries: Mexico, Bolivia, and Brazil. Most of the sums granted to Mexico were spent in efforts to eradicate the hoof-and-mouth disease that had attacked its herds of cattle. A major portion of the grants to Bolivia was for the purpose of ameliorating hunger. The grants to Brazil were large primarily because Brazil is a large as well as a needy nation, and, like the grants to the other republics, were mainly in the form of technical aid. Among the smaller countries, Guatemala, Haiti, Costa Rica, and Panama were especially favored. The largest loans—mainly through the Export-Import Bank—were extended to Brazil and Mexico. The former, of course, is the biggest nation in Latin America in both population and area and the latter has more inhabitants than any other except Brazil; moreover, both countries were strongly emphasizing manufacturing industries, as were Chile, Colombia, and a few others. The Dominican Republic utilized no United States government credits; its long-term dictator had ample revenues. Having comparatively large income from petroleum, Venezuela utilized only a few millions, while six other countries, five of them in Central America, made use of only a few hundred thousand each. The borrowings of Bolivia and Haiti responded to peculiarly urgent needs for outside capital.

The Department of Commerce's Office of Business Economics, in the publication referred to above, took no account of the contributions of the United States government to the Inter-American and related highways. It included these, however, in a subsequent report.[2] The highway total for the period under inspection amounted to $24,123,000, distributed as indicated in Table 21.

Most of the contributions to roads went to Central America for the construction of the Inter-American Highway, which runs from the northern boundary of Mexico to the Panama Canal, and for building the Rama Road, which will eventually extend from that highway across Nicaragua to the vicinity of the Caribbean Sea. These grants, and much larger ones authorized by the United States Congress in 1955, attracted little public attention in the United States or South America.

The United States government also granted during the decade in review slightly more than $3,974,000 to the Organization of the American States, to be expended in regional technical-aid projects in Latin America; and this contribution amounted to

TABLE 21

Contributions by the U. S. Government to the Inter-American and Related Highways, Fiscal Years 1946-1955

(In Thousands of Dollars)

Country	Contribution
Bolivia	$ 79
Colombia	13
Dominican Republic	7
El Salvador	619
Honduras	908
Nicaragua	6,479
Peru	55
Brazil	9
Costa Rica	6,641
Ecuador	126
Guatemala	6,576
Haiti	31
Panama	2,580
Total, Latin America	$24,123

approximately $4,551,000 by the end of calendar year 1955. The latter sum was no less than 70 per cent of the aggregate grants made by the members of this Pan-American organization. Table 22 will indicate the sums paid in by the Latin American governments.[3]

The contributions of even the largest of the Latin-American republics to this OAS technical program were only a small percentage of the grants made by the United States. But just as the United States government appropriated more than 70 per cent of the aggregate fund, so five of the Latin-American governments provided over 70 per cent of the Latin-American contributions. Mexico and Peru appear to have been somewhat remiss. Cuba and Uruguay were the most magnanimous of the smaller countries.

The case of the OAS technical cooperation funds is almost typical, so far as the United States is concerned, of the budgets of the various Pan-American organizations. The Washington government, during the first postwar decade, paid from 65 to 75 per cent of their total expenses, although it had managed to

TABLE 22

CONTRIBUTIONS OF THE LATIN-AMERICAN COUNTRIES TO THE OAS PROGRAM OF TECHNICAL COOPERATION, CALENDAR YEARS, 1951-1955

(In Thousands of Dollars)

Country	Contribution
Argentina	$ 463.7
Brazil	684.4
Colombia	172.3
Cuba	85.5
Ecuador	28.2
Guatemala	27.0
Honduras	19.3
Nicaragua	19.0
Paraguay	15.0
Uruguay	79.9
Bolivia	14.8
Chile	139.2
Costa Rica	15.6
Dominican Republic	30.0
El Salvador	25.1
Haiti	10.0
Mexico	73.8
Panama	16.1
Peru	31.5
Venezuela	105.7
Total, Latin America	$2,056.1
(Total, U. S. A.	$4,550.7)

reduce its share of the burden before the end of the period—under pressure from the appropriations committees of the House and the Senate. Comparative assessments for the year 1956[4] are set forth in Table 23, which shows that the share levied against the United States was still 65.15 per cent. The most expensive of these institutions were the Pan American Union, the Pan American Sanitary Bureau, and the Inter-American Institute of Agricultural Sciences (with its plant and experimental farms in Costa Rica).

The United States government extended very substantial aid to Latin America during these years through the United Nations and its affiliated special agencies. World-Bank loans aggregating $579.2 million were made to several countries of the region dur-

TABLE 23

SCALE OF ASSESSMENTS, INTER-AMERICAN ORGANIZATIONS, FOR THE YEAR 1956

Organization	The United States Assessment	%	Latin America Assessment	%
Pan American Union*	$2,630,311	66.00	$1,355,009	34.00
Pan American Sanit. Bureau	1,386,000	66.00	714,000	34.00
Inter-American Institute of Agricultural Sciences*	210,000	69.68	89,485	30.32
Pan American Institute of Geography and History*	49,260	39.41	75,740	60.59
Amer. Internat'l Institute for the Protection of Childhood	10,000	28.69	24,850	71.31
Pan Amer. Ry. Congress Ass'n	5,000	39.91	7,528	60.09
Inter-Amer. Indian Institute*	4,800	17.39	22,800	82.61
Inter-Amer. Radio Office	5,682	25.51	16,592	74.49
Total	$4,301,053	65.15	$2,306,004	34.85

* For fiscal year 1957; the other items are for calendar year 1956.

ing fiscal years 1948-55,[5] and the United States not only supplied a major part of the capital of the bank but also influenced its loan policies. Grants allocated by the UN Technical Assistance Board to Latin America during 1950-1955 totaled $19,725.4, and the United States government contributed indirectly more than 51 per cent of this sum. Grants bestowed by the UN Children's Fund's Executive Board aggregated some $15,865.4, of which the United States government supplied over 67 per cent. Latin America's share of these two indirect grants from the big neighbor amounted to approximately $21 million, and Latin Americans probably would not have received the rest without its leadership and largess. Of course, the Latin-American governments made gifts to the two central funds from which they received aid. Their total contributions to the UN Children's Fund amounted to nearly 23.5 per cent of their grants, and their contributions to the UN Technical Assistance Board aggregated 28.8 per cent of their grants. But some countries, as one might expect, contributed much more than others to these two world organizations. In fact, payments to them exceeded grants from them in four instances—Argentina, Cuba, Venezuela, and Uruguay—almost tallied in the case of the Dominican Republic, and ran from approximately 33 per cent of the grants in the cases of Chile and Colombia to nearly 57 per cent in the case of Brazil. The other republics, however, made only token contributions to UNCF and UNTAB. Net benefits received by Latin America as a whole from these global organizations amounted to some $26,180,900. Table 24 shows the distribution of these grants among the various countries.[6]

TABLE 24

ALLOCATIONS TO LATIN AMERICA BY UNCF AND THE UN TECHNICAL ASSISTANCE BOARD FROM THE BEGINNING THROUGH 1955

(In Thousands of Dollars)

Country	UNCF	UNTAB
Argentina	$......	$ 15.3
Bolivia	539.3	1,227.6
Brazil	3,167.1	2,229.9
Chile	1,251.8	1,279.7
Colombia	913.4	1,086.0
Costa Rica	409.6	588.3
Cuba	.....	80.3
Dominican Republic	158.4	237.3
Ecuador	983.7	1,545.0
El Salvador	730.0	938.0
Guatemala	697.2	620.0
Haiti	1,101.8	984.6
Honduras	323.6	348.0
Mexico	3,412.5	1,288.4
Nicaragua	513.5	281.3
Panama	183.3	424.5
Paraguay	337.3	1,010.2
Peru	1,063.1	634.9
Uruguay	79.8	213.1
Venezuela	.....	312.0
Regional	.....	4,381.0
Total	$15,865.4	$19,725.4

It should be noted further that Latin-American assessments in connection with the regular budgets, largely administrative, of the United Nations and its affiliated special agencies were very small in comparison with those paid by the United States, which were more than four times larger than theirs for calendar year 1956 and five or six times larger during the early part of the decade under consideration. As in the case of the Pan-American agencies, Latin Americans shared the benefits of these world organizations—whatever these benefits were—at a low cost because the government and the people of the United States carried a heavy portion of the expense. Table 25 offers a general comparative view of assessments for calendar year 1956. Although individual assessments for each of the Latin-American republics are not tabulated here, it is noteworthy that with the exception of Brazil in the case of ICAO and of both Brazil and Argentina in that of the ITU not one of these countries contributed as much as 2 per cent to any of the regular budgets of these global institutions. In fact, the combined assessments of

TABLE 25

THE UN AND AFFILIATED SPECIAL AGENCIES: ASSESSMENTS AGAINST THE U. S. A. AND LATIN AMERICA, CALENDAR YEAR 1956

Organization	U.S.A. Amount	Per Cent of Total Budget	Latin America Amount	Per Cent of Total Budget
United Nations	$16,108,389	33.33	$2,720,979	5.63
United Nations Educational, Social, and Cultural Organization	3,152,574	30.00	542,242	5.16
Internat'l Civil Aviation Organization	891,729	33.31	258,605	9.64
World Health Organization	3,410,140	31.64	604,270	5.56
Food and Agricultural Organization	2,034,900	31.50	458,015	7.09
International Labor Organization	1,848,932	25.00	509,566	7.01
Internat'l Telecommunications Union	484,000	8.95	924,000	17.11
World Meteorological Organization	59,660	15.48	34,540	9.13
Total Assessments	$27,990,324	30.44	$6,052,217	6.58
(Total UN and Agency Budgets			$91,943,032)	

eleven of the nations—the smaller republics—usually amounted to less than that percentage and were little more than token payments.[7]

Such were the main ways in which the United States gave economic and technical assistance amounting to a total of around $1.7 billion to its Latin neighbors during the ten years following June 30, 1945. There were also a few others, but the magnitude of the aid given through them cannot be assessed with precision, either because information from Latin America is lacking or for some other reason. In connection with the cultural exchange programs, for example, Latin Americans certainly received far more than they gave, although the difference cannot be ascertained without full access to their expenditures on such programs. Latin Americans attended numerous "American-sponsored schools" during this period—elementary and secondary schools which received total grants of more than $1,332,000 from the United States government—but these educational institutions (operating in Latin America) were given this assistance in part, or even mainly, with the view of providing better accommodations for the children of citizens of the United States residing in the region, especially the children of members of the various foreign services; so that even after inspecting statistics of total costs and total enrollments it would not be easy to apportion the benefits accurately among the various recipients. A similar problem is likewise involved in measuring the benefits accruing to Latin America from the Gorgas Memorial Laboratory, which was established in Panama City in 1928 on the presumption that it would be financed by all of the members of the Pan American Union, but was supported by Latin America only to the extent of nominal cash contributions (in 1929 and 1931, respectively) from Ecuador and Venezuela and a building and some land from the Republic of Panama.[8] Its official support during fiscal years 1946-1955 came solely from the United States government, which appropriated to this research laboratory an aggregate of close to a million dollars.[9] Devoted to the investigation of tropical diseases and their cure, the laboratory no doubt made some discoveries of significance to tropical Latin America.

2.

Probably not fully aware of the extent and variety of the contributions that flowed out to Latin America from the United States, or of the magnitude of the Soviet danger as viewed by their large neighbor, the Latin-American leaders continued to complain. Disposed to compare the aid they obtained from the government in Washington, D. C., with the assistance that the war-harried and Soviet-imperiled nations of Europe received from the same source, rather than to measure their assistance in terms of the aid granted by the United States to countries with problems similar to—and in some instances much graver than—their own, they felt that they had been relegated to a minor place in the esteem of their big associate in North America. Perhaps they would feel somewhat less aggrieved if they could view their needs and handicaps in the light of those of several of the African and Asian countries; such, for instance, as the nations dealt with in the tabulations which will conclude this survey.

Table 26, compiled from data supplied by the Department of Commerce's Office of Business Economics, summarizes the assistance (again excluding military aid) extended by the United States government to 18 underdeveloped nations of Asia and Africa. Seven of these—Iraq, Israel, Jordan, Lebanon, Liberia, Libya, and Syria—have small populations comparable to the populations of Uruguay, Paraguay, Ecuador, Bolivia, the six republics of Central America, and the three little island nations in the Caribbean. Saudi Arabia's inhabitants, around 7,000,000, corresponded roughly with the 5,440,000 of Venezuela, similarly rich in petroleum. Afghanistan's numbered 12,000,000; Colombia's 12,108,000. Burma's totaled 19,045,000 and Argentina's 18,393,000. Ethiopia's population numbered 16,104,000; Thailand's 19,556,000; Iran's 20,253,000; the Philippine Republic's

21,039,000; Egypt's 21,935,000. The aggregate for Mexico was 28,052,000, but the total was only some 9,035,000 for Peru and 6,072,000 for Chile. India's inhabitants probably numbered no less than 372,000,000; Pakistan's 75,842,000; and Indonesia's 78,163,000. In contrast, Brazil, the most populous country of Latin America was occupied by 55,772,000. The total for Latin America was 166,075,202; the total for the 18 Asiatic and African countries listed in Table 27 was 678,621,000.[10] But these Asiatic and African nations received *direct* economic and technical assistance from the United States government amounting to only $2,473,164,000 during the first postwar decade, while Latin America, with hardly a fourth of their population, received $1,507,313,000; and the Philippine Republic and Israel, both special cases because of unique circumstances, account for

TABLE 26

U. S. GOVERNMENT AID TO SEVERAL COUNTRIES OF ASIA AND AFRICA, FISCAL YEARS 1946-1955

(In Thousands of Dollars)

Country	Grants	Credits Utilized	Total
Afghanistan	$ 2,909	$ 23,734	$ 26,643
Burma	20,505	5,043	25,548
Egypt	21,451	17,934	39,385
Ethiopia	6,932	3,399	10,331
India	131,459	232,391	363,850
Indonesia	109,218	145,136	254,354
Iran	157,884	64,384	222,268
Iraq	5,945	889	6,834
Israel	231,363	140,440	371,803
Jordan	21,038	.....	21,038
Lebanon	11,926	1,550	13,476
Liberia	5,609	23,287	28,896
Libya	15,370	.....	15,370
Pakistan	121,639	15,136	136,775
Philippine Republic	745,462	133,329	878,791
Saudi Arabia	4,383	19,112	23,495
Syria	949	.....	949
Thailand	26,103	7,255	33,358
Total	$1,640,145	$ 833,019	$2,473,164

the difference. India, with far more than double Latin America's population, was the beneficiary of no more than $363,850,000.[11]

The United States was not linked with these countries by ties like the Organization of the American States and its associated agencies. Such additional aid as its government gave to Asiastic and African nations was indirect, channelled through various global institutions. But assistance donated through the United Nations Children's Fund and the UN Technical Assistance Board was considerably larger than the sums indirectly channelled through the same agencies to Latin America. The total for the 18 Asiatic and African countries was approximately $75.6 million, of which the United States contributed nearly $45 million; the total for Latin America was approximately $35.6 million, around $21 million being the portion donated by the United States. Details are presented in Table 27.[12] It should be

TABLE 27

ALLOCATIONS TO SEVERAL COUNTRIES OF ASIA AND AFRICA BY UNCF AND THE UN TECHNICAL ASSISTANCE BOARD FROM THE OUTSET THROUGH 1955

(In Thousands of Dollars)

Country	UNCF	UNTAB
Afghanistan	$ 621.3	$ 1,957.2
Burma	1,715.3	2,320.6
Egypt	1,503.2	1,759.1
Ethiopia	261.0	1,187.1
India	13,390.2	3,646.5
Indonesia	5,039.1	2,826.8
Iran	1,406.6	4,215.6
Iraq	1,146.1	1,828.0
Israel	1,109.0	1,734.3
Jordan	1,149.6	840.7
Lebanon	93.4	732.1
Liberia	352.3	1,030.5
Libya	328.5	2,801.1
Pakistan	4,402.9	3,905.6
Philippine Republic	2,510.2	1,406.7
Saudi Arabia	.....	525.7
Syria	497.8	1,371.1
Thailand	1,930.4	2,407.8
Regional (estimated)	.....	1,650.0
Total	$37,456.9	$38,146.5

noted, however, that these more distant nations, like those of Latin America, made contributions to these two global agencies —their aggregate grants to them amounted to over $10.7 million—which brought their own net receipts down to somewhat less than $65 million.

It will be recalled that World-Bank loans extended to Latin America through fiscal year 1955 amounted to a total of $579.2 million. Loans made by this bank to the 18 Asiatic and African nations—only Ethiopia, India, Iraq, Pakistan, and Thailand obtained loans[13]—aggregated a bit less than $24.5 million.

The contributions of the governments of these 18 countries to the regular budgets of the UN and affiliated special agencies during this decade were very small, only a trifle larger than those paid by the Latin-American governments. The data laid out in Table 28 will reveal their comparative insignificance.[14]

TABLE 28

THE UN AND AFFILIATED SPECIAL AGENCIES: SCALE OF ASSESSMENTS OF CERTAIN ASIATIC AND AFRICAN NATIONS, CALENDAR YEAR 1956

Organization	Amount	Per Cent of Total Budget
United Nations	$3,175,281	6.57
ICAO	212,231	7.91
FAO	543,286	8.41
ITU	624,800	11.54
UNESCO	626,311	5.96
WHO	685,220	6.37
ILO	525,837	7.11
WMO	37,671	9.78
Total	$6,430,637	7.00

(Total UN and Affiliated Budgets . . $91,943,230)

Comparison of the aid which these underdeveloped countries of the Old World received from the United States government during the decade immediately following the termination of the second World War with the assistance Latin America obtained from the same source appears to indicate that the Latin Americans ought not to assume that they have suffered grievous neglect. But whether they made the comparison or failed to make it, they did not cease to complain about their treatment. They probably preferred and would continue to prefer to be associated with Europe in connection with the "mutual-aid" programs; and they were most likely to appeal, as in the past, to the sentiment of Hemispheric Solidarity. Moreover, as they entered the second decade of the postwar era they seemed to be winning their case. The Eisenhower administration recommended in both fiscal year 1956 and fiscal year 1957 that they be granted larger assistance than usual, and in both years Congress voted bigger sums than the administration requested.[15]

No attempt will be made at this time to evaluate the efficacy of these multiple forms of assistance. The task will be left to others who are already busy with it.[16] The numerous experts employed by the several agencies, national and international, engaged in technical assistance and economic development seemed for the most part to be working with enthusiasm, if not always with prudence, as they tackled problems of public health and education, agriculture, irrigation, mining, manufacturing, electric power, transportation, public finance and administration, taxation, and even various others. The danger, as always, is that their enthusiasm will sag and they will no longer be dedicated missionaries of progress but mere bureaucrats primarily interested in the perpetuation of their jobs. They should be efficient; they are the highest paid missionaries the world has ever seen, and a few of them had been missionaries of the church before they became missionaries of the state. Nor should one fail to observe that private philanthropic organizations of the United States were never so busy or so prosperous. They not only received private gifts; they also received much larger gifts from the United States government in farm commodities and transportation costs.

The people of the United States were living—and might continue to live for an unpredictable period—in an era of compulsory charity. The relief distributed by these "Voluntary

Agencies" and others was by no means entirely voluntary. Their philanthropy was supported—probably would continue to be supported—mainly by contributions exacted from taxpayers of the United States, although it is unlikely that Latin-American or other recipients were—or would ever be—fully aware of that fact. Perhaps their unawareness will do no serious harm. It merely tends to enlarge their concept of American generosity, and particularly the generosity of the staffs of these so-called voluntary agencies, some members of which have become expert lobbyists in Washington. But this writer cannot avoid asking himself whether all these forms of compulsory benevolence—some of it imposed, of course, with the objective of promoting the security of the United States, but all of it closely linked with the personal interests of the distributors and those who profit from subsidized exports—will ever cease or even be much reduced, and to what extent such expenditures will eventually depress the levels of living of citizens of the United States engaged in cultural pursuits as well as the living levels of other low-income groups who must pay more than a fifth of their net incomes, less small allowable exemptions, in Federal taxes (not to mention state and local taxes, ever on the increase, or the drain of perpetually rising prices).

CHAPTER 6 THE INTER-AMERICAN HIGHWAY

THE Inter-American Highway is the remnant of a grandiose project, originated in the 1920's, that once envisaged an automobile road extending from the northern boundary of Mexico to the southern part of South America and, in some minds, northeastward from Argentina through Uruguay, Brazil, and the Guianas to a convenient point in Venezuela, perhaps Caracas. First thought of as a Pan-American Highway, the project probably represented no more than the transformed vision of a Pan-American Railway that had thrilled James G. Blaine and Andrew Carnegie and driven Hinton Rowan Helper stark mad.[1] By the early 1930's however, this 10,000-mile dream had been reduced to a more modest 3,300 miles or so, the approximate distance between Nuevo Laredo and Panama City. In fact, the part in which the United States was to become involved through the State Department embraced only the some 1,600 miles stretching from the northern boundary of Guatemala to the Canal Zone, for the Mexican government soon gave assurance that it would look after its more than 1,700 miles either with its ordinary revenues or with funds borrowed abroad (namely, in the United States).[2]

No overwhelming task of research is required to determine who these highway enthusiasts of the 1920's were. By the exercise of average imagination they might even be identified without investigation. But it is usually advisable to buttress imagination with facts. And the facts clearly indicate that the main promoters of this highway project, whether in its grandiose or in its more restricted form, were the business interests and public officials of the United States: (1) The National Automobile Chamber of Commerce, representing the producers of automotive vehicles; (2) manufacturers of rubber tires; (3) the American Road Builders' Association; (4) the Society of Automotive Engineers; (5) the Society for the Promotion of Engineering Education; (6) State highway commissioners and engineers; (7) manufacturers of road-building machinery; (8) producers of materials such as steel and cement used in the construction of highways; (9) the United States Army Engineers; (10) the United States Bureau of Public Roads, called for a time the Public Roads Administration and shifted during the decades under consideration from the Department of Agriculture to the Federal Works Agency and then to the Department of Commerce; (11) investment bankers who hoped to profit as salesmen of highway bonds. Representatives of all these interests were among the conspicuous promoters of both the larger and the smaller highway schemes.[3] Their activities illustrate the dynamics of business enterprise. Students of advertising could examine their methods with profit.

The promoters utilized Pan-American congresses and conferences, brought Latin-American officials, businessmen, and engineers to the United States to inspect its best highways, persuaded those already in the country for other purposes to make inspections, induced journalists to champion their cause, and solicited the support of chief executives and cabinet heads, of senators and congressmen.[4] A few of the legislators were given free trips to Latin America as delegates to various Pan-American assemblies; others, especially if they were from Michigan or Ohio, centers of the automobile and rubber industries, either needed no persuasion or could easily be convinced of the importance of the highway.[5] At first, the promoters financed themselves. They asked the Federal Government for no money. They merely requested a little of the time of influential officials: the President, secretaries or assistant secretaries of administrative departments[6] and bureaus, the director of the Pan American

Union. When they began to ask for appropriations, they requested very small sums: $15,000 in 1925 to pay the expenses of a delegation to a highway congress at Buenos Aires and another $15,000 in 1927-1928 for the expenses of a delegation to a highway congress that finally was held in Rio de Janeiro in 1929. Friendly road resolutions at other Pan-American assemblies cost the United States Treasury almost nothing; representatives were sent to these for many other purposes. By 1929, however, the promoters were urging Congress to appropriate $50,000 for a "reconnaissance survey" from the Panama Canal to the southern boundary of Mexico.

These small appropriations encountered little opposition. Fears that they might be used as a precedent for much larger sums in the future were allayed by the assurance that not one dollar would be taken from the United States Treasury to build a single mile of highway in Latin America and that private enterprise would take care of the financing.[7]

Assurance of high regard for the taxpayer is always a safe and sane procedure. Planners of raids on the United States Treasury should never reveal to Congress at the outset the full magnitude of an enterprise, all the problems that it might encounter, or an even approximate estimate of ultimate costs. It is always better to exert pressure on legislators very gradually, step by step. Perhaps the truth of the matter in this instance is that the original promoters did not intend to request much more than this $80,000 from the national government. They probably supposed that they could depend upon private financing for the rest. They were none too familiar with the climate, topography, and meager public revenues of Latin America. At any rate, no further funds were solicited from the Republican administrations of the period.

Meantime the program of "highway education" was given full swing. Latin Americans were feasted, junketed, publicized, and organized.[8] Friendly senators and congressmen inserted their speeches in the *Record* (and probably franked them out to constituents).[9] Presidents and cabinet officers were quoted in support of the project.[10] It may be that the most persuasive arguments employed by the promoters were to the effect that the great highway would stimulate United States exports and provide opportunity for investment; but those most emphasized were arguments calculated to stir emotions and stimulate the pride of long vision and grand achievement. The memory of Blaine and his magnificent railway idea was revived. The glory of ancient Rome was recalled. Was not the permanence of the Roman Empire based upon good roads whose remains could still be seen in Europe? For many centuries no other country had constructed such highways. Little progress in this art had been made since Rome fell. But now the turn of the United States had come. The United States had no desire to rival Rome in the realm of empire, but it could easily surpass the Romans in the construction of highways. By building long hard-surfaced ribbons at home and promoting them abroad, it could perpetuate its fame for five thousand years. By promoting the construction of this Inter-American Highway it could also cultivate the friendship of its neighbors.[11]

In the meantime, likewise, the reconnaissance survey through the length of Central America was in progress. Started in June, 1930, it was completed in May, 1933. Army aviators participated in several sections. But Franklin D. Roosevelt already had turned Herbert Hoover out of the White House before the engineers and aviators came home.

2.

The survey report of the Bureau of Public Roads, transmitted to the President by Secretary Cordell Hull, to whom it had been transmitted by Secretary Henry Wallace, was promptly published as *Senate Document* No. 224, under the title of "Proposed Inter-American Highway." It contained several passages of purple prose composed by Henry Wallace or Thomas MacDonald:

"The idea of an inter-American highway from the United States to Panama stirs the imagination.... It will cross the trails of conquistador, buccaneer, filibusterer, missionary, and settler, associated with all the glamour of empire building on a magnificent plan, of sordid gold hunting, of human slavery, governmental inefficiency, and finally revolt, independence, and a slow and difficult struggle against the fortuitous events of an unkind history."

Again, vaulting imagination and glowing humanitarianism:

"One of the unique advantages of the North American Continent is that it embraces both the Temperate and the Tropical Zones, and that between the two there are no mountain or water barriers.... The highly developed areas of the north and central portions ... are contiguous to the potentially rich but less developed areas of the south, and direct overland communication between them in feasible.

"This is the basic economic fact presented by the proposed inter-American highway. To perfect the connection between these two complementary regions ... only highway transportation is lacking. With road connections established, the resultant benefits in exchange of goods, in development of natural resources, in growth of tourist traffic, in higher standards of living in areas hitherto barred from economic progress by lack of communication, and in interchange of ideas and international amity, appear manifest.... As a missionary, a highway has no equal. Good roads make for good neighborliness."

Finally, a long view and a further suggestion of national interest:

"This highway has been thought of as an automotive sales outlet, as a tourist attraction, and as a trade-in-general stimulator. It would be all of these, no doubt.... But the possibilities do not end here. Throughout a very long period ... we have been dependent upon the Far East and the Antipodes for many commodities. . . . Among these may be mentioned hard rice, tea, cinnamon, and other spices and condiments, camphor, quinine, and other medicinals and drugs, rubber, copra, many . . . vegetable and essential oils, . . . copal . . . , abaca hemp, and insecticide plants. . . . What could be more prescient than to encourage, induce, and expand these commodities . . . in the Central American countries, engender versatility in agriculture, and help [them to] abandon the one-crop system? The consummation of such a program would . . . raise their standards of living to a salutary level."[12]

With the arrival of the "New Dealers" in Washington, ideas regarding the financing of the highway changed and bureaucrats began to replace businessmen as chief promoters. Private financing and private enterprise were no longer lauded. "Tax and tax, spend and spend" may not be an accurate description of New Deal economic policy, but Roosevelt and the men around him were determined to use the contents of the Treasury in a mighty effort to lift the nation out of the economic depression and abate the miseries of the unemployed; and one of the many schemes which invited their interest as offering relief was the building of the Inter-American Highway. Granted the permission of Mexico, the Central American countries, and Congress, they would have spent tax money to help with the construction of the entire 3,300 miles between Nuevo Laredo and Panama. The Mexican government, however, was still determined to build its own roads, and Washington legislators were reluctant to unlock the vaults of the Treasury. Asked in 1934 for an appropriation of $5 million, Congress grudgingly granted only a fifth of that sum, mainly for the construction of bridges.[13] Nor did the national legislature make further appropriations of much consequence during the years preceding Pearl Harbor. It merely allowed the Public Roads Administration to utilize some of its administrative funds to keep a few engineers in Central America to aid and encourage its highway bureaus. Total expenditures of the United States on the Inter-American Highway before this country entered the "shooting war" late in 1941 amounted to less than $3 million.[14]

But the war crisis blew the Treasury wide open. Before the end of 1941 Congress authorized the expenditure of $20 million on this highway, on two conditions: (1) the Central American governments must agree to expend at least $10 million and (2) the entire $30 million must be spent under the auspices of the State Department and under supervision of the Public Roads Administration of the United States. One of the inducements for legislative liberality was the assumption that this $30 million would finish the project. Another was the allegation that the road might be required for military defense.[15] By July, 1943, however, the Federal Works Agency, pleading the cause of the State Department and the Public Roads Administration, was asking for $12 million more to be expended on the construction of a "particularly difficult gap" through the rough and rainy mountains of Costa Rica, the "excessive cost of which was not foreseen."[16] And Congress responded once more. Thus, within a period of about eighteen months, a total expenditure of $32 million was authorized, and most of this sum was actually appropriated by the time World War II terminated.[17]

Nor was this all, by any means. The War Department was voted so many billions that it could not miss a few millions; and the Army Engineers, supposedly operating in collaboration with the State Department and the Public Roads Administration, promptly undertook the construction of a "pioneer road," which really meant a military road, or rather the completion in a rough manner of the Inter-American Highway. Although this would require the building of scattered sections adding up to an aggregate of over 900 miles, the Engineers set to work in 1942 with the ostensibly optimistic expectation of finishing the task by May of 1943. They surveyed and constructed for considerably more than a year, spent a net of over $36 million, built only 347 miles of shoddy road, and then abandoned Central America. They probably wasted at least $23 million, and their haste and waste boomeranged. Investigation by a Senate committee in 1946-1947 suggested that the recommendations of high army officials had been either doubtful, equivocal, or adverse, and that the Army Engineers, long associated with the "pork-barrel," had foolishly rushed in where wiser men had feared to tread and fouled a project that had been implemented slowly and gradually in the dry seasons that prevailed in Central America during only half of each year. To work during the rainy period and at the height of preparations for a terrible war was to work expensively and under impossible handicaps: mud, landslides, low priorities for machinery and materials, scarcity of shipping facilities. The most efficient construction companies were uninterested. Companies which showed an interest laid down hard terms and exacted exorbitant contracts. It was all very depressing.[18]

3.

To secure appropriations to finish the highway proved very difficult. No large sums were obtained for the fiscal years ending June 30, 1948, 1949, and 1950. Congress went no further than to authorize the spending of $100,000 of Public Roads Administration funds every year or so in order to prevent complete interruption and deterioration.

Then, in 1950, the Departments of State and Commerce—the Public Roads Administration, resuming its title of Bureau of Public Roads, had just been shifted to the Commerce Department—executed a clever maneuver. They consolidated their request for funds for the Inter-American Highway with their request for funds for domestic highways, for which large sums were needed because of neglect during the war period. The success of such tactics in peacetime had already been demonstrated, at least to some extent, in 1934, when the request for $5 million was buried by Harry Hopkins and Harold Ickes in huge requests for relief and public works. Moreover, in 1950, Dennis Chavez, always a champion of large expenditures for highways and always eager to extend a helping hand to Latin-American relatives whose language he spoke, was chairman of the Senate Committee on Public Works. The two executive departments primarily concerned now summoned the courage to ask the committee over which Senator Chavez presided for an authorization of $64 million to be spent during the following eight years, under the supervision and direction of the State Department and the Bureau of Public Roads, for the completion of a highway that originally was expected to cost the United States only a trifle but had already taken from the Treasury at least $71 million!

The maneuver was not entirely successful. Eight million dollars were authorized for the next two fiscal years, but only a total of $7 million was appropriated for the biennium. The maneuver was repeated in 1952, with even less success. The appropriation for fiscal 1953 fell slightly short of a million and for fiscal 1954 and fiscal 1955 the appropriation was no more than a million each year. The promoters had asked for an aggregate of $64 million to be expended over a period of eight years. They had been voted a little less than $10 million during the first five years of the period. In addition, they were permitted to extract $100,000 annually from the administration fund of the Bureau of Public Roads. But they would still need far more than $54 million to finish the highway, and they probably would not be able to complete it before 1965 unless they could manage to obtain much larger appropriations. A period of 35 or 40 years would be required and an aggregate of at least $136 million, probably as much as $140 million, would have to be expended in order to finish a project which originally envisaged a time-span of something short of a decade and a contribution of only a few hundred thousand.[19]

As of April 1954, the state of the Inter-American Highway

was as follows: Mexico had finished its part, but the long stretch through Central America, currently estimated at 1,590 miles, was far from complete. Less than half of it, no more than 719 miles, was in satisfactory condition. Three segments, amounting to a total of 186 miles—Guatemala, 25; Costa Rica, 147; Panama 14—were impassable. The mileage of all-weather road was 1,368, with only 484 of this described as "paved" and with only another 235 said to be "good." And the word paved did not necessarily signify concrete; it only meant that some of the 484 miles was probably made of concrete and that the rest was merely graveled and oiled. Moreover, there was the further problem of maintenance, the cost of which the United States might have to share.[20]

Such had been the role of the new and benevolent Rome in Central America, not an inexpensive role. But no doubt the highway would be completed some day. The United States would spend more money to salvage what had already been spent and describe the expenditure as "technical aid."[21] For purposes of highway construction and repair, Central America (if not Mexico) had become a part of the national domain of the United States, with the State Department as the negotiator and superviser and the Bureau of Public Roads as the construction agency. This expansion of a roadbuilding enterprise had been, and would continue to be, hard on the new Roman taxpayers. Compared with the other burdens thrust upon them by the Washington government in these austere days, however, the load might seem light. The State Department must hold a key to the Treasury in order to achieve its objectives. Until the arrival of calmer times and better diplomats, diplomatic brains and capacity to persuade must be supplemented by gold.

So far, if heavy expenditures are subtracted from the profits of trade, the highway had been of little economic value to the United States. Its commerce had increased since the 1920's with the countries which the road traverses, but for other reasons in the main. When completed, the road probably would not be much used for military transport to the Canal Zone. A single bomb exploded on almost any section of it, particularly on any of the mountainous sections of Guatemala and Costa Rica, would interrupt traffic, and the "Berlin lift" of the early postwar period had clearly demonstrated the superiority of air over land transportation. The highway had perhaps stimulated the economic development of Central America, although the extent of the stimulus cannot easily be assessed, and would contribute even more to such development when finally finished. Whether this economic development would help to "keep the Communists away" was not entirely certain, for poverty may not be the sole seed-bed of Communism. No matter what benefits this expensive highway had brought to the United States and its near neighbors in the past, no matter what mutual benefits it might confer in the future, these could never justify the waste of the Army Engineers, the deceptions of the highway's promoters, or the slipshod estimates of eventual costs.[22]

In a letter dated March 31, 1955, President Dwight Eisenhower recommended an appropriation of $74,980,000 to complete the construction of the highway during the next three years. The letter was addressed to Vice-President Richard M. Nixon, who transmitted it to the Senate shortly afterward. The President declared that the highway would have political, economic, and strategic value and urged its prompt completion. Ignoring the haste and waste of the Army Engineers, he stated that the government of the United States had expended $53,723,-000 on the project.[23]

Two Senators, George Malone of Nevada and Dennis Chavez of New Mexico, commented enthusiastically on the President's message the day it was received. Malone, who had never voted for any grants by the United States to the non-American world, not only favored the completion of this road but advocated the completion of the Pan-American Highway all the way to Chile and Brazil. Chavez, an enthusiast for automobile roads anywhere in the Americas and one of Latin America's most devoted friends in the Senate, contended that the leaders of the region wanted help, not mere promises, and described in glowing terms the economic, cultural, and political benefits the highway would eventually confer.[24]

The next day (Pan-American Day), April 14, Representative Brooks Hays of Arkansas made an address in support of Eisenhower's recommendation. Dwelling on arguments similar to those presented by Chavez and the President, Hays contended that "prompt favorable action" should be taken. And it was on the same day that the House of Representatives voted an appropriation to continue the construction of Nicaragua's Rama Road.[25] Malone, Chavez, and Hays all mentioned trips they had made over the Inter-American Highway. Such junkets, usually at the expense of taxpayers, may not be unimportant in gaining votes for appropriations. Congressional action on President Eisenhower's recommendation for the highway was rather complicated. The sum of $74,980,000, to be expended during 1956-1958, seems to have been authorized with the view of securing appropriations of around $25 million each year for three fiscal years with the hope of finishing the road; but in the end the appropriation was reduced to $62,980,000, to be available until expended, on the theory that more leisurely construction would be less expensive but that this entire sum should be voted in 1955 in order to give assurance to Central America.[26]

The presumption was that the highway would be finished within four or five years instead of three. But completion would depend upon additional expenditures amounting to $20 million or more by the Central American governments, and it was unlikely that they would make this supplementary money available without additional grants or loans from the United States government. Although both the State Department and the Commerce Department were aware of this difficulty by virtue of previous experience, neither said a word about it during the entire period of discussion—at any rate no statement from them appears in the record.[27]

Moreover, upkeep will be a problem. Little risk is assumed in making the prediction that the United States will be urged to share the expense of keeping the road in good repair. Nor is serious risk involved in the predicting that the United States will be prodded into the appropriation of funds for the Pan-American Highway, of which the Inter-American is a part, from the Canal Zone to southern South America. Pressure will be exerted in Washington both by the Latin Americans and by interested groups in the United States: construction companies, manufacturers of automotive vehicles and equipment, ardent opponents of Communism, and diplomats who insist on utilizing the contents of the Treasury to facilitate their negotiations.

CHAPTER 7 THE LEVERAGE OF THE
CANAL ZONES

CONTROL of two Canal Zones in Central America, one in Panama and the other in Nicaragua, has cost the government of the United States many millions and seems destined to cost millions more. The original sum paid to Panama for the utilization of the zone across her territory was $10 million, to which was later added $25 million, contributed to Colombia as a sort of appeasement for Theodore Roosevelt's aiding and abetting the secession of Panama shortly before the canal concession was acquired from the latter in 1904. The perpetual option secured from Nicaragua in 1916 occasioned the expenditure of another $3 million, and the agreement with Panama provided for a perpetual annuity of $250,000 a year, payable in gold dollars. These are well-known facts. But the continuous pressures by officials of these Central American governments are not so familiar to the general public in the United States. The utilization of the Panama zone and the retention of the option on the Nicaragua zone provide the two countries with leverages which they wield in times of crisis to pry open the United States Treasury—or rather with effective self-serving arguments, which they employ as often as favorable opportunities permit.

Panama exacted a heavy toll—more than a million dollars—during World War II for the use of airfields outside of the zone by the United States government in the defense of the canal and incidentally of the Republic of Panama itself. Acting on the unfounded assumption that the United States government acquired the zone in Nicaragua for the purpose of building another canal and not with the objective of *preventing* the construction of another such means of interoceanic communication, the Nicaraguan dictator insisted during the war period that additional payment should be made to his government to compensate for the damage suffered from the failure to open the canal across his country. In both instances the use of the lever was effective. When would it be used again? Would such intermittent payments turn out to be unending? Would the United States, so generous in its spending in other parts of the world, succumb to pressures from these and other countries of the Western Hemisphere until its expenditures in the New World came to equal those made in the Old?

Would Panama try to follow the example of Egypt in respect to Suez? Contending that the Suez Canal and the Panama Canal "had fundamental analogies," the Panamanian government complained in August, 1956, at the failure of the United States and Great Britain to invite it to send representatives to the conference convoked to consider the problem of the seizure of Suez by Egypt's dictator.[1]

The bounty bestowed upon Panama by the terms of a treaty signed with the United States on January 25, 1955, and approved by the United States Senate on July 29, 1955, amounted to some $39 million—real estate valued at $27 million and other favors calculated to cost the big neighbor $12 million—without including the eventual costs of placing Panamanian workers in the Canal Zone in the same status as American employees in respect to wages and retirement benefits, or the costs of raising the canal annuity from $430,000, to which it had been elevated shortly after the United States devalued the dollar in the 1930's, to $1,930,000—an exact million and a half each year, granted in perpetuity.

No difficulty was encountered in securing the Senate's consent to this treaty, although some members seemed to be troubled for one or more of the following reasons: (1) Panama would be left free during the next international crisis as in that of World

War II to charge the United States a heavy price for the use of airfields beyond the Canal Zone; (2) coverage of aliens under the United States Civil Service Retirement List would involve unpredictable expenses; (3) senators friendly with the shipping interests of the United States feared that the canal tolls would soon be increased. Regarding the employment of the lever by Panama the Senate disclosed no resentment.[2]

2.

The Rama Road was planned and partly constructed as a war secret. Its existence was not revealed to members of Congress until 1946. The motives of its projectors and builders were not fully disclosed even a decade later, but the highway had ceased to be a mystery by 1952, when Congress finally decided to authorize appropriations to extend it toward its destination.

Senator Homer Ferguson, member of a special committee set up to investigate the national defense program, had his curiosity aroused in the summer of 1946 while inspecting the work of the Army Engineers and the United States Public Road Administration in Central America. Driving with his special assistant, George Meader, along the Inter-American Highway some 22 miles north of Managua, he spied a spur road running away toward the east. He asked a representative of the Public Roads Administration in Nicaragua some embarassing questions and obtained rather unsatisfactory, if not evasive, answers. He learned enough, however, to conclude that this spur was the work of the Public Roads Administration or of Nicaraguans under its supervision—and that construction costs were being paid by the United States Treasury.[3]

Ferguson and Meader returned to the United States with the determination to shed more light on this mysterious highway. The first witness they examined on the subject was Edwin W. James of the Public Roads Administration, Inter-American Regional Office:

"Senator Ferguson. Explain the Rama Road.

"Mr. James. I don't want to explain the Rama Road.

"Senator Ferguson. But I want you to. You are building it down there now. . . .

"Mr. James. All right, Mr. Senator. So far as I know that was an allotment of defense funds by President Roosevelt. . . .

"Senator Ferguson. Do you know when this agreement was made to give this $4,000,000? . . .

"Mr. James. As I recall it, we must have gotten the money on the Rama Road early in 1942 and the circumstances were peculiar. . . . You remember when President Somoza came to the United States about . . . 1939 and was received by a military cortege. . . . At that time a commitment of some kind must have been made and the White House probably made it. . . .

"Senator Ferguson. In other words, he wasn't only received with military honors, but with monetary honors. . . .

"Mr. James. That is what I have in mind exactly, a commitment of some sort was made and I have been told that the State Department knows nothing about it, and it is not protocol, when the White House does not volunteer information, to be asked for the information. . . . The Rama Road starts from San Benito . . . and extends to the town of Rama . . . at the head of navigation on the Escondido River. . . . San Benito to Rama is approximately 288 kilometers. . . .

"Senator Mitchell. What is there at Rama? . . . It could be a seaport?

"Mr. James. It could be. . . . The interruption is at the bar at the entrance to the Bluefields Lagoon. . . .

"Senator Ferguson. Do you know what it will cost to dredge that?

"Mr. James. I haven't any idea. . . .

"Senator Ferguson. Were you ever consulted as to what it would cost to build that road?

"Mr. James. We were. . . . Our first estimate . . . was $2,000,000 because they asked us what it would cost to build a road to the ordinary standards that Nicaragua was accustomed to build on her own account. . . . We envisaged an ordinary country road down there with water-bound macadam or gravel. Perhaps even a one-way road. . . . Before the matter was developed to the point where funds were made available we learned to our astonishment that somewhere a commitment was made to build a road to approximately the standards of the Inter-American Highway. . . . When they said that to us we protested . . . and we compromised on a highway narrower than the Inter-American. . . . The compromise was with the officials of the State Department . . . Mr. John Cabot and Mr. Phillip Bonsal. . . .

"Senator Ferguson. Now, maintenance is pretty heavy on that road? . . .

"Mr. James. It is pretty heavy on a road in a tropical country."[4]

Another witness, a retired officer of the Army Engineers named C. P. Gross, placed the road project in a longer perspective:

"Mr. Gross. . . . I was down there from 1929 to 1931 on a ship-canal survey. Having been 2 years in Nicaragua on that survey, the recommendation was . . . a third set of locks at Panama. That disappointed the people of Nicaragua greatly. They apparently appealed to the State Department over those years [1931-1939], and there was some desire . . . to please them. A request was made from Mr. Somoza's government for a survey of a barge canal, and I was sent down with a group to make a survey and a report. I was there some 3 months and left a small party to complete certain field work. . . . The estimate was so high and the commerce that it would develop so nebulous that it looked like money over the dam. . . . I made the recommendation that for the purposes they wished to achieve, to get their friendship, to do some good, . . . they could do far more by building a road, and I recommended the Rama Road.

"Senator Ferguson. Then, we were buying friendship by building the Rama Road.

"Mr. Gross. That was my recommendation. . . ."[5]

The mystery was beginning to dissolve. But Senator Ferguson could not convince himself that the President and the State Department of the United States had the right to use the money of American taxpayers to purchase the friendship of foreign countries. Moreover, he doubted that friendship could be bought once for all time. Such policies might involve repeated outlays and a permanent drain on the Treasury. He therefore continued to probe. Calling a third witness, a diplomat named John Cabot, then or recently a staff member of the State Department's Caribbean and Central American Affairs Division, Ferguson asked him what the Rama Road had to "do with the military emergency" and what legal obligation the State Department had assumed in respect to this highway. Cabot's testimony did not completely satisfy Ferguson, but it banished some of the clouds that had concealed the origin of the road project:

"Mr. Cabot. In 1916, the so-called Bryan-Chamorro Treaty was signed [ratified], by which we . . . had a permanent option to build a canal across Nicaragua and had certain other considerations given us, and we paid them . . . three million dollars. . . .

"In 1938, President Somoza began to complain that . . . we had this permanent option on what was probably the most valuable asset which Nicaragua possessed, but we hadn't used it, and, in effect, we were blocking the development of Nicaragua by our failure to do anything about it.

"There was a certain amount of equity in that, and when Somoza came to Washington in 1939, he took the matter up with President Roosevelt. . . .

"It was agreed and published at the time[6] that a survey would be made by the United States Engineers of the possibility of a barge canal. . . .

"When the army estimate came in, it . . . was thirty-five or forty million dollars, and obviously . . . the usage of the [barge] canal would not justify such an expenditure.

". . . There seems to have been some slight misunderstanding as to exactly what was said between President Roosevelt and President Somoza. Somoza had publicly declared in Nicaragua that President Roosevelt said that there would be a barge canal built."[7]

Here, then, was one of those executive agreements—or disagreements. Whether the compact was oral or written, Ferguson did not inquire; and the cautious Cabot answered no questions that were not asked. Noting, however, that James of the Public Roads Administration had attempted to shift responsibility for the decision to build an expensive highway to the State Department, Cabot sought to fix the blame on that powerful Federal bureau. Asked to state when the decision was reached to appease Somoza by constructing the highway, Cabot handed the investigators two "classified" documents: a letter by Assistant Secretary of State G. Howland Shaw, dated May 28, 1942, to Budget Director Harold D. Smith and a long enclosure which revealed that the Public Roads Administration had recommended this type of highway and presented several arguments in support of the project. Shaw, accepting the advice of the highway engineers, had requested a total of $4,555,000 from the President's Emergency Fund, stating that $4,500,000 would be expended on the Rama Road and $55,000 would be required to pay the cost of a survey from Rama, the eastern terminus of the projected highway, to El Bluff on the Caribbean Sea, and had remarked further that the highway would be surveyed and constructed by the Public Roads Administration, or under its supervision, with State Department collaboration. But the final sentence of Shaw's letter did not suggest any great emergency that might be served by the road. "It is estimated," wrote Shaw, "that the construction of the highway will require approximately 4 years, and it will therefore be necessary to continue the unexpended balances available from year to year until the highway is completed."[8]

Neither this letter nor the memorandum that accompanied it quoted any official documents that constituted a firm commitment to construct the road. The memorandum stated, however, that Roosevelt and Somoza had exchanged letters which had obligated the United States to make a barge-canal survey and suggested that the State Department had assumed certain obligations beyond that. The State Department's version of what had occurred between May 1939 and May 1942 was as follows:

"In May of 1939 when President Somoza of Nicaragua visited Washington he had certain conversations with the President of the United States about the desirability of linking the east and west coast regions of Nicaragua. As a result of these conversations letters were exchanged on May 22, 1939, in accordance with which this Government undertook the survey of a canalization and highway project to link the eastern and western regions of Nicaragua. The surveys of the barge or light-draft canal project led to the conclusion that the benefits to be derived would not be commensurate with the cost, which was estimated at about $30,000,000. However, in view of the commitment of the United States to cooperate in a practical manner in the establishment of communications between the two sections of Nicaragua, it now appears that in the opinion both of the Nicaraguan Government and of the Department the cooperation in question could be best rendered through the construction of a road. Such a road would branch off from the Inter-American Highway at a point known as San Benito, about 22 miles north of Managua, and would proceed in an easterly direction toward the river port of Rama. The length . . . would be about 172 miles (270 Km.). From Rama to El Bluff on the Atlantic Ocean, there is a distance of 60 miles which is navigable for vessels with less than 12 feet draught, so that barge communication is entirely feasible."[9]

A definite obligation is thus asserted, but who made the commitment? Was it contained in this exchange of letters by the two chief executives? Was it embodied in a letter written by the Secretary of State? The State Department was not yet ready to make a full disclosure. It appears, however, that some high official, or officials, had assumed an obligation that would eventually cost taxpayers of the United States at least $12 million, perhaps considerably more.

For what purpose? The enclosed memorandum was careful to assert a military objective: "It has been indicated by the War Department that this road would have a very definite military value in relation to hemisphere defense." But it is hard to take this assertion seriously. It seems to be merely a necessary justification for an allotment from Roosevelt's Emergency Fund. A road to be completed in no less than four years and to be reached when finished by no other means than barges on 60 miles of a muddy river in a rainy tropical jungle could not have been planned to serve any pressing military need. The long quotations from the Public Roads Administration included in the memorandum indicate that the main objectives were to stabilize the political situation in Nicaragua by supporting Somoza,[10] to confirm the friendship of the dictator and his associates, to promote the economic development of the country, and to expand its trade with the United States.

Work on the highway had gone forward slowly. The executive allotment had been reduced to an even $4 million. Surveys by the Public Roads Administration had not begun until near the end of the year 1942 and construction was not initiated until several weeks later. The western half of the route traversed a region of alternating drought and flood. Annual precipitation in the eastern section ran from 100 to 250 inches. Efficient work was possible only during the dry seasons and there were almost no dry seasons in the major part of this eastern area. With the highway hardly half finished, construction stopped in June, 1948. The funds had been exhausted. If the highway was to be completed, its promoters would have to request appropriations from Congress. Somoza would never finance it as long as he could hope for further aid from the United States. The Public Roads Administration's estimate for its completion was $8 million.[11]

3.

Promoters of the Rama Road asked Congress for no appropriations in 1947 or 1948. It was a period when the Truman Doctrine was being promulgated, when Greece and Turkey and France and Italy were demanding financial assistance, and when the Marshall Plan was being adopted for Western Europe. Moreover, the Republicans were in control of the national legislature. It was therefore clear that this was no time to ask for money to complete a road through the tall rain-forests and thick jungles of Nicaragua. Even after Truman was elected in 1948 and the Democrats regained control on Capitol Hill, it proved impossible to push the request for an appropriation through the committees to the floors of the two chambers. This was tried in vain in 1949.[12] Moreover, another effort in 1950 fell short of success, even though the promoters brought their influence to bear on the Senate Committee on Public Works, headed by Dennis Chavez, always an enthusiast for highways and always eager to assist his Latin-American kinsmen. The bill dealing with Federal aid for highways and containing a section authorizing $8 million to finish the Rama Road reached the floor of the Senate; but the item had little support other than that given by Chavez and was stricken from the bill on motion by Senator Ferguson, who scolded Somoza for forcing the building of a spur road to his plantation, denounced Nicaraguans for stealing road materials, and castigated the New Deal and the Fair Deal for extravagance all over the world.[13]

The State Department, however, in this second effort to obtain an appropriation for the Rama Road, threw further light on the secret project. The Assistant Secretary of State for Inter-American Affairs, Edward G. Miller, flourished a $12 million letter written by Sumner Welles to the Nicaraguan Minister of Foreign Affairs under date of April 8, 1942, and signed as Acting Secretary of State. Here, at last, was a definite commitment, provided that Congress could be committed by a document transmitted without previous consultation, for Welles said:

"With reference to conversations which Your Excellency has held with officials of this Government and to conversations held by His Excellency President Somoza during his visit to Washington in 1939, I have the honor to inform you that careful and sympathetic consideration has been given by the appropriate officials of this Government to the matter of developing communications between the eastern and the western sections of Nicaragua. In this connection, I refer particularly to the Nicaraguan Legation's memoranda of November 30, 1939 and August 10, 1940, and to the exchanges of views with regard to the possible canalization of the San Juan River.

"I regret to inform Your Excellency that these studies have clearly shown that the construction of the proposed barge canal is economically impracticable and that, therefore, I consider the project to be one to which the two Governments will wish to give no further consideration. However, my Government is fully aware of the importance of linking the east coast regions of Nicaragua with the regions of the interior and the Pacific coast. The matter is one which has been frequently discussed by representatives of our two Governments. It has now been agreed that the most promising method of achieving the objective would be the construction of a road from San Benito on the Inter-American Highway north of Managua to Rama on the Escondido River, from which point river communication to El Bluff and Bluefields on the Atlantic is available.

"It is the opinion of my Government that the existence of the road mentioned would have, under present circumstances, a very important bearing upon the defense of the hemisphere.

"Therefore, taking into account the spirit of the communications which were exchanged on May 22, 1939, between President Somoza of Nicaragua and President Roosevelt of the United States, my Government is willing, at its own expense, to carry out the following:

    (a) The construction of a highway between San Benito and Rama.

    (b) The survey and recommendation of a route of a highway from Rama to El Bluff; the construction and financing of such a road being a matter for the decision of the Nicaraguan Government, in the light of the survey, and no obligation in regard thereto being contemplated by this Government."[14]

The letter went on to suggest that both the survey and the construction should be carried out in agreement with the Public Roads Administration of the United States. Moreover, Welles added a note of caution: "The construction of the road from San Benito to Rama and the survey from Rama to El Bluff will, in the opinion of my Government, constitute a complete execution by my Government of any obligation which it may have incurred particularly under numbered paragraph I of the aforesaid exchange of letters of May 22, 1939." Welles evidently hoped to settle the problem of the canal option definitively. But would this be the result? A payment of $3 million in 1916; now another $12 million or more; what next and when?

Perhaps the release of other secret documents in somewhat calmer days might induce legislators to appropriate funds which they had refused to vote in 1950, so near the beginning of the distressing "police action" in Korea. At any rate, a procedural precedent had been set. Authorization for money for the Rama Road had been sought through the Senate committee that dealt with Federal aid to highways in the United States, appropriations for which were authorized for two years at a time. Preparations were now made to persuade Congress to concede in 1952 what it had refused to authorize in 1950. "Justifications" were industriously compiled; and, even more, the State Department decided to reveal two additional documents calculated to increase Congressional sense of obligation to Nicaragua. They were significant documents, none other than the Roosevelt-Somoza exchange of letters of May 22, 1939, so tantalizingly alluded to in previous years. After a decade, the Rama Road mystery was about to be solved.[15]

Somoza made the following appeal to FDR:

"Adequate transportation facilities are a prime requisite to the development of the production and trade of a nation. It is the opinion of the Government of Nicaragua that it is of paramount importance to link together the productive regions of the east coast of Nicaragua with the more densely populated productive regions of the interior and the Pacific coast and to provide a more direct channel of communication between Nicaragua and the United States. This objective could effectively be attained by canalization of the San Juan River for vessels of moderate draft, and, if possible, by a complementary waterway from Lake Nicaragua to the Pacific. I desire to inquire whether the assistance of the Government of the United States might be extended to assist my Government in the realization of this project. Specifically, it would be necessary in any event as a first step to have precise surveys and estimates, and I am hopeful that it will be feasible for the Government of the United States to send engineers of the United States Engineer Corps for this purpose."

Somoza thus asked for only a survey and an estimate, but one could find in the letter a possible hint that further help might be expected later. Roosevelt's reply seems to contain a somewhat more definite suggestion of assistance over and above a survey and an estimate. Note especially the last sentence in each of the two paragraphs of his letter.

"Regarding your suggestion for the canalization of the San Juan River for vessels of moderate draft, I have been pleased to instruct the United States Army Engineer Corps to make the necessary studies and surveys of a canalization and highway project to link the eastern and western regions of Nicaragua. I am impressed with the thought that such a project would greatly facilitate and expedite communications between your country and mine and, by opening new areas to the production of complementary noncompetitive products, would provide new bases for an increase in commerce between those areas and the United States. Moreover, it is obvious that, should the occasion arise, the existence of such a waterway would have a very important bearing upon the defense of the hemisphere.

"As soon as the necessary financial arrangements can be made in this country, a board of four officers of the Corps of Engineers, accompanied by an official of the United States Engineer Department and an officer of the Medical Corps, will be sent to Nicaragua. It is expected that the board would leave for Nicaragua next July and would be able to carry out the studies for the project within a few months. Upon the basis of their reports we can take such further action as seems in the common interest of our two countries."[16]

These and other documents were laid before Congress in 1952 in a second request for $8 million to complete the Rama Road. But neither the members of the Senate nor those of the House seem to have given close attention to the most elaborate "justification" presented by the State Department. This had been prepared by Capus M. Waynick several months before, while he was still ambassador to Nicaragua. A diplomat apparently in dire need of help, he wrote out a long plea for this appropriation:

"1. Nicaragua believes that she should trust absolutely a formal ... commitment by our President and State Department. I believe it would be unwise to shatter this confidence.

"2. The President of Nicaragua ... regards the road as a substitute for the canalization of the San Juan River ... and he regards the whole undertaking as tied in with our continuing canal rights.

"3. Despite our military occupation of Nicaragua some years ago, friendship for us has persisted there. Nicaragua declared war on our enemies in 1941 the day following our own declaration.... At a time when communism is infiltrating the Isthmus ... it would be particularly unfortunate for us to destroy confidence there in the integrity of our executive pledges.

"4. Nicaragua is geographically central in the Isthmus between Mexico and South America and a logical place, I believe, for an air base for defense of the Panama Canal and other strategic areas....

"5. While I do not attempt to justify the building of the Rama Road for direct benefit of the United States, I do believe that a system of roads ... can be of great substantial value to the United States as they pave the way to ... development of commerce ... [and] dependable Pan-Americanism....

"7. Our pledge to Nicaragua was not a specified sum of money to apply on the Rama Road. It was to build the road. I believe it should be honored in full, regardless of any differences of opinion as to whether greater caution should be observed in making such commitments without a saving clause...."[17]

The appropriation for the Rama Road was warmly debated in both houses of Congress in 1952. The leading antagonists were George Meader in the lower chamber and Homer Ferguson in the upper. The proponents did not obtain all they desired, but they got an authorization of $4 million for the biennium and later managed to secure appropriations of a million each year for fiscal 1954 and fiscal 1955. Perhaps it will not be amiss to illustrate the arguments of 1952.

Both Congressman George Meader and Senator Homer Ferguson asserted, in effect, that Roosevelt and Welles should not have admitted any obligation to Nicaragua in connection with the canal option and that their executive agreements should have no weight with Congress.[18] Meader declared:

"The remarks about a treaty in the debate here have been misleading. Some who have spoken ... have indicated that it is as a result of a treaty that the Rama Road is to be built, at a cost of $12,000,000. There is nothing of the kind. The 1914 treaty [ratified in 1916] gave the United States an option to build the canal if it wanted to."

Ferguson asserted:

"I find nothing which indicates that we owe any further money for the right to build the canal. We paid $3,000,000 for the right in 1914 [1916]. We paid for the perpetual right. . . .
"What I am trying to figure out today is how to accord fair play to American taxpayers. We are talking about fair play for everyone else, but when we suggest ... fair play for the American taxpayer we are criticized for it. . . ."

Ferguson's was one of the few expressions of sympathy for the harried taxpayers that was made during the debate.

Several Congressmen spoke in favor of the measure. The main arguments were that pledges had been made and must be kept in order to avoid the loss of the confidence and friendship of the Latin Americans; that when the United States was spending billions elsewhere it ought not to object to an outlay of a few millions in the neighboring countries; that further expenditures must be made in order to prevent the jungle from swallowing the $4 million already spent; and that funds used to build highways would eventually return profits. "Good roads," declared Fred L. Crawford of Michigan, "bring people together and promote good will and peace and commerce." The leading proponents in the Senate were Dennis Chavez and Spessard Holland, the one from New Mexico and the other from Florida. Chavez declared:

"I feel that if we asked for the right to build the canal and were given the right to build it, we obligated ourselves to build it. . . . I think . . . [the Rama Road] is a pretty good business proposition. . . . It would have cost $800,000,000 to build that canal."

Holland stated his position very carefully:

"I claim that this obligation was undertaken by President Roosevelt to cause an abandonment on the part of Nicaragua of its claim that we were obligated to dig the second canal, rather than being merely permitted to do so, as we contended. . . . Under the settlement made, our interpretation, rather than that of Nicaragua, prevails. We are not obligated to dig the canal, but we have the right to do so if we so elect."[19]

Affirmative action by Congress in 1952 was conclusive. The Rama Road would eventually be completed, but not before 1960 or 1961, unless more than a million was appropriated each year. Nor is there any assurance that $12 million will finish it. That figure is based on an estimate of 1948, and costs have a way of exceeding estimates. As of April 1954, around 62 miles remained to be constructed, most of it running through a soggy rain-forest where work could be done for only a few months each year, and bituminous surfacing had to be applied to the entire length of the highway, then estimated to be 158 miles (a little shorter than had been anticipated in the early 1940's).[20] It was still too early to appraise its economic and social influence in Nicaragua or its contribution to inter-American friendship and trade.

CHAPTER 8   RUBBER-PLANTING FIASCOS IN TROPICAL AMERICA

INTERMITTENTLY for more than half a century citizens of the United States and their government have interested themselves in the cultivation of rubber in the Western Hemisphere. Their efforts have cost investors and taxpayers many million dollars—probably well above a hundred—and have produced almost no rubber. Attempts to grow rubber in the American tropics began in the 1890's with a speculation spree that lasted more than a decade. They were resumed in the 1920's, after an interval of recovery from losses and disappointments, in the hope of finding a means of escape from the exactions of successful rubber planters of the Middle East. They entered a new phase in the 1940's amid the consternation caused by the Nazi invasion of Western Europe and the Japanese seizure of the Oriental rubber regions.

The first effort started with the wrong trees—*Castillas*, sometimes called *Castilloas*, instead of *Heveas*—and the wrong emphasis, and with too much haste. Excited by consular reports made under the direction of the State Department, reports that predicted a rubber famine and seemed to suggest large and comparatively easy returns from cultivated rubber, investors soon became the prey of speculators who bought or leased lands in southern Mexico and Central America and expended more energy in the "fleecing of saps" than in the cultivation of saplings. Land companies, rubber-planting companies, and rubber-tapping companies sprang up by the score in half the states of the North American Union. Prominent men whose intelligence and honesty were likely to be taken for granted were listed as members of administrative staffs and boards of directors. Extravagant advertisements appeared in newspapers. Glowing prospectuses were distributed on farms and street corners. Salesmen of securities plied their trade. "Oldtimers" of the tropics, in phrases that seemed to exude caution, assured anticipated victims that they would make no mistake if they ventured their savings in rubber planting. Sir Thomas Lipton, well-known tea millionaire, was quoted in praise of tropical agriculture. Collis P. Huntington, Western railway magnate, was represented as advising that rubber held out better promise of enrichment than railroads. William Allen White, who had recently leaped to fame as a Kansas journalist, was quoted as expressing amazement at the speed with which rubber-tired buggies and automobiles were swarming over the West. Californians were told that Joaquin Miller, popular "poet of the Sierras," was spending his vacations on Mexican rubber *fincas*. The hard life of the "hot lands" was covered by a thick cloak of romanticism and glamour. The tropics were portrayed as delightful regions where Harvard men read Homer after the day's work was done.

Dividends of from five to fifteen per cent were promised immediately from "side crops," and much higher returns after the rubber trees began to pour forth their liquid gold. Big annual yields were predicted, as high as twenty pounds from each tree, within six or seven years. Rubber securities were offered on terms within the reach of all. They could be bought on installment for as low as two dollars a month. Attractive bonuses and discounts were included, along with insurance policies providing for cancellation of the rubber debts of the deceased and transmission of their holdings to designated heirs. Little businessmen, farmers, clerks, policemen, firemen, teachers, preachers, all the world's hard driven, were offered a chance to escape from their bondage of toil and anxiety.

Enticing nomenclature was employed. Californians with a

veneer of Spanish culture, Scandinavians residing in Minneapolis and St. Paul, men of many races and languages in Chicago and New York, Anglo-Saxons from Oregon and Texas to Maine and Massachusetts were soon pronouncing and mispronouncing Spanish names. Chiapas, Tehuantepec, Socunusco, Campeche, Oaxaca, Aztec, Montezuma, Chamelicón, Escuintla, Matagalpa, San Pedro Sula, Zacualpa, Dos Ríos, Rubio, San Juan Bautista, Tierra Blanca, Santa Lucrecia, Lolita, Doña María, Buenaventura, Colombia, Esmeralda, Esperanza—these and many more became familiar to thousands who invested their savings or emerged triumphant from repeated encounters with sharp and aggressive salesmen. A few of the promoters preferred, however, to give English names to their plantations, such as Yale, Iowa, and Tennessee, or Philadelphia, Chicago, Manhattan, and Daytonia.

Full confidence and high optimism were necessary in order to induce little investors to keep up their installment payments. They were told that they could well afford to risk a few dollars more even without immediate dividends in order to secure in return a comfortable income for the rest of their lives after the rubber trees reached maturity. Presumably reputable individuals, sent out frequently to inspect the plantations, usually returned with glowing reports of progress. Effective use was made of photography: luxurious tropical vegetation; rubber trees in the foreground (probably of the wild species); barefoot *peones* under big *sombreros* engaged in clearing or tapping while smiling plantation managers astride mustangs looked on with approval.

Installments continued to stream into corporation offices and new companies continued to be organized in spite of warnings from the State Department and the Department of Agriculture, and despite bankruptcy in some instances and revelations of fraud in others. The financial panic which began late in 1907 caused a number of liquidations and reorganizations, and still the rubber enthusiasm held up. Thousands of seedlings were planted as late as 1910. In fact, the rubber-plantation boom, as already intimated, continued for more than ten years.

The aggregate of stocks, bonds, and "rubber-harvest" certificates purchased by the people of the United States during these years has not been precisely determined. The authorized capitalization of the more than a hundred enterprises organized for the purpose of speeding rubber's return to the New World where it originated probably amounted to well in excess of $100 million; but the promoters and salesmen did not succeed in marketing all of their securities before the final collapse. First and last, probably forty or fifty million *Castillas* and a sprinkling of *Heveas*, sometimes called *Parás*, were planted at the cost of fully as many million dollars. Lands acquired in one way or another in southern Mexico and Central America reached a total of several million acres, but only a few hundred thousand were actually cleared and planted in rubber before the failure of the effort was convincingly revealed. Perhaps a larger area was devoted to other crops and to grazing. Jungle, some of it exploited for various forest products, remained on the rest.

A very violent revolution in Mexico, accompanied by intense "Yankeephobia," expelled even the most determined and honest planters and compelled their workers to join insurgent armies. Milder political disorders and dismal failure to produce rubber at competitive prices finally terminated the effort in Central America. By no means all of the enterprises were fraudulent or even purely speculative. Perhaps even the majority of the promoters were conscientious and industrious. Some employed genuine rubber experts and others trained them. From the practical standpoint, however, the character of owners and managers and the capacity of scientists were of little moment. The effort was doomed from the outset by the selection of *Castillas* instead of *Heveas*. But investors, managers, and scientists made at least one very significant discovery. They discovered that *Castillas* were scanty producers.[1] Lush jungle soon spread over the plantations and choked the rubber trees, but millions of them were still in fairly good health a decade and a half later when attempts were made to renew the plantation effort and when exploring parties from the United States inspected the region.

2.

These parties had been sent out by Herbert Hoover, then secretary of commerce, who in retrospect seems to have been unduly alarmed by attempts of foreign producers and governments to restrict the output and export of a number of raw materials which were required by American industries and ultimate consumers. Still apparently convinced of the soundness of his views and the effectiveness of his measures, Hoover referred to the problem in his *Memoirs*, recalling that the Department of Commerce had obtained an appropriation of half a million dollars in 1923 "to investigate these activities and to conduct a battle against them." "The worst example," he declared, "was the British rubber control originated by the energetic Secretary of State for the Colonies, Winston Churchill. It was organized in 1922 to reduce rubber production and steadily advance the prices. The prices were forced up from 13 cents per pound to $1.21 a pound by 1925." Hoover and his associates countered by organizing "a nation-wide campaign to reduce imports by conservation and by substitution of reclaimed rubber," by urging the Dutch government to "maintain reasonable prices" and stay "out of the combination," and by encouraging "American manufacturers to plant rubber in non-British territory." The price of rubber fell to 59 cents a pound by March, 1926, and to 40 cents per pound by the following June, and Hoover claimed credit for the reduction.[2]

Meantime Hoover's exploration teams and the agents of some of the big rubber manufacturers had been investigating rubber plantations and prospects for rubber cultivation all over the globe. As it turned out, only Henry Ford centered his plantation efforts in Latin America. Other manufacturers directed their attention to Asia and Africa. But failure to give more stress to the Western Hemisphere was not the fault of Hoover or his staff.

Julius Klein, director of the Bureau of Foreign and Domestic Commerce, was not lacking in enthusiasm when he submitted the report on the Amazon valley. "The population of this region is estimated at 1,500,000," he observed. "Under present conditions . . . a total of 30,000 laborers might be procurable . . . for rubber-plantation projects—a force sufficient to plant and care for an area of at least 150,000 acres." Regarding the character of the workers, Klein declared: "As a rule the laborer of the Amazon is of good physique, inured to exposure, and under proper incentive capable of long-continued effort. Man for man he could probably be classified as superior to the Indian and the Javanese labor[er] used on the rubber plantations of the Orient and at least equal in efficiency to Chinese labor."[3]

Klein's letter submitting the findings of the team which explored northern tropical America was rather persuasive: "On account of its near-by location and the common wish for increasing prosperity throughout Latin America, many Americans would prefer to see the rubber-plantation development in tropical America rather than in other parts of the world. This report will show that conditions are favourable to rubber culture in more than six million acres in northern tropical America." Labor appeared to be somewhat scarce, but workers could be shifted from some of the Caribbean islands or imported from the Orient. The world's need for rubber was increasing at a rapid rate. "It would obviously be to the advantage of interested American capital and to the United States as a nation to have the necessary new plantations as near to our shores as feasible. . . ."[4]

H. N. Whitford, the Department of Commerce's administrative head of the crude-rubber survey, was perhaps a little less confident and convincing early in 1926 when he presented the problem to the House Committee on Interstate and Foreign

Commerce. "In tropical America, except Haiti, labor is not abundant," he said. "Where organized agricultural development already is in existence, as is the case with the fruit companies..., it is believed the capital costs can be kept below the usual level of such costs for new areas in the Middle East." The fruit and other companies might be induced to "plant small units in strategic places and encourage peasant plantings around these units." The natives could gain experience "from working on the company's farms." The various governments in areas where such companies were not operating might be persuaded to permit the importation of Chinese. Fairly large rubber plantations probably could be established in the Amazon Basin without bringing in labor from the outside. If the governments of the lands farther north objected to importation of workers, the future of plantation rubber in Latin America might have to depend upon the small farmers who, while growing rubber, could also grow "good crops between the rubber trees." "I see no reason," Whitford concluded, "why it is not possible to encourage the nationals of the various... countries to plant rubber by the establishment of small demonstration plantations in each one of them." Whitford therefore urged Congress to set up a fund to be used for this purpose in cooperation with the Latin-American governments. This might stimulate plantings in each republic, and the total acreage "might be large." Assistance by the United States should be in the form of advice; possibly also in the way of furnishing seeds, or establishing nurseries. If big investors in this country wished to inaugurate large plantations in Latin America, "so much the better," but he had "found no capitalists willing to undertake this work."[5]

Harvey S. Firestone said that he had desired to plant rubber in Panama, Mexico, and Central America but had turned elsewhere because of adverse topography or the risk of revolutionary violence.[6] Richard O. Marsh, civil engineer and representative of the American Association for the Advancement of

Science, declared: "I have talked to nearly every great financial concern in this country. They have all told me plainly in effect, 'Mr. Marsh, we will not invest hundreds of millions of dollars in a rubber development in any other part of Latin America except Panama, because we have no faith in the political security of such investments. We have seen a billion dollars of American money in Mexico ... jeopardized by unstable government....' " Marsh was an extreme enthusiast for Panama, where he alleged that well over two million acres adapted to rubber planting were available. He made a special plea for a rich valley in the Darién region, where he said he had discovered 1,600,000 acres perfectly suited to rubber culture. The supply of native labor would not be adequate, but workers could be shipped in from the Caribbean islands or from the Orient.[7]

Thus problems of labor shortage, wages, and political instability had to be reckoned with. And there was also the problem of disease. The survey teams had noted that "leaf blight" was prevalent in some parts of South America and in the Island of Trinidad. But the mistake of planting *Castilla* trees would not be repeated. The experience of the early years of the century had not been forgotten, and subsequent tests had confirmed the impression that *Castillas* would yield much less latex than *Heveas*.[8]

3.

There were no productive rubber plantations of any significance in the Western Hemisphere at the beginning of World War II. Nearly all previous efforts had proved futile. Production and export of rubber were again under restriction in the Orient. Control under the Stevenson Plan, inaugurated on November 1, 1922, had been lifted on November 1, 1928. The world economic depression of the 1930's had motivated another effort at restriction, however, an attempt more effective for a time than the one advocated by the Stevenson Committee and adopted by Churchill. An International Rubber Regulation Committee had been created in 1934, with a membership that included a few representatives from industrial consumers; but prices had moved up from a low of a few cents a pound to more than twenty cents. In the words of Jesse H. Jones, president of the Reconstruction Finance Corporation and later secretary of commerce: "The International Committee, set up by the British and Dutch governments, had for years controlled the flow of raw rubber into the world markets."[9]

Alarmed by Nazi victories in Europe, Congress passed and the President approved two rubber acts near the end of June, 1940. One authorized the RFC to procure, stockpile, and distribute rubber; the other appropriated half a million dollars to the Department of Agriculture to encourage the cultivation of plantation rubber in Latin America. RFC became the sole purchasing agent for all the crude rubber imported into the United States, selling some of it to manufacturers at cost plus carrying charges. The Department of Agriculture became the exclusive agency for the fostering of rubber planting in Latin America.[10]

After the Japanese attack on Pearl Harbor further steps were promptly taken under congressional and executive direction. RFC was given authority to finance synthetic rubber plants and a program of rubber cultivation in Haiti and to stimulate the collection of wild rubber in Latin America. The Department of Agriculture was voted appropriations for the cultivation of *guayule* rubber in California and elsewhere in the United States. RFC's rubber stockpile was still far too small at the time the nation entered the second World War, only some 630,000 long tons where annual consumption required nearly twice that quantity. The Rubber Development Company, which shortly became the Rubber Development Corporation, was organized to cope with the crisis, and a "Rubber Tsar" was appointed to expedite the process. Rubber Procurement Corporation would have been a better name for the new agency, since it merely financed and managed the collection of wild rubber in Latin

America, paid the costs of the Haitian plantation project, and purchased rubber from Liberia, India, and Ceylon.

The main solutions adopted were conservation, reclamation, and the production of synthetic rubber in plants which cost $700 million. But synthetic rubber without a mixture of from 25 to 30 per cent of natural rubber was not a satisfactory raw material, so that more natural rubber was needed than could be acquired from Latin America or elsewhere. The total output of India and Ceylon was no more than 115,000 tons per annum. Only 65,000 tons of crude and 20,000 tons of latex were obtained from the Firestone plantation in Liberia, and only 153,545 long tons, mostly wild rubber, were acquired from Latin America during the war period. The average price paid for Firestone's crude was 30 cents a pound while twice that sum was paid for rubber purchased from Latin America. Not more than a third of the natural product so badly needed was to be had. The plantation fiascos of earlier years in the Western Hemisphere were keenly felt by citizens of the United States.[11]

Moreover, two additional failures of planting efforts, and possibly three, were to be suffered during the fifteen years following 1940. The Haitian project, which involved an attempt to cultivate the *cryptostegia* vine and extract rubber from it was an utter failure, and so likewise was the *guayule* program. The first produced 5.5 tons at a cost of nearly $7 million, or $546 per pound; *guayule* rubber proved to be potentially cheaper, but its average actual cost was probably not less than $100 a pound!

Blaming Vice-President Henry Wallace, member at the time of the Board of Economic Warfare, for the *cryptostegia* fiasco, Jesse Jones later wrote scornfully: "One plantation his bright young disciples originated in Haiti (against the advice of the qualified rubber authorities recruited by our organization) succeeded in spending nearly $7,000,000 to produce about enough rubber to fill a large truck."[12] Representative W. R. Poage of Texas, chairman of a subcommittee of the House Committee on

Agriculture appointed to investigate both the *cryptostegia* and the *guayule* programs, reported on the former as follows on January 2, 1945: "The only extraction method known so far is to clip the end of each vine. When this is done, one or two drops of white juice flow out. This must be caught in a vessel." "It is easy to see," Poage continued, "that the tremendous amount of hand labor incident to the collection of the latex makes this a most inefficient method of producing rubber." The Texas Congressman reported that the program had recently been discontinued because it had become "apparent that rubber could not be produced from *cryptostegia* in the quantities that had been expected."[13] Some 43,000 acres had been planted.

Pressure exerted by the California delegation in Congress and by the farm block was mainly responsible for the authorization of the *guayule* project early in 1942. The law provided for a planting of 75,000 acres, and 500,000 acres would have been permitted if President Roosevelt had not interposed his veto.

The Department of Agriculture's scientists were clearly in league with the farm group, and at least one of the rubber manufacturers offered a helping hand. Elmer W. Brandes, Bureau of Plant Industry, declared in January, 1942: "I believe the whole program could be effectuated at practically no cost to the Government if the present price of rubber is maintained."[14] Rubber was then selling at 22.5 cents a pound. Assuming that the price would not fall below that figure, Loren G. Polhamus, staff member of the same bureau, estimated total net costs to the government of the 75,000-acre project at $11,290,000 through fiscal year 1948.[15] Brandes asserted that strains of *guayule* containing from 16 to 19 per cent of rubber had been developed by the Intercontinental Rubber Company, which was eager to sell its assets and its scientific discoveries to the United States government. William H. Mason, an official of the General Tire and Rubber Company, declared that the rubber content of this shrub had been raised from 12 to 22 or 23 per cent by the experiments of Intercontinental, and that he thought it might be increased to 30 per cent.[16] Members of the House Committee on Agriculture, spurred by the analogy of the sugar program adopted in 1934, were eager for further profits for the farmers at the expense of taxpayers and consumers. Harold D. Cooley of North Carolina, R. H. Murray of Wisconsin, H. P. Fulmer of South Carolina, and Edward O'Neal of the American Farm Bureau Federation all agreed with the following view expressed by Congressman H. B. Coffee of Nebraska: "I think we can visualize this industry as something similar to the sugar-beet industry. We recognize . . . the necessity of having sugar produced on the continent because of a threatened shortage of supplies from the offshore areas," even though "sugar can be produced more cheaply in the tropical islands."[17] Congressman Fulmer even suggested a tariff as well as a subsidy. But both the B. F. Goodrich Company and the Goodyear Tire and Rubber Company, along with the Bureau of Plant Industry, opposed this scheme and advocated government operation of the program in the interest of industrial consumers, and this was the plan finally adopted.[18]

Making no reference to his optimistic statements of early 1942 and claiming credit for himself and his associates to which they were not exclusively entitled, Brandes summarized the sad story of the expensive *guayule* failure in 1948: "The project during the war was an action program of rubber production and the acreage was considerable because the endeavor was to produce as much rubber as possible as an emergency measure. . . . There were roughly 32,500 acres of *guayule* planted. . . . When the action program . . . was liquidated Congress directed that the rubber be plowed up. . . . There were about 14,500 tons of rubber in the ground that could have been processed but it never was." The plants were not uprooted and processed because the expenditure required could be utilized at much greater advantage in procuring rubber from other sources. Scientists, who are the miracle-men—and occasionally the medicine-men—of our time, are rather indifferent regarding expenditures of tax money

137

and reluctant to discuss such matters. Brandes finally admitted, however, that "about 200 tons" of rubber were actually extracted at a cost of from $30 to $40 million. Remarking that he was not in charge of this program "at that time" and that it was under the Forest Service of the Department of Agriculture, he noted that the plantings had recently been transferred to his bureau as a research project and then added: "A good deal of work was done during that production program in the way of scientific research on the *guayule* plant to improve it by breeding. . . . The improved plants have been preserved. . . . Some strains of plants . . . were increased . . . from 10 per cent of rubber up to 18 per cent. I think some of our analyses show that individual plants contained as much as 22 per cent rubber." Had Doctor Brandes forgotten the percentages of rubber content firmly assured early in 1942? Were he and Mason in error then, or had the plant deteriorated under scientific magic?[19]

4.

Already Brandes and his associates had been presenting glowing accounts to congressional committees of their work in connection with the *Hevea* cooperative program in Latin America. As early as January, 1942, Brandes had told the national lawmakers of the achievements that he and his associates had recorded:[20]

"The Government has a long-range program which contemplates the development of a very large plantation Para-rubber industry in the Western Hemisphere and the Government has been working on that . . . since July 1940, and has made a great deal of progress. By cooperative agreements with 13 Latin-American countries, the Department of Agriculture has established scores of nurseries and planted some eight to ten million trees and has obtained bud wood of these superior strains or clones . . . , high-yielding and disease-resistant material, which comes in the form of bud wood to be budded or grafted on these eight to twelve [*sic*] million trees, and that work has progressed very actively for 19 months, so that the prospects are that a good bit of the Hevea plantation rubber industry will be brought back to the New World.... The Goodyear Co. has planted rubber in Costa Rica, some in Panama; the Ford Motor Co. has planted on the Tapajoz River, which is one of the southern tributaries of the Amazon; the Firestone Rubber Co. has 70,000 acres of rubber planted in Liberia, half of which is now in tapping."

This was clearly a propaganda diversion. The subject under consideration was California *guayule*. Twelve million trees were a lot more than eight or ten million; Doctor Brandes was disclosing more than a little carelessness with numbers. His geography was also a bit confused, for he deftly listed Liberia along with Central America and Brazil. But by this irrelevant palaver and a cheerful remark to the effect that *Heveas* required only a year or two in the nursery and five years on the plantation in order to pour forth their latex, he was painting a bright future for harassed Congressmen dreaming of an abundance of plantation rubber in the Western Hemisphere, safe from the spoliations of aggressors across the oceans.

The appeal for an appropriation for fiscal year 1945 was made by Robert D. Rands, who stated that the latest figure on acreage actually planted was 9,298. If the average was 80 to 100 trees to the acre—and the number was probably no larger—the total would be much less than the eight million and far less than the maximum of twelve million recited by Brandes in January, 1942. But big plans were said to be under way; more than 33,000 acres would soon be added, not in vast tracts but in little patches all over lowland tropical America. "Now ... we are emphasizing the small-farm type of rubber planting," said Rands, "because that will be thoroughly competitive with the Far [*sic*] East after the war." This small-farm talk was beginning to have a familiar ring; it had cloaked and would continue to conceal the large bounties handed out by the government of the United States to the big farmers. Rands conveyed another false impression, with respect to the ravages of the leaf blight, when he stated that the "Ford Co." had "developed . . . resistant strains in Brazil."[21]

To solicit the appropriation for fiscal year 1946 Brandes showed up with his habitual enthusiasm. As the global war approached its end a special committee, he alleged, had agreed that the cooperative program in tropical America should be continued with the hope of attaining hemispheric self-sufficiency in natural rubber and of furnishing Latin-American countries "with a cash crop." "We actually now have nurseries and field plantings . . . amounting to . . . 20,000 acres," Brandes declared. "It is our conception that this . . . joint research and development program should continue with scientific control of every detail at least to the point where the producing plantations have reached tapping age, or until they reach economic maturity. . . . If this is done I think we have a right to hope that the program will be a success in terms of what we set out to do." He was thus slyly doubling the seven-year term for the program that he had suggested in 1942. Inserting a colossal *if*, he continued: "If planting should start now and be maintained at a rate comparable with the maximum rate of the formerly expanding industry of the East I should say we could count on getting a third of our requirements of genuine rubber within the next 15 years from tropical America." This third would probably necessitate an annual production of plantation rubber in Latin America of not less than 200,000 long tons, provided due allowance was made for the expanding requirements of the Latin Americans themselves. Responding to an inquiry by Congressman Louis C. Rabaut of Michigan about the leaf blight, Brandes made this firm statement: "That fortunately is one of the research jobs that has been carried on right from the beginning and we can say with complete assurance that the South American leaf blight will not be a limiting factor in the development of rubber plantations." Who had been carrying on this research job, the Ford Company which, according to Rands, had already developed "resistant strains" as early as 1944, or the scientists of the Bureau of Plant Industry? Brandes, like Rands, sponsored the familiar small-farm idea, but also hinted at the need for larger funds for another purpose: "In practically every one of our cooperations there is incorporated the development of the . . . family-size farm as a feature . . . but we . . . think somewhat larger plantations, either financed by the cooperating governments or by private agency, are necessary in the beginning as a demonstration. . . ."[22]

Brandes sang the same refrain the next year when he appeared at the hearings of the House Appropriations Committee to request funds for fiscal 1947. "The work has progressed fortunately," he affirmed, "toward the objective, with now something over 30,000 acres of plantations either newly developed or salvaged . . . by crown budding, developed cooperatively through our program." Asked again about the leaf-blight problem, he replied: "We have an answer to the practical problem of growing the rubber trees in spite of that disease, namely, the crown budding that I just mentioned. . . . We have . . . a large number of strains of the Para tree that are quite resistant to the disease." "In addition to that," he continued, "we are carrying on a long-term project of producing strains . . . that combine high yield and resistance to this disease. That is being done on the former Ford plantation on the Tapajos River in Brazil." The Ford Company had abandoned its Brazilian enterprise; but no explanation was given or asked. Perhaps it were better not to disclose the discouraging details.[23]

The drive for the rubber appropriation was spearheaded by Ross Moore in 1947, and progress was described in less confident terms. "Rubber is still largely a research problem," this new representative of the Bureau of Plant Industry admitted, in spite of the fact that the collaborative program had been in operation for seven years. He claimed, however, that "about 16,000 acres"

141

had been planted since the program's inception, "planted by small and big farmers in Guatemala, Mexico, Colombia, Peru, Ecuador, and so forth." Referring most likely to the Ford properties in Brazil, he said that "about 20,000 acres already planted but injured by leaf disease" had been "reconstituted by budding with resistant strains." Asked whether the rubber diseases had been eradicated, his answer was, "No; we have not eradicated the diseases." But Moore explained that a new technique had been worked out that would make possible the "commercial production of rubber in an area rife with disease." It was a budding technique which involved the planting of a seedling, the budding of "a high-yield clone to produce a ... trunk," and the budding of a "resistant top on top of that," thus finally producing a much-lauded "three-story rubber tree." Congressman Karl Stefan, Nebraska Republican, inquired whether the Ford plantation in Brazil had "closed down," and elicited the reply that it had been "turned over to the Brazilian Government." Pursuing the subject further, Stefan asked whether any other company was active in Latin America, and got the response that Goodyear was "still operating in Costa Rica."[24]

Back at the hearings of the Committee on Appropriations once more in 1948, Brandes claimed that he had said from the outset that 15 years would be required to "establish the nuclei of scientifically controlled plantation rubber industries in this hemisphere." It seems certain that he had not told Congress any such thing before 1945. He also claimed that the scientists of the Department of Agriculture had "salvaged" the plantation that Ford had discarded and felt sure that it would soon "become a success." As a matter of fact, Ford had owned two plantations—Fordlandia and Belterra. But nothing was said about the double fiasco. "We feel," Brandes declared, "that considering the difficulties that were involved ... progress has been measurable and satisfactory. Rubber has been planted in 12 different countries and in four of them on quite a large scale. . . . Altogether we estimate that there are about 35,000 acres. . . . There are plantings ranging... from 1 acre to 16,000 or 17,000 acres; the largest being in Brazil, Costa Rica, Colombia, and Mexico." (He seemed a little uncertain about Peru.) "One of the objectives... was to get these plantations started," he concluded. "I believe we can say that has been done."[25]

The most enthusiastic rubber promoter of them all was the late Henry G. Bennett, long-time president of the Oklahoma A. and M. College and first director of the Technical Cooperation Administration. He told Congressmen in 1951 that rubber was growing in sixteen Latin-American countries and that the Department of Agriculture was engaged in rubber-development work in ten of them. The program, he declared, was "vital to the welfare of our own nation as well as to the economy of the nations involved." Deprived of an opportunity to regale the House members with the epic of the tripartite miracle sapling, he managed to describe it to the Senate Committee on Foreign Relations. "Rubber has had two great difficulties in Latin America," he began, "one with the roots of the trees and one with the blight that attacks the leaves. You will find... in the northern part of Brazil [that] we have a great rubber experimentation. There on... about 10,000 acres they are demonstrating that the three-story tree can be grown, the base... from the Brazilian seed, and then the body [from]... the best of the East Indies trees, and the top, which is the second graft, ... resistant to blight. As the result of this cooperative research, I am... convinced that rubber can be grown in the hemisphere... from Vera Cruz down to Central Brazil... including Haiti and the Dominican Republic.... This three-story tree has been perfected to the extent that nurseries are set up, and it is in supply sufficient to be distributed to individual farmers and to larger plantation growers."

Sixteen cooperative experiment stations in as many Latin-American countries had demonstrated, Bennett said, that as good rubber could be grown in all of them as in the East Indies. Why not?

The kind of rubber tree that was then cultivated in every tropical region originated in Brazil and had gained world renown as *Hevea Brasiliensis*.[26]

5.

Following 1951, the funds for the cooperative rubber program in Latin America were merged in the billions appropriated for the Mutual Security Administration, later called the Foreign Operations Administration, and afterwards the International Cooperation Administration. Thus almost hidden from legislators determined to effect economies, balance the national budget, and reduce the national debt and federal taxes—if any such legislators still existed—the program received larger sums for its activities. Further concealment seems to have resulted on July 1, 1954, when the management of the program passed from the supervision of the Bureau of Plant Industry to the exclusive control of the Foreign Operations Administration.[27] But two members of the staff of that bureau had already begun work on a monograph summarizing fourteen years of achievement. Finally published in November, 1955, it was a rather dull and laudatory pamphlet. The industrious and scrupulous reader, however, might be able to make a fairly accurate appraisal. Rubber research centers had been established in three countries—Haiti, Guatemala, and Costa Rica—and cooperative projects, at one time or another, in at least thirteen: two in Haiti, one in the Dominican Republic, two in Mexico, two in Brazil, and one each in Guatemala, Honduras, Nicaragua, Costa Rica, Panama (the Canal Zone), Colombia, Ecuador, Peru, and Bolivia. The only independent tropical countries of Latin America not included in the program were Cuba, El Salvador, and Venezuela. Chile, Argentina, Uruguay, and Paraguay were, of course, not in the tropics and not expected to grow rubber.

The aggregate cost of the program borne by the United States during the fiscal years 1941-1954 was in the neighborhood of six million dollars. Several of the Latin countries had lost interest and ceased to participate. Rubber statistics at the end of the year 1953 for the eight nations still active follow:[28]

Country	Clonal Trees in Production	Acres Planted
Bolivia	none	125
Brazil	800,000	37,125
Colombia	1,500	775
Costa Rica	190,000	2,960
Guatemala	37,000	2,000
Haiti	104,000	1,400
Mexico	72,300	3,070
Peru	1,000	745
Total	1,205,800	48,200

It should be noted that this tabulation, copied from the monograph mentioned, does not indicate *commercial* production, as the careless reader might naturally assume. The truth is that very little rubber from Latin-American plantations had been marketed by the end of fiscal year 1954. The information presented by the Department of Agriculture's scientists is very scanty and vague on this specific subject. No rubber had been produced in Bolivia, as the table reveals. Nor had any been placed on the market from the Peruvian or the Colombian plantations. Only a few hundred tons yielded by the Haitian plantings had been sold, hardly any more from those of Costa Rica and Guatemala, and only a few thousand tons from the plantations of Mexico and Brazil. Production had seldom gone beyond the stage of experimental tapping. The story of the first fourteen years of the collaborative program is not a story of profits but a narrative of battles with disease.

The experts of the Department of Agriculture seemed to be

proud of the victories they had won, and would probably be sad when there were no more battles to fight. Wittingly or unwittingly, they appeared to be saying that the contests with the enemies of the rubber tree and the development of many hybrid species were more important than the production of commercial rubber. But from time to time and near the end of their report they assured any legislator or taxpayer who chanced to read it that the future of rubber planting in tropical America was no less than brilliant. The plantations would eventually produce all the natural rubber required to meet the needs of the Western Hemisphere, they declared, and they therefore advised that the program be supported by the United States until that goal had been reached. Let officials, investors, and taxpayers stop counting their dollars. Another hundred million or so and another decade or two would advance the program to its destination.

With or without the approval of the supreme authorities in Washington they declared: "The United States objective is to create a 'living' stockpile within our defense zone. . . . Latin-American objectives are principally (1) self-sufficiency of rubber for internal consumption, and (2) to grow rubber as a cash crop on the undeveloped lowlands by colonists and settlers from the overcrowded highlands." The maintenance of the "dead" stockpile by the United States was requiring the expenditure of $28 million annually. Investment in a "living" stockpile "would be self-liquidating, and eventually provide great savings to the taxpayer." Association with an official of the Goodyear Tire and Rubber Company and some of the worried Solons of the Senate during the Korean Crisis had sent the rubber experts to the "crystal ball," and this was the vision it disclosed: rubber trees growing on thousands of family-size farms and on numerous demonstration plantations, publicly or privately financed, which were serving also as centers for plant distribution and the processing of latex.[29]

Congressional committees should subject this program to more careful scrutiny. Perhaps they might discover that the propensity to experiment had been retarding and could continue to retard the production of much-needed rubber. A distinguished head of a medical school once remarked, without conscious humor, that "research sometimes must be interrupted in order to give adequate attention to the cure of patients." Maybe the emphasis in this collaborative rubber program should be shifted from the laboratory to the field. If the suggestion seems to reveal ignorance or lack of appreciation, and if a tone of sarcasm has crept into this narrative, apologies are now offered. Pleaders for appropriations in a day of extravagant phrases probably do not dare to disclose any lack of confidence. They must "puff and blow" in order to "wangle" their funds. But it is not easy to forget taxpayers if one is a taxpayer himself and not also a bureaucrat—and let it be remembered that natural rubber is still on the Defense Department's list of critical raw materials.

Reporting on March 15, 1954, to a Senate committee investigating "Miscellaneous Strategic Raw Materials of Agricultural Origin," the Department of Agriculture stated that the minimum strategic requirement for natural rubber in the Western Hemisphere, exclusive of Canada, was in the neighborhood of 300,000 tons per annum. "There are now approximately 48,000 acres of planted rubber trees in the American tropics," the department went on to observe. "When this rubber comes into bearing it should produce 20,000 tons of rubber annually. . . . To reach the minimum need . . . would require the planting of an additional 500,000 acres of rubber trees. . . . The present interest in rubber planting in Latin America would indicate that if there is no serious setback . . . the Latin-American countries can be self-sufficient within 10 years and can produce sufficient rubber to meet also the needs of the United States within 20 years."[30] Such was the prospect after more than five decades of effort and the expenditure of well over $100 million. It must have disappointed the needy Latin-Americans. The goal envisaged by the agricultural scientists was still 20 years in the future and probably more than another $100 million would be required to reach it!

CHAPTER 9 SUGAR AND OTHER COMMERCIAL PROBLEMS IN INTER-AMERICAN RELATIONS

INTERNATIONAL relations, hemispheric and global, are characterized by the interaction, by the discords and harmonies, of ideologies and material interests. Economic disagreements often threaten cordial relations based upon common ideals. Involving methods rather than long-term objectives, inter-American disputes regarding barriers to trade, investment, and other economic activities have not been infrequent. The sugar trade will serve as an example.

All the independent countries of Latin America except Chile and Uruguay, and practically all the dependent territories of tropical America as well, produce cane sugar; and most of them could expand their production if larger markets were available. In spite of government limitations on plantings in some of the countries, total output of sugar in this part of the world rose from an annual average of less than 8 million short tons, raw value, in the 1930's to a yearly average of nearly 14 million short tons in the early 1950's.

The natural foreign market for the sugar of the region, especially the immense portion of it lying north of Chile and Paraguay, is the United States, the world's biggest consumer of sugar. With a per-capita utilization of almost 100 pounds per annum during recent decades, the people of this country consumed over 157.2 million short tons, raw value, during the years 1934-1955, an annual average in excess of 7 million short tons; and they might have consumed considerably more if they had not been hampered by individual rationing during the war period and by other limitations. Aggregate consumption for the years

1956-1962 is estimated at 62.6 million short tons. Growers and processors of beet sugar in nineteen Far-Western States (extending from Wisconsin, Nebraska, and Kansas to Washington, Oregon, and California), and in Ohio, Michigan, and Indiana on the Great Lakes supplied nearly 35.5 million of the more than 157 million short tons consumed in the United States during the 22 years following 1933. Producers of cane sugar in Louisiana and Florida supplied in excess of 9 million. Hawaii furnished approximately 20 million. The Philippine Islands and a few other distant lands accounted for an additional 13.6 million. The share of Latin America and the dependent territories and colonial possessions of the Western Hemisphere was approximately 59 million short tons, a total far below potential capacity,[1] for which they were paid over $4 billion.

Senator Paul Douglas, trained economist as well as politician, declared on January 17, 1956: "I think there can be no question that the Caribbean area is far better adapted to the production of sugar than the United States; that the yield, not only per acre but per man, would be much higher there; and that therefore if we could organize . . . upon rational principles, the most economic use of labor and capital would be to have the sugar consumed in the United States grown primarily in the Caribbean area. . . . But I know . . . that because of past mistakes and the pressure both from the cane regions [of the United States] and the beet-sugar regions we have built up . . . powerful producing interests. . . . I would urge you . . . to be as sensible as possible and to consider the consumer . . . and try to get as much sugar as we can from the areas that can produce that sugar more cheaply."[2] Thomas Jefferson, reflecting the views of Adam Smith, had stated the case very concisely long ago: "Could every country be employed in producing that which nature has fitted it to produce and each be free to exchange with others natural surpluses for natural wants, the greatest possible would then be produced of those things which contribute to human life and human happiness."[3]

But "natural law" and "rational principles" have never been

allowed to operate as determining factors in the sugar market of the United States. Since July 4, 1789, man-made law has compelled consumers in this country to pay tariffs, excise taxes, and subsidies on the sugar they have used; and consumers have also been subjected to individual rationing during wartime and to national, though not personal, rationing (except during 1942-1947) since 1934. While there have been no extreme oscillations in the price of sugar for more than two decades, a steady rise in the retail price has occurred—the annual average was 5.2 cents a pound in 1933 and 10.4 cents per pound in 1955—and market interferences have reduced Latin-American trade with the United States to the extent of many millions of dollars annually.

Free-trade policy no longer prevails anywhere, perhaps least of all in respect to most products of farms, forests, and mines. International commerce is throttled by almost every conceivable barrier, actually or ostensibly erected in the interest of national security or prosperity, or for the purpose of according favors or relief to national groups, large or small. Advocates of the removal of such barriers, or some of them, have in mind the exporter rather than the consumer, who is now the "forgotten man." The rigidities and insecurities of the modern world, human greed, sympathies for producers, and aspirations of individuals and cliques barricade the free market. "Natural law," although admittedly efficient, is considered impractical, or dangerous, or cruel rather than benevolent.

Attitudes in respect to free trade in the United States, even the attitude of the traditionally low-tariff party, were well illustrated during the hearings that preceded the adoption of the current sugar program in 1934. Secretary Henry Wallace remarked at that time: "Sugar furnishes an extraordinary example of what happens to a commodity when the various governments of the world take an interest in the application of tariffs and bounties and other artificial devices.... The result has been to distort the judgment of producers ... ; ... everywhere ...

production has been built up . . . behind the government walls . . . only to overflow those walls and produce a world-wide chaos in the commodity." Asked by a friend of the beet growers if he might be planning the ultimate extinction of that industry in the United States, Wallace replied: "With the human situation as it is . . . I would not retire it at any time in the next 10 years. If I were speaking from a purely . . . logical point of view, if I were in the position of an autocrat, working from the standpoint of a hundred-year period, I would begin gradually, and if I had a truly satisfactory relationship with . . . those places where sugar can be produced efficiently, I would gradually shift over to . . . producing the things we could efficiently here . . . and getting in exchange therefor the goods they can produce."[4]

In similar fashion A. J. S. Weaver of the staff of the Agricultural Adjustment Administration pointed out that if expansion of production should continue in the United States, this nation would be "saddled, possibly forever, with a high-cost industry, which is not a fair thing to contemplate for the consumers." When Congressman Fred Cummings, a Colorado Democrat, asked whether the purpose of the administration was "to give us a shot in the arm and slide us out of business while we are partly unconscious," Weaver, his brain befogged and his ears "dimmed" by an overnight trip on an airplane, first stammered "Yes" and then "Certainly not."

This response caused excitement among the sugar men, who assumed that the purpose of the Roosevelt administration was to destroy their industry, and led to administrative efforts to placate them. Rexford Tugwell, at that time an official of the Department of Agriculture, offered the following consoling remark: "So far as this bill goes, there is no commitment to any future policy." The purpose of the government at the moment was to try to make the domestic sugar industry profitable; and if this could not be done, to see that it did not "expand further."[5]

In his message of February 8, 1934, Franklin D. Roosevelt went into somewhat more detail. "I do not at this time recommend placing sugar on the free list," he said. "I feel that we ought first to try out a system of quotas with the threefold object of keeping down the price of sugar to consumers, of providing for the retention of beet and cane farming, and . . . of providing against further expansion of this necessarily expensive industry."[6]

The objectives of the program expressed in the basic sugar acts were not quite so explicit in respect to protection of the consumers and prevention of the expansion of a "necessarily expensive industry." "To include sugar beets and sugarcane as basic agricultural commodities under the Agricultural Adjustment Act, and for other purposes" was the rather vague language employed by the Jones-Costigan Act of May 9, 1934. The Sugar Acts of September 1, 1937, and August 8, 1947 (the latter called the "Sugar Act of 1948") were more complicated in their descriptions of objectives. Using identical language, except for the omission of the phrase "to raise revenue" in the law of 1947, both contained this declaration of intentions: "To regulate commerce among the several States, with the Territories and possessions of the United States, and with foreign countries; to protect the welfare of consumers of sugars and of those engaged in the domestic sugar-producing industry; to promote the export trade of the United States; and for other purposes."[7]

These basic acts authorized the use of quotas as an instrument of control. They gave the Secretary of Agriculture a mandate (1) to determine the quantity of sugar needed in each calendar year to meet domestic requirements at prices equitable to consumers and profitable to producers; (2) to allocate among the various supply areas, domestic (both insular and continental) and foreign, specific shares of the market based upon the relative supplier position of the respective producing regions prior to the imposition of controls; and (3) to award subsidies to domestic producers (continental and insular) in payment for compliance with quotas and with the terms prescribed for the benefit of farmers and workers. Crop and disaster insurance were provided by the government. The sugar tariff was gradually reduced from two cents to half a cent per pound on Cuban raw sugar and from a somewhat higher rate to 0.625 cents a pound on raw sugar imported from full-duty countries, with an additional import tax of half a cent a pound on imports of refined ("direct-consumption") sugar. At the same time, however, an excise tax of half a cent a pound was levied on all sugars consumed in the United States.

Minimizing the burdens imposed upon the consumer and the taxpayer, the proponents of the program have repeatedly declared that it has not cost the Federal Government "one dime." It is impossible to determine even probable differences in prices under the program and without the program, but prices would certainly have been lower most of the time if the program had not been in operation. Annual costs to the consumer in increased prices have been estimated at from $250 million to $400 million. Excise taxes collected during 1934-1955 amounted to nearly $1.4 billion; duties on raw sugar and import taxes on the refined product aggregated some $700 million. Administrative expenses ranged from a million to a million and a half per annum. Compliance payments to domestic producers exceeded a billion dollars during the 22-year period. Excise taxes, some of which were returned to the insular governments, more than reimbursed the Federal Treasury for its expenditures in connection with the program, and might well be reduced if the domestic beneficiaries were not expecting larger doles and if Federal finances were in a better condition.[8] Had larger quotas been assigned to the various tropical countries of the hemisphere, exporters, as already suggested, might have taken advantage of the larger markets resulting from Latin America's expanded purchasing power.

Congressmen and Senators from the sugar-producing states have been steadfast in their support of the program and successful in their efforts to obtain larger quotas for the continental beet and cane areas. Members of the farm bloc have enthusiastically approved it in the hope of securing more benevolent treatment for other farm commodities. Their attitude may be illustrated by the remarks of the chairman of the House Committee on Agriculture in 1955. Harold Cooley, head of this important committee, made it clear that he endorsed the sugar policy because it had operated without causing public agitation and because he felt that it might be used as an argument for high and rigid supports for cotton, peanuts, and other farm produce. Mr. Cooley, June 22, 1955: The sugar program "has operated so . . . successfully and . . . so smoothly through the years that the ordinary housewife is not even aware of the fact that we have a program in operation."[9] Again, July 30, 1955: "The program has operated so well . . . and so smoothly that the average housewife is not . . . aware . . . that we have a sugar program. Even the average Congressman is unaware of the fact that we have a sugar program."[10]

Such was Mr. Cooley's tender regard for consumers and taxpayers. He favored this program of surreptitious plunder because it seemed painless. Nor did he reveal any practical devotion to the much-lauded free-enterprise system so far as farmers were concerned. He assumed that they were willing to exchange a share of their liberty for government largess. Discussing this phase of the sugar program with True Morse of the Department of Agriculture on June 23, 1955, the North Carolina Congressman remarked: "We know—all of us know—that sugar can be produced in offshore areas at far less cost than we can produce it here. All of us know that this program is . . . saturated with subsidy and control and regimentation and all of these unholy and un-American things that we have been told of from day to day. . . . You fix the amount that a man can grow, the amount that he can market—the amount to be refined . . . and you pay a tremendous subsidy to the producers. . . . Here is a bill, if there ever was a program on earth that had . . . all of these things that Mr. Benson has been denouncing, this is it. [Yet] I am for it. He is for it. The President is for it." At this point Congressman Poage of Texas added his bit of sarcasm: "Surely they could not be asking for all of the regimentation you described, because

Mr. Benson is opposed to all regimentation. He told us that." Laughter resounded in the corridors.[11]

Continuing his discussion on July 14, 1955, and directing his remarks to Secretary of Agriculture Ezra Taft Benson in person, Mr. Cooley said: "Both you and President Eisenhower have approved the Sugar Act. . . . And yet in this program it seems to me that we have everything that you disapprove. I mean you have . . . enslavement of agriculture, you have subsidy, almost unlimited, and you have wage controls even in the beetfields and the canefields. You have crop insurance. You have disaster insurance. . . . You have complete and utter regimentation from the seed to the table. . . . You have got your producers up to 93.5 per cent of parity and are holding them there. That is all right." Mr. Cooley's heckling was clearly intended to promote equally high subsidies for producers of other crops.[12]

The general public may have been largely unaware of the sugar program and its costs, but this had been by no means true of its various beneficiaries. The program's operation had been characterized by a greedy scramble for quotas that had caused no little vexation among administrative officials, all of whom were thoroughly conscious of the program's complexities and the violent clashes of producer and other interests that it had periodically aroused. In fact, the struggle had intensified with the passing years. The State Department, the Department of Agriculture, and the Interior Department had all been harassed by lobbyists in search of market shares and bounties. Months were wasted during the initiation of the program. Secretary of Agriculture Wallace described the clamor as "one of the most astounding exhibitions" he had "ever seen."[13] Almost every year —excepting the war period, when allotments of acreage were not in force and when larger profits could be obtained from the production of other farm commodities—efforts were made by various beneficiaries to gain advantages over their competitors. Some of the public officials even involved themselves in the scramble. Members of the staff of the Reclamation Bureau, for instance, championed the beet producers in return for the latter's support of new irrigation projects,[14] and officials connected with the Sugar Division of the Department of Agriculture were so friendly that they soon became officials of the sugar companies.[15]

President Roosevelt was frequently disturbed by the sugar lobbyists in Washington and by the deft operations of the sugar rivals. In a press conference of June 15, 1937, he said: "I don't think there will be any [sugar] legislation until these lobbies get out of town . . . the most pernicious of all lobbies since any of you people . . . have been alive."[16] He tried in vain to prevent discrimination against domestic insular producers and producers active in the independent countries of the Caribbean, and signed the sugar bill of 1937 with reluctance.[17] Again, in April, 1939, he complained that "sugar lobbyists" were "pressing for drastic amendments . . . which would disrupt the balance established in the existing legislation as between the opposing interests of the various groups concerned," and not only "further burden consumers for the additional benefit of producers" but "seriously impair one of the principal markets for our export crops, and establish discriminations among various parts of the United States."[18] A year later he urged the House Committee on Agriculture to refrain from recommending "any bill that would impair the foreign outlets for our surplus products, run counter to the Good Neighbor Policy, discriminate among various groups of domestic producers and processors, or increase the burden on our consumers and taxpayers."[19] No changes were made in the basic law of 1937 until 1947, but the representatives of the mainland sugar interests were busy with self-serving schemes in 1941 and might have had them adopted if the Second World War had not intervened.

Not only were pressures relaxed during the war and early postwar years because other profitable farm products diverted interest from sugar but, for the same reason, the Secretary of Agriculture was able to bring the mildly conflicting groups into essential agreement before Congress considered new legislation on the subject in 1947. Nor was there any very unseemly activity in 1951 (Korean War) when the Sugar Act of 1948 was extended for a period of four years beyond 1953. But the contest was resumed with renewed vigor in 1955, when 30 sugar bills were introduced in the House of Representatives and a bill signed by no less than 49 Senators made its appearance in the Senate. With farm prices allegedly depressed, the continental sugar men were determined to enlarge their quotas at the expense of offshore producers. "The town has been literally throbbing with lobbyists and lawyers," declared Congressman Cooley on July 30, 1955, as he began to press for speedy passage of the sugar bill through the House. The feat was accomplished within little more than an hour. A few remonstrances were made in behalf of Puerto Rico, Cuba, Mexico, and the Philippine Islands; two or three members expressed concern about exports; one speaker mentioned the consumers; and then the bill was approved by a vote of 194 to 44, without recording the "yeas" and "nays" and with hardly a quorum present.[20]

The hearings of the House Committee on Agriculture preceding the introduction of the bill by Mr. Cooley had kept its members busy for ten long days. Cane men from Louisiana and Florida; beet growers and beet Congressmen from the West; representatives of the seacoast cane-sugar refiners of nine states; attorneys for Puerto Rico, the Hawaiian Islands, the Philippines, and Formosa; lobbyists for Peru, Mexico, Cuba, the Dominican Republic, and Haiti; a Guatemalan diplomat who served notice that his country would expect soon to send sugar to the United States; domestic molasses companies and producers of alcohol; policy officials representing the Federal Government; bakers, candymakers, manufacturers of chocolate and ice cream and bottlers of soft drinks; exporters, shippers, and foreign investors; labor leaders and workers in the big sugar ports—more than a hundred witnesses appeared, made their pleas, exhibited the cleavages in our competitive society, disclosed the increasing problems of public planning and management, and left this writer in a pensive mood. Only the consumers diffused in millions of private homes throughout our land were absent—the diffused consumers and the diffused taxpayers, many of them little people struggling to provide for their families, who were carrying not only the burdens of the sugar program but also the burdens of growing paternalism and expanding government operations in the economic realm.

The civilian bureaucracy of the Federal Government now numbered over two and a half million. How enormous would it be at the end of the next decade? Would all imports, as suggested by scores of bills introduced in 1954-1956, eventually be subjected to quotas? Would all production eventually be aided by subsidy? Would a two-price system finally be adopted for every commodity, with the benefits of lower prices restricted to foreign purchasers subsidized by the consumers and taxpayers of the United States? Would Adam Smith's sovereign ultimate consumers, supposed to determine the quantity, character, and trends of production, become the mudsills of our economic system? Would the pure consumers—those who neither turn out nor distribute material goods, those who are presumed to form the cultural apex of civilization—would these become the paupers of our country while its political and economic leaders were boasting about national prosperity? Only the well-organized consumers requiring sugar in the manufacture of other commodities were heard by the Committee on Agriculture, and even these were not heeded.

Every argument—sound or not—calculated to promote special interests was used. War veterans were said to be moving west in great numbers in order to buy farms and grow beets on expensive irrigation and reclamation projects (to be offered later as exhibits for even more expensive projects while the rich lands of the rain belt were more and more excluded from cultivation). The friendship of Latin America and the fate of the Point-Four Program were said to be at stake: foreign countries must be given a larger share of our sugar market in order to prevent the spread of Communism. Nations ruled by dictators and near-dictators should have their quotas reduced in the interest of the more democratic countries. Sugar quotas must be made to depend upon concessions to exporters and to American investors in foreign lands. Countries nearest to the United States must be favored for strategic reasons. Sugar production at home should be rapidly expanded in behalf of national security. High levels of production and employment must be maintained in the United States at whatever cost. Only by increasing exports could the nation prosper: "The margin we export represents the difference between domestic prosperity and depression." The quotas we send across the seas will "return to us in many ways." A rich and powerful nation, we must ever be conscious of our influence and responsibilities. "We are like Gulliver in Lilliput. We must be always aware that ... what appears to us as a slight shift in position may well prove to be an earthquake to one of our friendly neighbors." Even the argument of more or less collaboration with the United States in recent wars and in the United Nations was employed.[21]

Although the first session of the 84th Congress adjourned before the Senate considered the House bill, the guardians of the mainland sugar men, eager to complete the sugar legislation before the contest for general farm legislation began, acted promptly in 1956. The Senate Committee on Finance held only two days of hearings; its chairman introduced a sugar bill on February 7, and the bill was passed the next day, without amendment and without a recorded vote. Efforts were made to shift some of the quotas among the offshore countries and to effect changes in the allotments of refined sugar in some cases, but the only serious opponent of the measure was Senator William Fulbright, who mentioned the exploited housewife but was primarily interested in expanding the export of Arkansas rice.[22]

The differences between the House bill and the Senate bill were mainly these: (1) the House was more generous, among offshore countries, to Peru, the Dominican Republic, and Mexico, while the Senate was more liberal in its treatment of Cuba; (2) the Senate made even greater concessions than did the House to the demands of the mainland beet and cane areas. Franklin D. Roosevelt's "necessarily expensive industry" was not held in check. It would be permitted to expand more rapidly than ever —at the expense of the taxpayers, consumers, and exporters of the United States and to the detriment of the Latin-American neighbors, even including the commonwealth of Puerto Rico. Expansion of production in the mainland areas during the years 1956-1962 may amount to as much as 1.7 million short tons, which probably will be sold for over $300 million at wholesale prices. Cuba's share of the aggregate consumption of the United States during the period—a little short of 21.1 million tons—will be more than 2.5 million tons, worth over $250 million, seaboard wholesale, less than it might have been if the Sugar Act of 1948 had not been thus changed. The new legislation will permit no more than comparatively minor expansions of the shares awarded to Peru, the Dominican Republic (although the quota was doubled for this tyrant-ridden country), and Mexico, since the combined increase for these three suppliers—the major Latin-American participants other than Cuba and Puerto Rico—is not likely to be in excess of 147,000 short tons. Of the estimated consumption of some 62.6 million short tons by the people of continental United States during 1956-1962, mainland producers are expected to supply some 17.8 million tons, or more than 28.5 per cent. If no change had been made in the allotments stipulated by the Sugar Act of 1948, their share would have been 16.1 million tons, or a little over 25.6 per cent.[23]

2.

Sugar is only one example of the use of the quota system in the United States since the early 1930's. The Secretary of Agriculture has been endowed with legal authority to impose quotas on the import of almost any farm product deemed to be in surplus supply: raw cotton, linseed oil, butter, wheat, flour, rice, peanuts, cheese, flaxseed, live cattle, dressed beef (temporary or permanent embargoes on the last two). Such quotas limit or prevent Latin-American exports to this country. In many other respects, however, Latin Americans have easy access to the markets of their big neighbor. Coffee, bananas, cocoa, tin and most of the metals and minerals, various forest products, and several other commodities are either on the free list or charged with very moderate tariffs or excise taxes. Rates rarely exceed 50 per cent ad valorem; the average is hardly more than 10 or 15. Among the higher rates are the following (ad valorem equivalents): fuel oil, 30 per cent; linseed oil, 24; canned beef, 20; tuna fish, canned in oil, 45; mica, 12 to 25; tungsten, 19; mercury, 16; fresh tomatoes, 22 to 44; wool, 14 to 40; straw hats, bodies, and braids, 6.5 to 90. There is, however, a growing sentiment among farmers and little industrialists for various types of trade barriers. Whether this sentiment will lead to extension of quotas and increasing of tariffs and excise taxes only the future can reveal. These farmers and small businessmen will be opposed by powerful groups—big industrialists engaged in mass-production and looking for export markets and owners of the merchant marine, for instance—whose profits, capacity, and influence have been enormously expanded by recent wars and programs of government aid to foreign countries,[24] and who may count upon the support of such doctrinaire economists as attribute peculiar virtues to exporters. Congressman C. M. Bailey of West Virginia described the rival economic forces with essential accuracy early in 1955: "The history of the tariff in the United States has, in the past, been principally the story of a conflict between manufactured goods and farm products. . . . Today that is not the conflict. The differences of view are between the great units of mass production . . . and the small manufacturer."[25] For several years Bailey, along with Congressman Richard M. Simpson of Pennsylvania and numerous other associates and collaborators, had been advocating quotas or higher tariffs on crude petroleum and not a few other minerals and metals as well as on scores of manufactured products such as pottery, tile, textiles, leather goods, clothes pins, hats, caps, gloves, rugs, and bicycles, some of which were imported, or might be imported, from Latin America. No matter which side wins, consumers—especially those engaged in cultural activities and neither producing nor selling material goods—are not likely to reap the benefits. Exports often tend to maintain or increase prices, and imports will not reduce prices if they are upheld by government action or manipulated by producers and middlemen.

Although Latin Americans are never free from worry with reference to future commercial relations with the United States, their trade with their big neighbor had been large and relatively satisfactory in the recent past. For more than a quarter of a century they had been selling from almost a third to nearly a half of their total exports to its purchasers. The percentage was 29 in 1929, nearly 33 in 1935, more than 44 in both 1940 and 1951, in excess of 49 in 1952, and only a little less in the years 1953-1955. And during the same period Latin Americans were purchasing a slightly larger share of their imports from the United States; in fact, a little over half of them during the fifteen years beginning with 1940.[26] President Eisenhower's International Development Board, in its report published in September, 1954, wrote enthusiastically of the significance of trade relations with Latin America. "It is the largest market for our exports," the Board declared, "and the largest source of our imports. It is an indispensable and irreplaceable source of our vital raw materials, not only critical minerals for war and defense but foodstuffs as well." Attempting to penetrate the years ahead, the Board predicted that Latin America's population would be "twice that of the United States and Canada put together" in less than half a century and observed that it was not necessary to "spell out the importance of this growth" in view of our prospective share of at least 50 per cent of the region's imports. Finally, the Board made this strong recommendation: "The sporadic but recurring attempts to shut out from the United States market the products of the Latin-American countries by quota or by tariff or excise tax increases should be discouraged and a firm national policy against such measures should be clearly enunciated."[27]

A firm national policy with respect to quotas, embargoes, tariffs, and excise taxes would placate Latin-American exporters, but it would not satisfy all of their trade aspirations. They would like to have the United States reduce its emphasis on the development of alternate sources of supply in Asia and Africa and on the domestic production of synthetics as well; maintain high prices for their foods and raw materials; decrease its exports of such commodities; and furnish them with cheaper manufactured goods. And they would like to have all of these favors while they continue to protect their home markets and trade balances by means of tariffs, excises, exchange controls, multiple exchange rates, and every other device that seems effective, for they are strongly determined to expand and diversify their manufacturing establishments and they claim special privileges on the ground that they are only at the beginning of their industrial career. They could easily be quoted at length on this subject, but perhaps it will suffice to quote instead Friedrich List's sarcastic statement regarding Great Britain during the second half of the nineteenth century in order to illustrate Latin America's attitude with reference to highly developed nations which advocate the removal of trade barriers. In this connection List wrote:[28]

"It is a very common clever device that when anyone has attained the summit of greatness, he kicks away the ladder by which he has climbed up in order to deprive others of the means of climbing up after him. . . . Any nation which by means of protective duties and restrictions on navigation has raised her manufacturing power and her navigation to such a degree of development that no other nation can sustain free competition with her, can do nothing wiser than to throw away these ladders of her greatness, to preach to other nations the benefits of free trade, and to declare in penitent tones that she has hitherto wandered in the paths of error, and has now for the first time succeeded in discovering the truth."

There is almost no limit to what Latin Americans expect of *Tío Samuel*—and two decades of benevolent words and deeds by this bearded philanthropist's emissaries are partly to blame for the Latin-American state of mind. *Tío Samuel esta muy rico,* they say, and should share his wealth with his poor hemispheric kinsmen whose increased productivity and purchasing capacity will eventually repay him, especially in times of political and economic stress, by supplying his growing needs for critical raw materials and tropical foods and by furnishing larger outlets for the products of his expanding manufacturing plants (provided that such products do not compete with theirs).

But magnanimous Uncle Sam is not omnipotent. He cannot resist the demands of domestic sugar producers and various other farm blocs, or of the shipping interests, or of any other well-organized, powerful, and persistent domestic group. He cannot compel private investors to send their capital to Latin America unless they feel that it will be safe and yield at least as high returns as may be expected from other regions. He cannot compel importers to make their purchases in the dearest foreign markets. He may not be able forever to ignore taxpayers, consumers, and poorer citizens in the United States if he continues to permit them to cast their ballots in national elections and throw their weight around in the process of choosing personnel and determining policies. Nor is it certain that he can persuade his constituents to tolerate permanently the substitution of official and compulsory benevolence for traditional private generosity. They have not abandoned the doctrine of separation of church and state or their claim to freedom to manage their economic affairs without political interference (although they are seldom reluctant to call for government aid when they feel that it will serve their private interests). Artful propaganda, however, and astute action by the Latin Americans, if accompanied by deterioration in investment prospects and terms of trade in and with the tropics of the Old World, might result in greater devotion on the part of the United States to the tropics of America.

In spite of some trade barriers on each side, Latin Americans, as suggested earlier, have had a large share of the market of their big neighbor, and not only during the two world wars of the twentieth century but also in more recent years, supplying not merely sugar, coffee, petroleum, copper, and various other minerals and metals but many other products as well. During the decade beginning with 1946 the United States purchased more than a third of its imports from this region. The average was 35.5 per cent during the first five years of the period and 31.5 per cent during the second five years. The United States imported more from Latin America during these ten years than it imported from Canada, or Europe, or the rest of the world excluding Canada and Europe. In no single year during this first postwar decade did this country buy as much from Europe, or Canada, or all Asia, Oceania, and Africa combined as it bought from the Latin-American countries.

But the reverse of the story is different. In the course of the ten years starting with 1946 the United States sold far more of its exports in Europe than in Latin America (owing mainly to huge grants and loans made to the European countries), sold slightly more of its products to Asia, Oceania, and Africa than to Latin America, and exported a little more to Canada than to the Latin-American republics during 1953 and 1955, but considerably less during each of the other eight years. Latin-American markets absorbed during this postwar decade only 23.5 per cent of the exports of the United States.[29] Latin America needed larger and more efficient production in order to increase its capacity to buy the exports of its big neighbor—either greater productivity, or higher prices, or more grants and credits as in the case of Europe!

CHAPTER **10** FISHERY TROUBLES

BOTH the fishermen and the government of the United States have been disturbed by fishery troubles for a decade. The subject has attracted surprisingly little public attention,[1] but a rather serious problem had arisen in inter-American relations, and it remained unsolved.

The problem centers on tuna fish—yellowfin and skipjack—and the small fish used as tuna bait, but whale and other species are involved to some extent. The International Law Commission of the United Nations has been investigating the subject since 1951 and the General Assembly of that organization gave it serious consideration in 1956-1957. The problem was before the Organization of the American States on at least three occasions; and the State Department of the United States has been engaged in fishery negotiations with most of the eleven Pacific-Coast countries of Latin America since 1949 without satisfactory results.

The tuna industry of the United States, which has grown rapidly since 1946, is owned mainly by residents of California, Oregon, and Washington. Their investment is reported to aggregate some $125 million, including the capital in processing and canning as well as in fishing. The fishermen of these three states have been selling their annual catch of tuna for approximately $50 million in recent years. The annual wholesale value of the processed and canned tuna is reckoned at some $113 million. Taxes paid by the industry and the consumers of its products are said to exceed $52 million per annum.

Numerous schools of yellowfin and skipjack tuna inhabit the eastern Pacific Ocean from the Southern boundary of California to Peru, and roam in an area extending from three hundred to five hundred miles from the shorelines. The waters surrounding the Galápagos Islands, a possession of Ecuador, provide one of their favorite haunts.

The tuna fleet of the United States is composed largely of clippers, but a good many other vessels, most of them small, also engage in the industry. The fishermen number from four thousand to some ten thousand, depending upon the season. The processing and canning industry employs another eight thousand. The business is organized in a score of companies, associations, and unions, the majority of them in southern California. Among the California organizations are: the French Sardine Company, California Fish Canners' Association, the Tuna Research Foundation, the High Seas Tuna Packing Company, the American Tunaboat Association, the Fishermen's Cooperative Association, the Seine and Line Fishermen's Union, the Cannery Workers' Union, the Cannery Workers' and Fishermen's Union, and the Union of Clipper Engineers. Among the organizations in the other states are the Trans-Pacific Shipping and Packing Company and the Arctic Maid Company, both in Seattle, Washington, and the Columbia River Salmon and Tuna Packers' Association of Astoria, Oregon.

The tuna clippers lure the fish by means of live bait—anchovetta, mackerel, and other small species—and bring them in with large hooks attached by strong cords to short, stout poles. Other boats use nets and seines to capture the tuna, and nets and seines are the main equipment employed in fishing for bait. The tuna are large fish, weighing from 35 to more than 85 pounds, and are seldom found near the shore. But the habitats of the small bait fish are almost entirely within the familiar three-mile limit.

Since the bait-fish are taken from the generally acknowledged territorial waters of the Latin-American countries, permits to catch them are obtained from the various governments, which are paid from two to three million dollars annually for the privilege. If none of these governments laid claim to jurisdiction over waters beyond the three-mile limit, no licenses and no fees would be required to engage in tuna-fishing because the tuna seldom leave the waters customarily defined as a part of the high seas. But several of the Latin-American governments have attempted to assert their sovereignty far out from their shores—Honduras, El Salvador, Costa Rica, Ecuador, Peru, Chile, and probably some others have claimed dominion for a distance of two hundred nautical miles—so that fishermen from the Pacific Coast of the United States have had to encounter these governments in fishing for tuna as well as in fishing for bait.

Edward B. Wilber, budget officer of the United States Department of State, summarized the problem as follows on February 25, 1952:[2]

"The Latin-American countries do not at present participate in the tuna fishing except to a very limited extent, but they hope to do so in the future. They see the rapidly increasing United States tuna fleet harvesting large quantities of this natural resource which lies at their doorsteps and they fear the Americans are depleting the stocks, leaving little for the future. They also fear that the tuna-bait stocks, which lie in their territorial waters, are being depleted by the United States fleet. . . .

"These fears of the Latin-American countries have led certain of them to make conditions increasingly difficult for our tuna fleet—by extending the limits of territorial-water claims; by seizing our fishing vessels for alleged territorial violations; by enacting onerous regulations for bait fishing."

Costa Rica and Peru appear to have been the earliest of the group to become alarmed. The bait-fish disappeared from Costa Rica's Nicoya Bay late in 1947, and the government of that country, attributing their disappearance to the unrestrained activities of fishermen from the United States, refused to accept the explanation offered by these fishermen to the effect that the extinction of the fish resulted from the sudden appearance in Costa Rican coastal waters of a "red tide" of tiny poisonous animals which they greedily swallowed and which speedily caused the death of all the fish in the vicinity. Although Peru had proclaimed its control over waters extending out 200 miles from its shores as early as 1947, the Lima government remained fairly calm until early in 1952, when the tuna schools failed to appear within ten or fifteen miles of the coast as in former years. Contending that a host of American tuna-boats had depleted the stocks a few months before, Peruvian politicians complained bitterly; and they were further agitated by the attempts of the American tuna industry to obtain a tariff on fresh and frozen tuna and bonito imported from Peru and other foreign countries.

Although the United States Senate refused to approve the tariff bill passed by the House and the Tariff Commission also refused later to recommend such a levy, tension tended to increase. In a letter to Senator Pat McCarran dated March 12, 1952, Donald P. Loker of the French Sardine Company declared: "These countries are ... eager to obtain larger earnings from the operations of our fleet, larger earnings in fact than we can afford to pay and stay in business."[3] Appearing before the Senate Committee on Appropriations on June 10, 1952, and speaking for the entire California tuna industry, Loker observed further: "We have a problem with Ecuador, with Colombia, with Peru, with Honduras, with Costa Rica, and there are ten Latin-American countries that we have a definite problem with."[4] Writing to Senator Styles Bridges on May 1, 1953, Edward W. Allen, a Seattle lawyer representing the tuna interests, lamented the apparently unfriendly attitude of the Latin-American countries. "I have been thoroughly convinced," he declared, "that the millions of dollars which we have spent in Central and South America ... have been almost a total waste."[5] Grants to Latin nations bordering on the Pacific Ocean during the period from July 1, 1945, through the year 1954, for technical assistance and other purposes, including the Inter-American Highway, amounted to some $200 million; cheap loans and credits extended by the Export-Import Bank and other official agencies and actually utilized by these countries totaled more than $354.6 million;[6] and the fishery dispute might indeed nullify whatever sentiments of cordiality this benevolence may have fostered.

El Salvador probably expressed the view of most of the nations of Latin America's Pacific Coast regarding the subject of control of adjacent seas in a statement of December 20, 1954, made to the Law Commission of the United Nations, in which she declared: "The sovereignty of El Salvador extends to 200 miles of territorial waters and the corresponding territorial shelf, and it is wholly unacceptable for this country that in any international convention relating to the territorial sea, principles should be adopted which conflict with its political rights."[7] Already, at the Tenth International American Conference which met at Caracas, Venezuela, in March 1954, the government of Ecuador had presented a document that set forth its views and perhaps those of the majority of the Latin-American governments involved in the controversy. Ecuador's main contentions were: (1) That each state "must take the measures deemed necessary to exploit the natural resources in the areas under its sovereignty and jurisdiction in accordance with standards that insure prudent utilization"; (2) that such international sovereignty and jurisdiction should "include an area of 200 marine miles, reckoned from the outermost points of the coast, as the most adequate means of . . . facilitating the conservation and utilization of the natural resources of each state"; and (3) that each state must assume the duty of providing the "legal, regulatory, and technical measures" required for the "conservation and utilization of the natural resources . . . in the said areas under its sovereignty, for its own benefit" and the benefit of the "hemisphere" and the "community of nations."[8]

Meantime Ecuador, Peru, Colombia, and some of the other countries were seizing and detaining or penalizing numerous fishing vessels from the United States. The fines usually were limited to a few thousand dollars for each boat, but in one instance nearly three million dollars were exacted as fines from five whalers.[9] A Federal law of August 27, 1954, even went so far as to authorize the Treasury of the United States to reimburse American owners for fines imposed by countries asserting claims to jurisdiction over territorial waters beyond the three-mile limit. "We think the controversy is now coming to a head," said Warren F. Looney, special assistant to the Under Secretary of State, on February 17, 1955. "In fact," he added, "we know it is."[10] But Mr. Looney turned out to be a false prophet. The dispute was still unresolved more than three years later.

The views of the United States on the issue were clearly announced during the first half of the year 1955. In a public address in New York on May 13, 1955, Herman Phleger, legal adviser to the State Department, declared: "The principle of freedom of the seas is as valid today as when it was established.... We cannot return to the days of the Barbary pirates when the coastal states exacted tribute for the rights of navigation." This was certainly a vigorous statement. But Phleger hastened to add: "Nor can we return to those days when strong and enterprising states appropriated the resources of the seas by appropriating the seas themselves."[11] A few weeks earlier, on April 25, 1955, the State Department had published a memorandum which set forth the contention of the United States with precision:[12]

"The United States Government is convinced . . . that the most satisfactory avenue for the solution of the growing conflicts of interest over fishery resources lies in the development of conservation agreements among interested States. It is likewise convinced that continuous efforts by coastal States to extend unilaterally their jurisdictional control over . . . high seas cannot fail to aggravate existing international disputes and create new ones."

With the advice of the tuna industry, the State Department had evolved a plan to deal with the problem as early as 1949 and had signed an open convention with Costa Rica on May 31 of that year providing for a joint commission to investigate the subject thoroughly and recommend rules and regulations. Other nations of Latin America's Pacific Coast were expected to give their adherence to the agreement, which contained no commitment with respect to national jurisdiction over adjacent seas, and to appoint representatives on the commission. But only Panama did so, and not until the summer of 1953.

The new agency, called the Inter-American Tropical Tuna Commission, was organized in 1950, shortly after the outbreak of the Korean War, and for three years it had to operate on a very small budget, a total of only $132,500 for the period. Whether this circumstance aroused distrust and became a factor in preventing other countries from collaborating, as some citizens of the United States engaged in the tuna industry later charged, is not definitely known.

Officials of the United States and some of the leaders in the tuna industry of the Pacific Coast were optimistic for a time and reported a similar mood in Costa Rica. "The Government of Costa Rica," declared William O. Hall of the State Department on June 25, 1951, "has hailed the Commission as a great step forward in the harmonious development of the fisheries and the elimination of friction. Costa Rica has invited other affected nations to join in this cooperative project and several have evinced a strong interest."[13] Speaking for the tuna interests on July 27, 1951, Donald P. Loker wrote: "It is safe to say that already—since the . . . negotiation of the treaty—there has been a notable diminution of . . . the frictions which have developed in the past."[14] In a letter to Senator Pat McCarran dated March 12, 1952, Loker was still hopeful. "I am convinced," he declared, "that if we get sufficient funds . . . each and every one of these . . . countries will jump on the band wagon and we can amicably settle our bait, territorial-water, license, and all other problems of interest and importance."[15] Writing to Senator McCarran on March 11, Sam Crivello, president of the Tunaboat Association, observed: "Peru, Ecuador, Panama, and Mexico have all evinced official interest in joining in this work, but they have not done so because the United States has not yet begun to seriously fulfil the commitments it made to Costa Rica under this treaty more than three years ago."[16] Loker remarked enthusiastically on June 10: "This . . . is the most perfect type of Point 4 program, for it will aid the economic development of Latin America . . . and will benefit our citizens and one of our industries at the same time."[17] And as late as May 1, 1953, Edward W. Allen wrote from Seattle: "I know of no single move which offers better possibilities . . . than the expansion of the Inter-American Tuna Commission."[18]

The plan seemed to have attractive features. The United States, the principal beneficiary of the tuna industry at this juncture, would pay nearly all of the expenses; the Latin-American countries were assigned hardly more than token contributions, which were soon fixed at $500 for each country. The purpose of the commission was to maintain the tuna and tuna-bait population at a level that would "permit maximum sustained catches year by year." Each member country would have an equal vote. Each would help to determine policies and share the work. The commission would have an independent staff, responsible to no single government, and the findings of the staff would be published in both Spanish and English. It was therefore felt that Latin Americans would have confidence in the commission's investigations and recommendations as they "would not in work conducted solely by the [tuna] industry or by the United States."[19]

But these high hopes were not well founded. Instead of collaborating on this basis, Peru, Chile, and Ecuador formed in 1952-1953 a combination of their own for the purpose of asserting their claims to sovereignty over extensive territorial waters and formulating common policies in dealing with all aspects of the problem.[20] Unprepared as yet to engage in tuna fishing on a large scale and unwilling to collaborate with the United States,

Costa Rica, and Panama in efforts designed to maintain the tuna and tuna-bait population at a level that might insure and perpetuate "maximum catches," these three South American republics and others seemed to be determined to obtain larger incomes from the operations of the tuna fleet of the United States. The two or three millions collected annually for licenses for bait-fishing did not satisfy them.

Their policy promised more immediate profits than collaboration offered, but it was not a policy calculated to promote hemispheric or larger international harmony. A segment of the current global problem of control over the high seas and fair utilization of the resources therein, the American fishery problem probably could not be solved by the Organization of the American States. Could the United Nations provide a satisfactory solution? This question might be answered during the next year or so. Meantime either the taxpayers of the United States or the tuna industry and the tuna consumers may expect to continue their contributions to the Latin-American riparian governments. Whether such contributions should be described as tribute depends upon the point of view. The policy which demands such payments can certainly be appropriately described as nationalistic.[21]

CHAPTER 11 BOLIVIA: AN EXHIBIT OF THE PROBLEMS OF ECONOMIC DEVELOPMENT IN RETARDED COUNTRIES

"VIOLENCE shook Bolivia in September, but by month's end the government of newly-inaugurated Hernán Siles Zuazo seemed confident it had sufficient popular support to maintain itself in power. The President declared a nation-wide state of siege after armed rioters staged a hunger march in La Paz in which at least five persons were killed and scores injured. Mobs burned the plant of the official government newspaper, *La Nación*, and the government-owned Illimani radio station, and did more than $1 million damage before police could break them up. Counter-attackers then sacked the Falange headquarters and the home of Oscar Unzaga de la Vega, leader of the opposition Falange Socialista Boliviana. . . . Over 200 were arrested for participation in the riots, and Falange leaders sought asylum in the various Latin American embassies. . . . In protest against the burning of *La Nación* . . . workers led by Juan Lechín, head of the Central Labor Organization, seized the plant of the shut-down opposition newspaper, *La Razón*. . . . After an inventory of *La Razón's* facilities was taken, the Chamber of Deputies passed a law authorizing expropriation of the newspaper for official use, but at month's end the bill had not been passed by the Senate. In the midst of the political upheaval labor chief Lechín suddenly resigned as Senate president, giving as reasons poor health and Senate failure to obtain a quorum. However, it appeared that the firm stand taken by moderate officials on . . . *La Razón's* expropriation was also a factor."

So wrote the editors of *Hispanic American Report* in a recent survey of the Republic of Bolivia.[1] Economic conditions in Bolivia were likewise chaotic. Inefficient operation of the three big mining properties—those formerly owned by the Aramayo, Hochschild, and Patiño companies—political disorders, labor recalcitrance, confusion attending the redistribution of agricultural lands, drought, and unseasonable frosts had caused scarcities that had resulted in tremendous inflation. The *boliviano*, which had been pegged at 190 to the United States dollar a few years before, was selling in the free market at 11,000 to the dollar. Savings of the small middle and upper classes were melting away. Wages of the workers, though raised repeatedly, were not keeping pace with the rising costs of living. Farmers, planters, and ranchmen, whether white, mestizo, or Indian, were withholding their produce from the town and city markets. The government of the United States, operating under the law of 1954 (Agricultural Trade Development and Assistance Act), and the "Voluntary" Relief Agencies of this country, under authority of other legislation, were offered an opportunity to expand their programs of global benevolence and dispose of larger quantities of the agricultural surpluses that plagued politicians and crowded the storage spaces of the Commodity Credit Corporation. Bolivia was on the dole.

In fact, Bolivia had been on the dole for several years, and particularly since the "reform" party, the National Revolutionary Movement, seized the government in April, 1952, under the leadership of Víctor Paz Estenssoro, Juan Lechín, and Hernán Siles Zuazo. Taxpayers of the United States were financing most of Bolivia's relief. Grants made by the Washington government to Bolivia during fiscal years 1946-1956 totaled some $49,576,000; Exim Bank credits utilized by Bolivia during the same period aggregated $41,465,000. The grand total was approximately $91,041,000 for a country with a population of about 3,500,000. For fiscal years 1953-1956 grants amounted to $45,573,000 and credits utilized added up to $10,111,000, making a total of

$55,684,000.[2] In addition, the United States government was supporting the Bolivian mining industry, including the mining properties of the Big Three seized by the Bolivian government in 1952, by the purchase of tin and other minerals, said to exceed its needs, for its stockpile. Expenditures for these during fiscal years 1953-1956 were probably in the neighborhood of $105 million. Yet Bolivia seemed to be in a sadder state in 1956 than in 1952. The United States was paying for the programs and the mistakes of Bolivia's political and labor leaders who were trying to follow in the footsteps of the politicians and labor bosses of Mexico, especially during the years when Cárdenas and Lombardo Toledano were dominant and when the Mexican workers and peasants were armed to defy and intimidate the regular armed forces. Mexico eventually weathered the storm and attained approximate political stability and economic prosperity. But it would be hazardous to predict that Bolivia would eventually match Mexico's achievement.

Many and various factors would determine Bolivia's future: education, health, and birth rate; more or less efficiency in production, the extent of improvements in transportation, and the degree of honesty and prudence in government; the state of labor-management relations and success or failure in the creation of a climate favorable to investment of both native and foreign capital; world demands for Bolivian minerals and metals; continuation of grants and cheap loans from the United States; continuation in even larger measure than heretofore of technical aid by the United Nations and its affiliated agencies; the attitude and activities of the Aramayo, Hochschild, and Patiño interests which had been deprived of their properties without anything like adequate compensation; and probably several others. During all the long years since the Spanish Conquest, perhaps also during the preceding Inca epoch, and during the century and a quarter since independence, Bolivia had not been a happy or prosperous country; and it would be folly to expect the eradication of age-old evils within a decade or so.

Recent reports by the agencies, foreign and domestic, dealing with problems of education and health in Bolivia indicate some improvement in recent years. Alcoholism, however, was still very prevalent among the masses, the birth rate showed no tendency to decline, and almost nobody denied that production had sagged since 1952, in spite of efforts to prevent it by some Bolivians aided by numerous "experts" from both the United States and the United Nations. Two or three highways had been completed and several new roads were under construction, but the problem of maintenance had not been solved. Many felt that the reform government was neither honest nor prudent, and it may be that they were not mistaken. Labor-management relations were unbalanced, partly because the government was more disposed to placate workers and retain their support than to conduct government-owned business at a profit or create conditions favoring the successful operation of private enterprise. Although a few foreign corporations were revealing an interest in Bolivian petroleum, gold, and industrial metals, the atmosphere was filled with distrust and suspicion, and markets for tin, zinc, tungsten, and other such commodities were becoming less favorable. The Bolivian tin industry, in particular, was having difficulty in finding ready outlets for its relatively expensive output derived from low-grade ores. But assistance from the United States—both direct and indirect, through the Organization of the American States and the UN and its subsidiaries—probably would increase rather than taper off. For nothing short of a revolt of American taxpayers could remove Bolivia from the benevolent list of beneficiaries, and the leaders of the two major parties of the United States were in such complete agreement regarding expenditures to contain Communists and maintain high prices that the taxpayers of this country appeared to be utterly helpless in their hands. In fact, such of them as were profiting by extravagant government spending would probably vote for its continuance. As for the Big Three tin companies, it seemed unlikely that they would ever recover their mining properties or receive full payment for them unless the United States indirectly supplied the means of compensation. The small sums which the "reform" government was setting aside for that purpose were hardly sufficient to pay a meager rate of interest on the investment, and no agreement had been reached on the value of the holdings that had been taken from them. In view of these facts, therefore, it seemed reasonable to expect that either a fairly just settlement would have to be made or else these investors would continue to harass the government by every means in their power; moreover, they would probably be able to find supporters among Bolivians whose savings were being destroyed and whose means of subsistence were being wiped out by Bolivia's runaway inflation.[3]

2.

It is possible, as some writers assert, that Bolivia's greatest handicaps are a very unfavorable heritage of physical environment and a wretched state of mind. The climate of most of the country, as nearly everybody knows, is too cold or too hot, too wet or too dry, and the terrain is either too high or too low. The great majority of her people live on the lofty plateau or in the upland valleys and are loath to settle in the eastern lowlands where they think they would suffer from heat, flood, drought, and loneliness, and where they could only expect to be reduced to subsistence farming and stockraising, in all probability, for the rest of their lives. Nor would it be easy to induce immigrants from foreign countries to come in and develop this part of the national domain, since most of them would be people accustomed to a better mode of existence. Hitherto, all efforts to colonize these extensive lowlands, soggy in the north and arid in the south, have achieved small success, and it was not unlikely that more failures lurked ahead. In any case, the future of these regions must depend mainly upon the prosperity or poverty of

Bolivia's western highlands, since hardly any other markets would absorb their produce, except impoverished Paraguay, a few settlements in northwestern Argentina, and the scattered population of western Brazil. Bolivia has valuable natural resources almost everywhere, although they are probably not so rich as many Bolivians suppose and as some Bolivians would have the rest of the world believe; but their extraction and distribution would continue to be a baffling enterprise because of climate, topography, and distance from foreign markets.

A nineteenth-century writer once described Bolivia as a "beggar sitting on a throne of gold"—and thus penned a very damaging half-truth, injurious because the description stuck in Bolivian minds and tended to deform their mentality, creating envy, self-pity, and the conviction that they could not master their fate because they were the victims of a few shrewd and ruthless Bolivians and foreigners who prevented them from recovering from the poverty that afflicted the nation at the end of the colonial period. Alcides Argüedas, a Bolivian historian and novelist, published shortly after 1900 a book entitled *Sick People* in which he dwelt upon both the physical and the mental maladies suffered by his countrymen. They continued to suffer from those maladies in subsequent years, but their mental troubles were probably worse than their physical ailments.

The ideology of Karl Marx became one of their worst afflictions. Most Bolivians did not read Marx; in fact, from seventy-five to eighty per cent of them were illiterate. But literate or illiterate, large numbers of them became familiar with the Marxist dogmas. In October, 1955, technicians in Bolivia began their discussions with investigating Congressmen from the United States with some pertinent remarks about this malady. The counsellor of the American Embassy told them that labor leaders who "participated in the revolution [of 1952] . . . were largely motivated by Marxist ideology." A cultural affairs officer said: "I want to review very rapidly . . . the longstanding and deep infiltration of the Marxist thought pattern in intellectual and labor circles here. . . . They have been brought up on the class struggle and Lenin's theory of imperialism as the last stage of capitalism . . . ; so . . . we are starting out on a very intensive program of educational exchange." The chief of the United States Information Service in Bolivia declared that this ideology was something that his organization was making an intense effort to correct: "We go after them in the motion picture showings. We have projectors and projectionists in all the mining areas. We have mobile units that go into some of the mines. Motion pictures are one thing that an illiterate person can understand. Since not all the miners speak Spanish we are making sound tracks in Quechua and Aymara." Responding to a question by Congressman Porter Hardy about the use of the radio, he continued: "You can't use one big station to cover the country; you've got to use little stations. You can't use only Spanish; you have to put on your programs in Indian dialects and . . . you've got to put on programs when the . . . villages have their power on. . . . The generators are turned on only when it gets dark." Asked about the availability of receiving sets in Bolivia, he replied rather vaguely that the number was "very small."[4]

A conference assembled by Columbia University late in 1954 to discuss the subject of "Responsible Freedom in the Americas" witnessed an exhibition of the mentality of a Bolivian intellectual named Fernando Díez de Medina that almost caused apoplexy among some of the Foundation and business executives in the audience when they heard the following intemperate remarks:

"For many years [the United States] . . . has allowed the rapacity of its bankers and businessmen to undermine friendly coexistence with our nations through the exploitation of our human capital and the unfair seizure of the raw materials of the weak. . . . Unfortunately the United States has done nothing to counteract fifty years of penetration of a colonial type on the part of its own investors, who have often taken advantage

... of the low living standards of the South American worker, nor to improve the hostile psychological reaction this industrial exploitation has engendered in the nations to the south.... Does the United States know ... whether its investors have intervened in internal politics, overthrowing or bringing to power governments, dominating the emerging national economy by the weight of their monopoly on the purchase of raw materials?"

Probably referring to his own country and the revolution of 1952, Díez de Medina declared that revolts in Latin America were sometimes "an incensed anti-imperialist protest against that form of capitalism which treats free peoples like colonies."[5]

The mental condition of the Bolivian party leaders and chiefs of political factions may be illustrated by quotations from their recent platforms. The platform of the dominant party, the National Revolutionary Movement: "We demand the support of all in doing away with the great private monopolies and putting all smaller enterprises in the hands of Bolivians exclusively." Platform of the Party of the Revolutionary Left: "The governments [of Bolivia] are kept in power by the mine-owners and the agents of imperialism. If by exception a government comes to power which opposes their interests, it is quickly overthrown on orders from Paris, London, or New York.... Our program cannot be fully carried out until a new type of state has been created which is ... the expression of the interests of oppressed classes, that is to say, nine-tenths of our people." Platform of the Worker's Revolutionary Party: "Indo-America, and with it Bolivia, has been unable to govern itself ... ; its nations have lost their political and economic sovereignty, and have become reservoirs of basic materials and a market for North American products. All this has been achieved by imperialism through its financial policies ... buying in the open market the oligarchies that govern us, which have sold out to imperialism and could not stay in power if it were not for the economic support they receive." Platform of Juan Lechín's Federation of Mine Workers: "To the miners, class struggle means ... the struggle against that sector of Yankee imperialism which is our oppressor.... It is a farce to speak of democracy [in Yankeeland] when the United States is controlled by sixty families, and when those sixty families live like leeches on the blood of semi-colonial countries like ours." That some of the intellectuals are afflicted by the disease which preys on the workers and politicians is indicated not only by the utterances of Díez de Medina; it is also revealed by the following quotation from the platform of the University Federation of Bolivia: "Yankee imperialism, implemented by the political piracy of the dollar, has made itself the political overlord of the semi-colonies of America. Bolivia and other Latin-speaking colonies of the continent are mere factories for imperialism.... Imperialism began by buying the governing oligarchies, which, without this economic backing, could not have remained in power."[6]

3.

That Liberals and humanitarians in the United States sometimes share the sentiments of these radical Bolivians, is indicated by remarks made in May, 1955, in the course of hearings by the Senate on the Mutual-Security Bill. Senator George Aiken of Vermont: "Up until the time they nationalized the tin mines, the people of Bolivia were getting nothing at all out of that tin ... a few people living outside the country got everything and left nothing at all for the people who lived there." Edward J. Sparks, acting assistant secretary of state for Latin-American Affairs: "That is correct. I have never seen living conditions so deplorable as they are in Bolivia among the Indian population. ... Simón Patiño, the old Bolivian, developed the tin mines ... and then went abroad ... living in France. He spent a short time in the United States ... [where] he organized ... the Patiño Mines Consolidated.... It was a Delaware corporation ... organized for a part of his operations in Bolivia." Senator Hubert Humphrey of Minnesota; "I hope they [the expropriated companies] haven't gotten a nickel back. . . . We have the wrong people in jail." Secretary Sparks: "It has always struck me as very indicative that this man Simón Patiño started without a cent in his pocket and became almost the second richest man in the world." Senator Humphrey: "Is he in jail now?" Secretary Sparks: "He is dead. His son lives in Paris. He has been in the newspapers and social columns, mostly." Senator Humphrey: "Every time we hear of something that has gone wrong, the people behind it are at the French Riviera living off the fat of the land. If it is a Delaware corporation, that means we are in it too. . . . I want to know why our government has not looked into this."[7]

Journalists of the United States, wittingly or unwittingly, often join the Bolivians in their lamentations. Late in 1956, for example, Robert J. Alexander, forgetting that profits from traffic in tin come from the pockets of foreign purchasers as well as from mines in Bolivia, wrote: "For half a century, these tin companies had drained untold riches from the nation, leaving little behind."[8]

At the other extreme is journalist Willmoore Kendall who wrote at the same time of Bolivia's "twin demons of unreasonable resentment and unassuageable self-pity," predicted the early demise of the Paz Estenssoro-Siles Zuazo régime, and denounced the State Department of the United States for its financial support of this radical "Left." "It *cannot* contribute to the welfare of the Bolivian masses," Kendall declared, "or cope with the problems of the Bolivian economy, because resentment, unlike rebellion, can only destroy."[9]

"The MNR's real creator . . . was the Spanish poet who with the phrase 'Bolivia is a beggar seated on a throne of gold' has managed to capture—and poison—the minds and hearts of the politically active elements of the Bolivian population. For the sentiment the phrase triggers . . . is: 'Ah! see the misery we have endured!' . . . All this is, of course, quite mad from the standpoint of sound economics and politics; but my point is that in order to grasp the Bolivian problem we must understand that we *are* dealing with madness. If Bolivia's tin industry has been a curse rather than a blessing to Bolivia, if Bolivia is more the beggar today than she would have been without her throne of gold, the reason . . . has nothing to do with the sale of Bolivian tin to the United States, or with anything remotely describable as 'exploitation' from outside. These things [these sales abroad, these market manipulations of the Tin Cartel] have, on the contrary, accounted . . . for a veritable flood of imports that Bolivia would not otherwise have had and that only a madman would regard as having impoverished her. They did, however, create a situation in which the Bolivians in general could indulge certain incipient bad habits that have now become endemic. For one thing, not moving off that throne to develop the agriculture and industry that might have produced the goods that might have replaced all those imports. Again, levying upon the proceeds of the tin industry for government purposes without regard to the effect of the levies upon capital formation. Still again, indulging in more—and far more expensive—government than the nation could afford. And, finally, taking it for granted that the world somehow owes Bolivia a living.

"Bolivia has become Point Four Paradise; seventy American 'technicians' have descended on Bolivia like a swarm of locusts, chirping the credo of what Toynbee calls the nineteenth-century religion of Technology. The technicians . . . never had it so good.

"What makes the Bolivian case hopeless, and *ought* to be worrying the State Department, is . . . the absence . . . of a Right, and of the political and economic and moral ideas a Right would, if it existed, enunciate, and, above all, of the institutions upon which other societies depend for the custody, development, and perpetuation of these ideas. . . .

"What ought to be worrying Americans in general [i.e., non-bureaucrats], and what begins to make the American case look pretty hopeless too, is the State Department itself, and its notion that if you wish to accomplish something abroad you work through those who believe you can get something for nothing ... that is, through the Left ... —which ends us up keeping in power, as we have been doing in Bolivia, a government that defies American standards of public morality. And, finally, Americans ought to be worrying about Congressmen and Senators who vote ... the funds with which to inflict such idiocies upon the outside world."

Alexander views the MNR—Movimiento Nacional Revolucionario, or National Revolutionary Movement—with enthusiasm infused with fear that the forces which it has unleashed may prove uncontrollable. He describes it as the "most important social movement in Latin America since the Mexican Revolution forty years ago." Enumerating its achievements, he writes: "It established universal adult suffrage, nationalized tin mining, launched an agrarian reform, and began a large-scale educational program. . . . In addition to these social changes, the MNR government launched a program of economic development . . . : extensive road-building, raising agricultural productivity in the highlands, developing the vast agricultural resources of the almost untouched eastern half of Bolivia, harnessing the country's vast hydroelectric potential, expanding the hitherto small petroleum industry." But:[10]

"The fact is that Indians and miners who support the Government are armed ... [and] should there be an uprising in La Paz or some other city, armed militiamen might well descend upon the town. In that case, there could easily be a race war between the Indian peasants and the white and mestizo city people, leaving scars from which the country would not recover for decades.

"A revolt would thus put an end to the peaceful development of the Bolivian Revolution. This would be disastrous not only for Bolivia but for her neighbors—which have similar problems —and the whole fabric of Inter-American relations."

Kendall, in sharp contrast, could see no virtue in the MNR and only calamity over the Bolivian horizon:[11]

"The tin mines, which to begin with have virtually exhausted their workable ores, must from now on yield progressively less income because of progressively deteriorating equipment and inadequate exploration. The land reform has plunged the nation's agriculture into a mess from which it cannot possibly be extricated in time to affect the present government's longevity. The inflation has already created inequities and resentments that would remain even if the currency were stabilized. More importantly still, the general population *know* that present food shortages are due, in considerable part, to the fact that MNR has used allocations of food imports as rewards to its favorites —who have proceeded to sell large amounts of them abroad. And finally, the government will not even consider the one measure that could ... put the mining industry back on its feet, namely: invite the old mine-owners, who have the capacity and the know-how to operate the mines, to return to Bolivia.

"The post-blood-bath regime—its probable leader is Oscar Unzaga de la Vega—will not, alas, differ on any crucial point from the present one. While he would attempt, he says, to find a 'foreign private enterprise' that would come in and operate the mines, he has no ready answer to the question, 'Why should such an enterprise be willing to take the risk of expropriation by some future government?' He would solve the food problem— the essence of which is a curious refusal on the part of peasants to move to the areas where there is fertile land ... by 'immigration from abroad.' He would stop the inflation by setting up a stabilization board, for whose operations, however, he would hope to enlist American aid. He too, in other words, thinks that the world somehow owes Bolivia a living."

What conclusions should a mere historian venture regarding Bolivia's recent past and what predictions should a mere historian risk in respect to Bolivia's future? It is too early to hazard a positive statement regarding the long-run objectives of Paz Estenssero, Lechín, and Siles Zuazo. Time, one of the best friends of the historian, will have to reveal the truth if the truth is ever to be disclosed. Until it is laid bare by the years to come, silence seems to be the best policy. Politicians of Latin America, like some politicians everywhere, have often deceived historians as well as the people. How frequently have historians, in Latin America as well as in the United States, assumed that revolutions in countries to the south were humanitarian movements designed to ferry the people across the last river that separated them from Utopia, only to be compelled later to revise their texts! Although this writer hopes his pessimism on this subject is not beyond redemption, he must confess that he has been fooled too often to venture into the realm of prognostication. He almost regrets that he has already guessed that the Aramayo, the Hochschild, and the Patiño interests will never recover their properties and that the United States government will increase rather than curtail its economic and technical aid to Bolivia. But let those predictions stand. A new Atlas seems to have taken the place in this skeptical age of the old Atlas in the mythology of primitive peoples.

CHAPTER 12 CULTURAL RELATIONS, HEMISPHERIC AND GLOBAL: "THE VOICE OF AMERICA"

"The [people of the] United States [must] realize the ever increasing need of bringing together the two basic streams of Western civilization which have given the New World such a commanding place in the struggle for freedom and human betterment. The Latin Americans [must] also realize it. But neither [people] is . . . quite sure that the other does. It is a most worthy task to correct this misapprehension."

THESE are the words of Luis Muñoz Marín, chief executive of the new "Commonwealth" of Puerto Rico, who is an ardent friend of both Americas and eager to prevent any misunderstanding from hampering their cordial co-operation.[1] The primary purpose of cultural relations is to harmonize interests and ideals.

There are differences in the customs, patterns of value, and economic conditions of the two peoples of America and dissimilarities in these respects between the various Latin nations themselves. This, Muñoz Marín would be the first to admit. But he believes that no fundamental disagreement exists with reference to their major objectives of peace, security, progress, democracy, and personal liberty—only disagreement regarding the methods of attaining them and on points of emphasis, and doubts regarding the measure of devotion of each of the two major groups to their common ideals.

Like many others in similar circumstances, the Latins of America are said to be in the grip of a "revolution of expectations."

Promises to be fulfilled *mañana* or *mañana por la mañana* no longer satisfy their most impatient leaders. They demand a larger share of the world's good things *now*. The contention that many others are in greater need and more insecure leaves them unconvinced. These zealots of the Western-Hemisphere concept urge and implore the United States to give them special consideration because this country and theirs happen to be occupants of the same Hemisphere and to have a similar history. "The Americas first" has become their watchword.

Long accustomed to look to the state for assistance, less afraid than their northern neighbors are of the expansion of its functions and less reluctant to have it participate in economic activities, they are not frightened by state planning or even state socialism. Let the state control exports, imports, banking, currency; let it own and operate the public services, engage in production, and even dominate national economies. Production must be expanded and diversified in Latin America *immediately*. Democracy and liberty are important, they seem to say, but not so important as health, practical education, and material progress. They have almost inverted their former scale of values, stressing physical welfare more than spiritual achievement, contrary to the habit of their cultural heroes of the past.

Diplomats of the United States tell them that this country has not lost interest in them, that their fellow Americans in the North still hold them in high esteem and are dedicated to the Hemisphere's prosperity and all of their basic objectives:[2]

"We want good relations with our sister republics [they declare]. We want to cooperate with them. We want peace and democracy and continental solidarity and due process of law and sovereign equality and mutual assistance against aggression."

But the Latins doubt the sincerity of our diplomats. They think these diplomats really expect them to sacrifice their own interests and hopes for the benefit of others in more distant lands.

They say they want assistance and not smiles; cheap loans and grants and not promises of future aid. They say this on all occasions: in inter-American meetings at Caracas, Rio, Panama, Washington, Buenos Aires. More aware of our shift of emphasis than of theirs, they tend to magnify our transformation and minimize their own. They contrast the war years with the postwar decade. Technical aid to foreign peoples, international cultural exchange, subsidies for the development of retarded countries, special efforts to explain our foreign policies and to cultivate an appreciation of our way of life—all these new departures in the conduct of the foreign relations of the United States began with Latin America. But the big neighbor soon extended them around the globe, spreading them thinner in Latin America than elsewhere, leaving no more than a sparse veneer where formerly there was a thick layer of helpfulness and explanation, and glowing exhibits of a prosperous future already within sight.

This comparative neglect could be tolerated while the war was approaching its end. But the termination of the war left the United States probably more insecure than ever and brought no change in Latin America's favor. A global struggle of a different kind followed, and Latin Americans felt bereft. They began to complain and their complaints have persisted.

John M. Cabot, an official of the State Department of the United States, summarized some of the complaints he heard at Caracas, Venezuela, in 1954 during a meeting of the Inter-American Economic and Social Council, where he and other representatives of his government were "confronted by a series of more or less strongly expressed views."[3]

"Many . . . delegations [said Cabot] felt that their countries had been unfairly treated in terms of trade; that over a period of years the raw materials they produced had tended to fall in price in relation to the prices of manufactured goods they had to import. Others wanted to stop the development of synthetics which competed with their natural products. A number felt that it was unfair that the dollar reserves they accumulated during the war by selling to us should have dropped sharply [in value] after the war in terms of what they wanted to buy from us. You would probably say that these positions were unreasonable. Perhaps they were; but other points made by our Latin friends in Caracas were not so unreasonable. They complained of our customs barriers, which keep out their products and force them to send us raw materials rather than semi-manufactured products. They wanted us to give some tax advantage to American investments [in their countries] . . . to encourage such investments. And they frankly found it hard to understand . . . [why] we gave them practically no grant aid. I . . . think . . . they unquestionably felt that those who made a nuisance of themselves were better rewarded than those who co-operated."

With respect to trade barriers the Latins of America insist that they are not in the same category with the United States. Javier Márquez, a Mexican writer, gave utterance to their general convictions on this score when he declared: "On the one hand we have a nation which leads in industrial progress; on the other, countries that have hardly begun to industrialize. On the one hand we have a country whose international trade has a secondary place in the national income; on the other, countries where a prosperous trade means abundance and a depressed trade means acute crisis. . . . Can anyone be surprised that each [side] believes that prosperity may be achieved by different methods?"[4] Carlos Lleras Restrepo, a distinguished Colombian politician, expressed essentially the same view in different language when he wrote:[5]

"The United States . . . has developed its industries during a hundred years of protection; it has assimilated European technology; it enjoys abundant capital resources and an immense domestic market. How can it be held, in treating with tariff reduction, that the same standards should be applied to it as to countries that are not so well endowed and have scarcely taken the most elementary steps in industrialization?"

The Latins had become passionate devotees of protection, protection of their "infant industries." Although retaining the barricades that shield many of the products of its farms and pastures and some of the products of its mines, the United States was moving, and trying to move the world, in the opposite direction. The two Americas were thus not in agreement in respect to this means of reaching Hemispheric goals.

Neither were they in accord on the subject of private international investments. Most political and business leaders of the United States during the first postwar decade were never more confident that such investment could play a dominant role in the development of the economically retarded countries; many Latin Americans were doubtful.

Quotations from the dominant groups in the North would be superfluous. They pointed to Canada as a model of the mutual benefits of foreign investment. They contended that economic progress in the United States would have been much slower if this country had not received the stimulus of European capital. They exerted themselves to find ways of inducing investors to send their money abroad. They set diplomats to work negotiating investment treaties to improve the "climate" in foreign lands. Politicians and businessmen proposed that foreign investors should be granted a measure of tax exemption and insured by their government against every hazard except bad judgment and defective management. The merits of "free enterprise" (aided, abetted, and protected by the national government) were acclaimed louder than ever before.

But, in the words of the State Department official previously quoted regarding the Caracas meeting of 1954, the Latins in the South were asking themselves a sort of loaded question: "Will this investment . . . develop our economy and raise our living standards, or will it merely mean that greedy foreigners will despoil our national resources, gouge our people, and oppress... [our] employees?"[6] To repeat their statements at length would be useless. Brief excerpts from the remarks made by some of them at another Caracas assembly that met in the same year 1954 should be sufficient. A delegate from friendly Brazil:[7] "I am well aware that private initiative and private capital, both domestic and foreign, were and still are great pioneers of progress.... But... there are economic activities that must necessarily be carried out or controlled by the state, particularly in countries in process of development, and these are activities that are the basis of the economic organization of a country." A representative from turbulent and distraught Bolivia:[8] "There is no doubt that more capital has been exported from Latin America in the form of profit than has been brought to it. It is therefore evident... that the remedy of expecting it all to come from private investment is worse than the ills [the economic ills] themselves. Foreign private investments... are a constant drain...." The incumbent foreign minister of dollar-hungry Chile made a plea for cheap loans or grants from the United States. Insisting that decisions in economic matters be made at once, he called upon the United States for prompt assistance:[9] "It is necessary to know... [whether] we are or are not to expect cooperation in order to complement our national efforts, if on the difficult road ahead we are alone or accompanied, and if the well-being of our people is a national problem or one of continental concern."

It is obvious that not a few Latin Americans, especially public officials, preferred—and they still prefer—government-to-government loans in place of private foreign capital. And their readiness to expand the economic functions of the state, already alluded to, means that their attachment to private enterprise, particularly when it is alien private enterprise, is by no means as firm as it is among business groups within the United States, who welcome state aid but object to state interference or participation in management and operation. Quoting our distinguished Puerto Rican friend again:[10]

"There is nothing wrong with private enterprise. It is a great technique, and in the United States an eminently successful one. But it is not the only technique that can be used to conduct business under freedom. The belief that the capitalistic technique is inevitably and ... inextricably enmeshed with the great principles of democracy is ... a barrier to understanding in areas where experience with the backward forms of that technique has not left happy memories."

Although lamenting the lack of democracy and freedom "in a number of Latin-American countries" and urging all Americans who believe in popular government and liberty to make a vigorous effort to abolish dictatorship in this Hemisphere within a decade, he contended that democracy would not be promoted by attempts to make free enterprise "compulsory." It is likely that in expressing this view he thought of himself as mediator between the North and the South. "In helping to create the conditions favorable to democracy," he warned, "we must not hold forth a concept of static democracy but of a vibrant, living democracy, flexible enough to adjust to the needs of many countries and cultures, all different." Were Latin Americans on the point of convincing themselves that State Socialism is compatible with democracy and personal liberty? And would they eventually discover that they were mistaken and that socialism merely provides an additional bulwark of despotic oppression?

On another occasion Muñoz Marín clarified his views on this subject and at the same time disclosed an intense yearning for progress so typical of many of his kinsmen of the early postwar period that quotation is hard to resist.[11]

"Let us urgently devise the basic objectives in housing, in health, in education, in economic productivity, in communications, which may be attainable by different areas of the Hemisphere.

". . . Let us solemnly declare that our essential goal—the goal of all Americans, North and South—is . . . to wipe out extreme poverty in this Hemisphere within the lifetime of children already born. Let us encourage government and private initiative to share in a good partnership with a view to better distributive justice. . . . Let us not be doctrinaire either as to socialism or capitalism. . . . Let us give friendly support to all groups thinking in terms of a greater, truly hemispheric America. . . . An America to serve the world."

This Pan-American zealot, this dedicated enthusiast for the amalgamation of the cultures of the two Americas, is well aware that the major costs of his program will have to be borne by the people of the United States, but he deems it necessary to effect a more equal distribution of capital and opportunity in this Hemisphere; and since he seems to be serving as the mouthpiece of numerous Latins south of the Río Grande, he will be quoted once more:[12]

"Too great is the disparity between the wealth and industrial might of the United States and the economic insufficiency of Latin America. Even with a great fund of good will it imperils long-range understanding. To bridge the gap in the least possible time, with the most efficient techniques available, with the most effective partnership of *governments* and *peoples* is . . . the task of the inter-American system in this generation. How to help the powerful emerging . . . Latin-American aspirations to a future rooted in economic security and democratic freedom is the acid test of . . . American statesmanship, in the widest sense of the word 'American' and in the deepest sense of the word 'statesmanship.' "

2.

What can the United States do to placate its dissatisfied neighbors in this Hemisphere while this nation continues to respond to its more distant interests and obligations, its global aspirations and responsibilities? Private investment apparently will not suffice. Its flow is inadequate to meet the felt needs of these neighbors. It is not the kind of capital they prefer and they are not disposed promptly to adopt the policies calculated to expand and accelerate the financial stream. Grants for technical advancement, grants or cheap government loans for economic development, they like better; but again the flow has seemed too small to speed the progress they crave. Removal of all barriers to the import of their commodities, together with a pledge, politically most difficult to arrange, never to permit their erection again, would certainly please these American comrades, but this would not be enough. They would like to have guaranteed prices for what they have to sell and lower prices for what they wish to buy, both at the cost of the people of the United States, its consumers and taxpayers, who would have to pay the higher prices on the one hand and provide the export subsidies on the other. Further, the Latins would like to have this country take care of their surpluses, whether caused by overproduction or displacement by synthetics; and if the United States could afford to grant all they have asked, they would soon think of something else. To international benevolence, once begun with gallant fanfare, there appears to be no end—or call it "mutual aid" and the result will be the same if the mutuality is vastly modified by immense disparities in wealth, actual or assumed.

Does not wisdom counsel a careful estimate of the capabilities of the United States, a precise and continuous appraisal of methods and points of emphasis all around the world, and a rigid selection of helpful and dependable beneficiaries and allies? In spite of the complaints and divergent views that have been enumerated, the Latin Americans probably would not be damaged if this were done. On the contrary, it is possible that they would either receive increased attention or feel better if they got no more aid and other regions got less, even though they still might like to obtain additional help in one form or another. Has not the time arrived for our regular foreign service all over the globe and our nomadic Secretary of State to employ their persuasive talents to the utmost as a substitute for some of the drafts from our Treasury? And what are these novel auxiliary organizations for—this Office of Cultural Relations, this heavily-staffed and expensive United States Information Agency?

Are not those sent abroad by this new organization for cultural exchange sent as emissaries instructed to explain our aims and ideals and the burdens we bear and to serve as exhibits of our culture and good will? Do they act like millionaires, or live and conduct themselves in such manner as to suggest that most of us are hard-working people of moderate means? Are the people whom the Office of Cultural Relations brings into the United States imported only for the purpose of impressing them them with our riches—the luxurious equipment of our hotels, our banks, our grand mercantile establishments; our mass-producing industries surrounded by the parked automobiles of laborers bought on credit (though the mortgages are invisible); our campuses with conspicuous buildings and inconspicuous underpaid professors? Let them inspect our city slums; the homes of our poor farmers in the eroded districts and our rural tenants; our school teachers compelled to work overtime to paint, decorate, and repair their modest dwellings; the living quarters and meager fare of the majority of our writers, artists, and clerks, and our citizens too old and feeble to work. This procedure might expose some of the deficiencies of our society, some of the problems we still have to solve; but these sojourners in our midst would learn that by no means all of us are rich and that most of us do not find it easy to pay the tax-collector, the landlord, the grocer, the clothier, and the physician. By all means, let them see the mirror as well as the showcase in order to avoid envy and bankruptcy, even at the risk of having them conclude that the most efficient system of economic enterprise on earth has not yet reached perfection.

A recent pamphlet put out by the United States Information Service assures the reader that this agency performs four major tasks: "(1) Explains U.S. policies and objectives. (2) Counters hostile propaganda. (3) Demonstrates the harmony of U.S. policies with the legitimate aspirations of other peoples. (4) Presents abroad aspects of American culture which promote understanding of U.S. policies and objectives."[13] But does it ever portray our citizens as they worry about their bills or sweat over their income-tax returns? Does it inform other nations of the size of our national debt? Does it display our cabins and cottages as well as our mansions? It does not lack ample facilities. It utilizes the cinema, the radio, and television as well as books, periodicals, and newspapers.

USIA describes its radio programs as the "Voice of America." But they are merely the official voice of the United States unless they speak for all our people and the whole of the Western Hemisphere as well; and while this may be true at times and in some respects, it would have been better if a less presumptuous name had been adopted. The description would be appropriate not only for the agency's radio programs but for all of its operations *if* its numerous personnel could voice the sentiments and aspirations of the Hemisphere. But neither the United States nor the majority of the other countries of the New World speak with a single authoritive voice on a multitude of subjects. They are not monolithic like Soviet Russia and its satellites and associates. Any jesting Pontius Pilate could ask what the patterns of value, the goals, and the programs of the Western Hemisphere are with considerable confidence that nobody could respond with a sufficiently precise and inclusive answer to satisfy all those involved.

Yet the Western-Hemisphere concept in its full flower seems to have embodied ample common convictions, ideals, and objectives to bind the Americas together in a unique practical relationship. Perhaps the concept was always partly fictitious; but faith and trust have a way of transforming fiction into fact. No other large region of the world ever attained so harmonious a relationship among its component nations, nor has the United States ever achieved an equal cordiality with and among so many nations in any other region—not even those of Europe, to say nothing of the Near East, the Far East, or Africa. The misunderstandings, the confusion, that have arisen since 1945 are apt to continue until this concept is broadened with Latin America's consent so as to embrace the entire globe, or such parts of it as remain free from Soviet control, until Hemispheric consensus regarding methods and emphasis is effected, or until a return to the original concept is forced by the spread of Soviet domination or made possible by some less calamitous change in the atmosphere and organization of the world.

Both the traditional and the new agencies of our government *certainly have an abundance of hard tasks ahead*. Let them coordinate their efforts and concentrate on problems of supreme importance. Let them convince Latin America and the rest of the non-communist world—and peoples behind the despotic curtains if they can—that our global aspirations are in harmony with the best interests of all the regions they embrace. Let them convince retarded peoples everywhere that this nation is no modern Atlas capable of carrying the weight of the planet on its back; that no Utopia can be built in a decade or two; that Paradise was not lost by over-exertion; and that hard work by others as well as ourselves, and not self-pity and loud complaints, is the only means of regaining it. And let it never be forgotten that this Western Hemisphere, where our ancestors had the chance to make a new start, is our inner fortress and the only base of operations we have; that all would be lost if it were ever weakened beyond repair. Perhaps the Latin-American champions of the Western-Hemisphere concept should be reminded more than once of the meaning of mutuality: tactfully advised that consumers in the United States deserve consideration too; that they should treat business enterprises from the United States with moderation; that they should not expect to be pampered in these critical times, or ignore the tax load of their friends in the North, or forget the virtues of self-reliance; and finally, that they should industriously contrive methods of their own to counteract the siren voice of the sinister Soviets.

Damaging conflict between the Western-Hemisphere concept and the United-World aspiration, as already stated at the end of the first chapter of this volume, does not need to continue if both are carefully defined and prudently modified to fit these times of trouble. Hemispheric isolationism has never applied to travel, trade, and capital investment, although the New World has at times received preference in some of these respects. The Monroe Doctrine, whether unilateral or Pan-American, is not inflexible. Its prime objective was and is security. It may be expanded so as to embrace a larger segment of the globe if wise considerations of security require such expansion. The avowal of self-restraint it contains with reference to political affairs overseas does not have to be kept eternally, especially if governments overseas wish to have it forgotten. If the United-World concept can serve the New World, then let it be adopted to the extent that it promotes the New World's vital interests. If the Western Hemisphere can be developed into a model of harmony, prosperity, democracy, and liberty, let this be done for the benefit of the Hemisphere and the rest of the globe. But let no one either here or there expect too much too soon. The advocates of the two concepts, so understood and modified, should support each other and refrain from debilitating skirmishes which merely serve the cause of ambitious tyrants and multiply the tragedies of deluded peoples.

The disciples of both concepts should work together to remove the obstacles in Latin America and elsewhere to the survival and growth of democracy: poverty, illiteracy, frustrating social immobility, the dishonesty and lethargy of politicians and bureaucrats, and every barrier that stands in the way of progress toward the ultimate goal of government of the people, by the people, and for the people. And they should work together with the peoples of the retarded countries, especially those of Latin America, in a spirit of humility, with full appreciation of the immense difficulties of geography, climate, colonial heritage, and diversities of race and culture that such peoples have had to confront and still have to surmount, and with a dedication that obliterates selfishness and assumptions of superiority—which, after all, may be more a product of Dame Fortune than of innate capacity. The spirit of the giver is still more important than the gift. The size of the grants by the United States may not have to be increased—might even be reduced—if the agents who have charge of their distribution act with a full measure of tact and devotion, communicating hope and enthusiasm to their counterparts in Latin America and everywhere, building cooperative societies that will make repulsive and even erase the class hatreds utilized by the Communists, as in Guatemala and other countries, in their efforts to establish oppressive "dictatorships of the proletariat," instead of democracy, in place of the traditional dictatorships of oligarchies of family and wealth.

CHAPTER 13 FOREIGN AID AND THE PROBLEM OF NONINTERVENTION

A MAJOR problem encountered by the United States in its postwar foreign policy, a problem likely to cause increasing perplexities, has been the problem of attaining its objectives of peace, prosperity, and democracy without violating its announced principle of nonintervention. Present in relations with nearly all of the underdeveloped countries, this problem has recently become most conspicuous in the case of the Latin-American nations with which the United States has signed formal collective pledges against all types of intervention.

One of the important documents that embodies such a formal pledge—the Charter of the Organization of American States, signed at Bogotá in the spring of 1948 and ratified shortly afterward by the governments of twenty-one countries in the Western Hemisphere—is not free from contradictions. While some of its provisions forbid intervention, others encourage it. The long preamble of this charter expresses the alleged firm conviction of these governments that "the true significance of American solidarity and good neighborliness can only mean the consolidation on this continent, within the framework of democratic institutions, of a system of individual liberty and social justice based on respect for the essential rights of man"; and, further, that the welfare of these countries and their "contribution to the progress and civilization of the world will increasingly require intensive continental cooperation," the principles and details of which the same document sets forth at some length.

Article 5, for example, contains such declarations as these:

"The solidarity of the American States and the high aims which are sought through it require the political organization of those States on the basis of the effective exercise of representative democracy.

"Social justice and social security are bases of lasting peace.

"Economic cooperation is essential to the common welfare and prosperity of the peoples of the continent.

"The American States proclaim the fundamental rights of the individual without distinction as to race, nationality, creed, or sex."

Article 28 records this obligation: "The member States agree to cooperate with one another to achieve just and decent living conditions for their entire populations"—which Articles 29-31 elaborate in this fashion:

"The member States agree upon the desirability of developing their social legislation on the following bases:

"All human beings, without distinction as to race, nationality, sex, creed, or social condition, have the right to attain material well-being and spiritual growth in circumstances of liberty, dignity, equality of opportunity, and economic security.

"Work is a right and a social duty; it shall not be considered an article of commerce; it demands respect for freedom of association and for the dignity of the worker; and it is to be performed under conditions that ensure life, health, and a decent standard of living, both during the working years and during old age, and when any circumstance deprives the individual of the possibility of working.

"The member States agree to promote, in accordance with their constitutional provisions and their material resources, the right to education, on the following bases:

"Elementary education shall be compulsory and, when provided by the State, shall be without cost.

"Higher education shall be available to all, without distinction as to race, nationality, sex, language, creed, or social condition.

"With due consideration for the national character of each State, the member States undertake to facilitate free cultural interchange by every medium of expression."

These and other declarations and agreements included in the charter clearly commit the nations involved to total democratic regimes. But when these commitments are violated, serious problems are confronted. Effective collaboration requires consent, and will encounter formidable obstacles when full consent is not forthcoming. Collaboration as envisaged in this charter and in general, however, is an affair of governments, and the very fact that several Latin-American governments fail to comply with the terms of the compact is a clear indication that they will be very reluctant to assent to outside pressure intended to implement these democratic pledges. The truth is that the granting of economic and technical aid to any other than democratic regimes which permit free elections and devote themselves to the general welfare is repugnant to this charter, for such assistance tends to prolong incumbent despotic governments and injure opposition groups eager to share social, economic, and political benefits within the various recipient countries. Because of the sensitivities of Latin Americans and the leaders of the new nations of Asia and Africa, and because the United States has become the major benefactor of the underdeveloped countries, the promotion of liberty and democracy along with mass economic progress in such of these countries as are now autocratic and tyrannical is bound to be a peculiarly difficult and prolonged operation for the government and the people of the United States.

In the case of Latin America, the policy of assistance not only risks the wounding of national pride if directed toward all the goals envisaged in the inter-American charter; it also violates—or seems to violate—some of the provisions of this ambiguous document itself. Articles 15 and 16, for instance, declare:

"No State or group of States has the right to intervene, directly or indirectly, for any reason whatever, in the internal or external affairs of any other State. The foregoing principle prohibits not only armed force but also any other form of interference or attempted threat against the personality of the State, or against its political, economic, and cultural elements.

"No State may use or encourage the use of coercive measures of an economic or political character in order to force the sovereign will of another State and obtain from it advantages of any kind."

The extreme national sensitivity thus exhibited by the Latin Americans stems from their undemocratic governments, from their previous unpleasant colonial experience, and from the interventionist policies pursued by the great powers during the century following the winning of independence by the Latin peoples of the New World; and other underdeveloped countries respond to similar sentiments, magnified in many instances by more vivid colonial memories, arising from similar experiences.

The first epoch of intervention by the United States in Latin America, an epoch of vigorous interposition in some cases, began in 1898, terminated at the beginning of the 1940's, and embraced two types: (1) fiscal and military, motivated mainly by defense strategy, economic advantage, and humanitarian impulses; and (2) largely political, motivated by devotion to democracy and human rights. The first type resulted in the establishment of five quasi-protectorates by means of armed force; the second, which employed the device of refusal to recognize governments set up by means of military revolts or *golpes de estado* in the hope that such refusal would promote democracy, failed to achieve its objective and merely aroused bitter opposition. Initiated by Theodore Roosevelt in relations with the five republics of Central America as early as 1907, this second form of intervention was gradually extended to nearly all of Latin America in the course of the administrations of Woodrow Wilson, Warren G.

Harding, and Calvin Coolidge, but was finally confined once more to the Central American countries by Herbert Hoover, and entirely abandoned shortly before the inauguration of Franklin D. Roosevelt, who began the policy of granting assistance to foreign countries in 1939, at about the same time that he terminated intervention of the fiscal and military type that had been initiated by William McKinley and continued by McKinley's successors, both Democratic and Republican.

That foreign aid administered by the United States through the governments of foreign countries might be described as intervention, depending on political conditions and attitudes in recipient countries, was more than suggested in the course of the year 1957 both in the United States and elsewhere. It is likely that the main motives prompting the foreign-aid programs of the United States are political (the "containment of Communism"), economic (the stimulation of exports and the facilitation of access to raw materials), and benevolent (the promotion of democracy and the general welfare of the recipients). But in many instances, as already intimated, such aid tends to prolong despotic governments and presumably to delay reforms in the interest of the common people; and one of the results of the new policy has been the fostering of a demand—both in the United States among the "liberals" and in recipient countries among those opposed to incumbent dictators and tyrants—for the resumption of intervention against despots and in favor of groups supposed to be devotees of more democratic governments.

Latin-American opposition groups, many of whose members are in exile, voluntary or compulsory, in Western Europe, in other countries of Latin America, and in various parts of the United States—Miami, New York, New Orleans, San Francisco, Los Angeles, Chicago, Washington, D. C., and other urban centers—have been among the first to raise the issue of intervention in connection with the foreign-aid programs of the United States. And whether the opposition leaders in the various Latin countries of America demand intervention in their own behalf, or the cessation of intervention in support of dictators and oligarchies, or the entire abandonment of intervention in the form of these foreign-assistance programs or any other measures, they are naturally the major critics in Latin America of the Latin-American policy of the United States, either because they are persecuted or because that policy hampers them in their efforts to gain political power and economic benefits, or for both reasons. Their most conspicuous collaborator in the field of journalism in this country is the *New York Times;* their most sensational official supporter during the year 1957 was Congressman Charles O. Porter of Oregon.

The *New York Times* clearly revealed its editorial policy on the subject of dictators and democracy several years ago. On February 14, 1950, for example, the following statement appeared on its editorial page: "One of the things that the State Department can do in encouraging democracy in Latin America is to show favor and friendliness to those nations whose ideals and aspirations approximate our own, and to refuse to help antidemocratic regimes." On April 14, 1956, its editors remarked: "The greatest weakness of United States policy toward the Hemisphere has been its overt friendliness toward dictators." And on March 2, 1957, they declared: "Our duty as a great democracy is to foster democracy and encourage democrats in Latin America, not dictatorships and not tyrants." Many other similar statements could be quoted, but these three should suffice to illustrate the policy of this widely-read metropolitan newspaper.

The disappearance—probably the murder—of a member of a family living in Eugene, Oregon, apparently connected in turn with the disappearance—probably the murder—of a Basque expatriate residing in New York, was largely responsible for the activities of Congressman Porter. Jesús de Galíndez, who was at the time a member of the history staff of Columbia University, disappeared on March 12, 1956; Gerald Lester Murphy, the son of parents living in Eugene, Oregon, was last seen on December 3, 1956, in the Dominican Republic, where he was employed as a copilot by a government-owned aviation enterprise; and the Oregon Congressman strongly suspected that Generalissimo Rafael Trujillo, dictator of the Dominican Republic since 1930, was responsible for both crimes, as well as many others committed not merely in the country which he tightly controlled but in three or four others, including the United States. In fact, Porter seems to have been convinced that copilot Murphy, probably then unaware of the nature and significance of his act, had flown the airplane that conveyed the kidnaped Galíndez to an airfield in the Dominican Republic and to his doom, and that young Murphy—age twenty-three—had been murdered several months later at the instigation of Trujillo in order to silence a witness who might have dissolved the mystery of the vanished Galíndez, who had aroused the ire of the dictator by writing a Doctor's dissertation, based on information acquired while an exile in this island nation, on the Era of Trujillo, for which the Basque historian was on the point of finding a publisher.

The circumstantial evidence pointing to Trujillo as the culprit was first published with ample imaginary and other illustrations by *Life* magazine (February 25, 1957, pp. 24-31). Congressman Porter began (February 28, 1957) to hurl his verbal missiles at Trujillo from the floor of the House of Representatives a few days after the appearance of this issue of *Life*, and not only continued his assault intermittently throughout the first session of the Eighty-fifth Congress but gradually expanded his warfare until his utterances were directed toward all the dictators of Latin America, although he may have been unaware of some of them. As late as September 3, 1957, three days after Congress adjourned, Porter inserted this statement in the appendix of the daily *Congressional Record:*[1]

"I adhere to my position that dictators should be overthrown and ... favor their being toppled by revolution to bring justice and mercy back into government—peaceful revolution if possible. As for military advantages of dictator-run countries in Latin America, I am most willing to debate this issue...."

The second sentence quoted from Porter's declaration referred to the defense system of the Western Hemisphere in its relation to Communist aggression and subversion. The Oregon Congressman had contended repeatedly that international Communism was more likely to be served than hindered by arming dictators, for he believed that they would employ the military equipment furnished by the United States—allegedly valued at $6 million in Trujillo's case—to suppress their people and thus cause them to turn against the United States and perhaps seek the aid of Communists.

That his attack would be directed against more than one American dictator was suggested from the outset. His speech of February 28 concluded with this statement:[2]

"The dichotomy is not between the free world and communism. It is between the free world and tyranny, communistic or otherwise. I do not underrate the threat of the international communist conspiracy, but I suggest that our failure to call a spade a spade, a tyrant a tyrant, in the Dominican Republic hinders us in our efforts to light a torch of freedom and fair play for all the world."

He asked for the assistance of Congress not merely for the purpose of clearing away the fog that enveloped the murder of Gerald Murphy but also for the purpose of inducing the Eisenhower administration to "revise misguided official policies which distress friends of freedom and fair play throughout Latin America."

By July 15, 1957, the Oregon legislator was ready to set forth his policy in concrete detail. With respect to the Dominican Republic he urged:

1. The submission of the Murphy and Galíndez cases to the Organization of the American States.
2. The furnishing by the executive departments of the Washington government of full information to tourists on "real conditions in the Dominican Republic."
3. Reduction of the Dominican sugar quota designated for import into the United States, a step which would be felt by Trujillo, since he had "taken over all but one of the sugar companies."
4. Discontinuance of Exim Bank loans along with both military and technical assistance to the Dominican Republic.
5. Dismissal of Ambassador Manuel de Moya if he should persist in his refusal to retract his insinuations, contained in a speech delivered in San Francisco, calculated to damage Congressman Porter's reputation.

In reference to Latin America as a whole Porter insisted that the Eisenhower administration should adopt the following policies:

1. Instruct diplomats to maintain proper but cool relationships with dictatorial governments, avoiding all unnecessary identification with the dictators.
2. Encourage the democratic governments to send their high officials to the United States in order that they may be accorded public honors such as to reveal that the people of this country are "on their side."
3. Confer no medals or other honors on dictators.
4. Make no statement that can be interpreted as approval of dictators.
5. Make sure that every American who travels to Latin America "knows the nature of the government of the country he intends to visit."
6. Make no Exim Bank loans to dictators.
7. Give no military or economic aid to dictators.

In short, Congressman Porter urged the Eisenhower government to "seize the initiative in Latin America in the . . . battle for men's minds." "This means," he added, "openly condemning dictatorial regimes and praising democratic ones, . . . giving wholehearted support to those . . . who are striving to liberate [and improve the economic condition of] their countries . . . by democratic means."[3]

On July 19 he attempted to achieve a part of his program by offering two amendments to the bill authorizing "mutual-security" funds for fiscal years 1958. One provided that priority should be given to the more democratic countries in Latin America in distributing economic aid; the other proposed to terminate economic and military assistance to such Latin-American nations as the State Department determined to be governed by dictatorships. Although both amendments were roundly defeated—the first by a vote of 171 to 4 and the second by a tally of 168 to 7—the Oregon Congressman expressed the belief that their defeat could be attributed mainly to his inability to submit them beforehand to the House Committee on Foreign Affairs for the purpose of hearings, and indicated that he would persist in his efforts to effect a change in policy.[4]

At this time, as well as before and after, Porter stood almost alone in the House in his attempt to withhold assistance from the Latin-American dictators and confer special favors upon governments approximately democratic in character. No member of that body spoke in favor of his program. On the contrary, it was expressly opposed for different reasons by a score of Congressmen. Some were Roman Catholics aware that they were dealing with countries of that faith and seemingly influenced accordingly. Some pointed out that Trujillo had been kind to Jewish refugees and thus underlined the dictator's benevolence. Others appeared to reveal a disposition to support any tyrant, anywhere, who seemed to be an ardent anti-Communist, and even hinted—in some instances more than hinted—that the "unsophisticated Oregonian," who was only thirty-eight years old, was a dupe of the "international communist conspiracy." A few were probably influenced by loyalty to the Republican administration whose policy Porter was attacking. More were opposed to the amendments because they felt that they would result in a drastic departure from the nonintervention policy that the Franklin D. Roosevelt administration had firmly established (in theory if not actually in fact); and a few even went so far as to praise the government of Generalissimo Trujillo. Perhaps the following quotations will sufficiently illustrate their arguments during the course of the first session of the Eighty-fifth Congress:[5]

Daniel J. Flood (Democrat, Penn.): "The Dominican Republic has been honored by that great enemy of communism, Cardinal Spellman, for their [its] outstanding fight against this [Communist] menace.... I am certain that the agencies of this Government will not be influenced by inflammatory articles and statements issued by any person or persons on this subject."

Victor L. Anfuso (Democrat, N. Y.), who likewise confessed that he had been influenced by the views of the same Cardinal Spellman: "I cannot overlook the fact that the Dominican Republic is an ally of the United States, that she is part of our Western Hemisphere defense, that we do business with her.... In these critical times when the United States is engaged in a death struggle with a common enemy ... we cannot afford to insult an ally...."

John M. Robsion, Jr. (Republican, Ky.): "The United States is associated with the Dominican Republic in the Organization of the American States ... and the United Nations, and the two nations cooperate in plans for hemisphere defense.... Would it not be better if the gentleman from Oregon withheld his indictment of a friendly government and its head until the departments of the United States Government ... have been given full opportunity to develop all the facts and take whatever action that may be required?"

George S. Long (Democrat, La., and brother of the late Huey

Long): "It has been widely and loosely said that the Dominican Republic is a dictatorship.... I have learned by experience not to be taken in by the word 'dictator.' ... If indeed the Dominican Republic is a dictatorship, we have no proof of the fact that would stand up under a court of law of our nation. I cannot believe that these proud people would ever submit to a ruthless dictator. I can and do believe that they would . . . honor good and efficient public servants, even as they are so honored in our own land, by returning them to public office again and again for the glory and honor of their country and their God. ... The Dominican Republic and its chief of the armed forces [Rafael Trujillo] . . . and its President [Hector Trujillo] . . . have always and unequivocably been on the side of God and Christianity. They have been to us a vital and necessary bulwark against the encroachments of atheistic communism and its diabolical attempt to infiltrate and destroy our country...."

Such were some of the statements provoked by Congressman Porter's initial assault. Thereafter the battle, with the exception of the short debate occasioned by his amendments offered in July, was a sort of hit-and-run affair. Conspicuous among the Oregonian's antagonists were "Pat" Kearney (Republican, N. Y.), George S. Long, John W. McCormack (Democrat, Mass.), and Carroll Reece (Republican, Tenn.).

On April 5 Congressman Kearney, extending his remarks in the *Record*, firmly declared:[6]

"I speak from personal experience when I say that accounts of the terrorism and so-called brutal dictatorship in the Dominican Republic are best described as gross fabrications. Criticism of this type coming from official sources can be made by the communists to fit in with the picture they like to paint of the United States as the meddling, imperialistic menace . . . bent on destroying independence and freedom in Latin America."

On April 17 Louisiana's Long addressed the House at length. The following passage reveals the tone of his argument:[7]

"I . . . owe it to my country, to my God, and to myself not to stand idly by while an attempt is being made to destroy a small and friendly nation whose only crime is that it refused to knuckle down under the assaults of atheistic communism. . . . I care not what type of government is maintained in Ciudad Trujillo so long as it is not an atheistic communist government which would endanger our safety and security. . . . The type and form of government which . . . the people of the Dominican Republic choose to have, as well as the political leaders they choose to govern them, is strictly none of our business."

On May 8 Congressman McCormack, House majority leader, inserted some remarks in the *Record's* appendix. Mentioning the fact that four Jewish members of the House had recently visited the Hebrew refugee colony in Trujilloland and returned to Washington well pleased with what they had observed, this Roman Catholic politician continued: "Mr. Speaker, it is encouraging to note that four of my distinguished colleagues, in the course of a visit to the Dominican Republic, formed the same favorable impression of the broad, humanitarian policies of Generalissimo Rafael Leónidas Trujillo Molino, L.L.D., that have been entertained by numerous United States leaders and citizens throughout the last 27 years."[8] And on May 27 the appendix of the *Record* contained another statement by Congressman Long in which he asserted that the "gentleman from Oregon" was engaged in attacking "one of the great leaders of a democratic and progressive Republic" and declared further: "As a Christian I shall humbly pray that my young colleague . . . shall see the error of his ways and . . . be moved by God to turn his undoubted ability . . . to fighting our atheistic communist enemy."[9]

On June 11 Congressman Reece obtained the floor in order to protest against "unbridled and concerted attacks upon our ally and good neighbor the Dominican Republic." Enraged specifically by a *New York Times* report of an address which Porter had made in Puerto Rico in the presence of a "group of dissident, disjointed, and frustrated expatriates," the Republican from Tennessee continued his harangue:[10]

"In the course of this meeting, this United States representative is reported to have expressed sympathy with the revolutionary ambitions of this mob against the... government of the Dominican Republic. Words are not within my grasp to express the sickening, appalling horror that I felt upon reading of such action by a member of this body.... The Dominican Republic has risen ... to a position of material and spiritual well-being ... almost unequalled outside our borders ... [and has] supported our policies not only in the Western Hemisphere but throughout the world."

On July 12, anticipating the introduction of Porter's amendments to the bill authorizing funds for foreign aid, Reece remarked that the Oregon Congressman was seeking to destroy not only the government of the Dominican Republic but the Batista regime in Cuba, the Somoza government in Nicaragua, and the Pérez Jiménez administration in Venezuela, and went on to declare emphatically that the United States had "received no mandate to remake the world" in its "own image"; on the contrary, he asserted that "we are duty bound to observe the sovereign integrity of native governments of every complexion [in Latin America], no matter how repugnant they may seem to our concept." Moreover, Reece contended that the adoption of Porter's proposals would "have the effect of promoting instability in an area vital to the security of the United States," for if the Communists should gain a "foothold in the Caribbean, our far-flung defense system would be of no avail."[11]

Likewise in anticipation of the Oregon Congressman's amendments, Representative Long read into the *Record* on July 17 the address delivered by Manuel de Moya at the Commonwealth Club in San Francisco on April 5, 1957, in the course of which the Dominican diplomat suggested that Congressman

Porter had allowed himself to become the dupe of a Red conspiracy that had carefully planned "Operation Galíndez" and "Operation Murphy." The Louisiana Congressman interpreted Moya's address not as an effort to "smear" every reform group in Latin America but rather as a warning that the Dominican Republic was the victim of an attempt by Communists and their sympathizers to use this little republic as a "stepping stone" to impose upon the people of the United States "a brutal paganism" determined to liquidate "our individual liberties" and "destroy our Christian faith."[12]

Prominent among those who addressed the House on July 19 in opposition to the Porter amendments were: Donald L. Jackson and "Pat" Hillings of California; James G. Fulton and Daniel J. Flood of Pennsylvania; Victor Anfuso and Abraham Multer of New York; Barratt O'Hara of Illinois; and Clement Zablocki of Wisconsin.[13] Jackson, a Republican probably actuated in part by loyalty to the Eisenhower government, quoted some of the nonintervention provisions of the Charter of the Organization of the American States in refutation of Porter's quotations from the same document committing the signatory powers to the democratic creed in all of its implications, and bluntly declared that no distinction should be made among the Latin-American countries for any reason whatsoever—a declaration that contradicted the action of both the Chief Executive and the Congress of the United States in granting special economic aid to Haiti, Guatemala, and Bolivia. Reviewing some unpleasant history of inter-American relations, Jackson said:

"If you will think back . . . you will recall that . . . we [once] undertook to police the Western Hemisphere to judge the merits of its political forms and of its political leaders. It has taken us decades to build up some meaure of respect and understanding . . . as the result of our national conduct during that era."

O'Hara, ardent Democrat and warm friend of Franklin D. Roosevelt and Harry Truman, stated his position with precise brevity: "I am fearful that if we set ourselves up as judges of our hemispheric neighbors... we might end up with the sincere trusting friendship of none." Anfuso said he feared that the adoption of the Porter proposals would "sever" the United States "from friendly nations who had joined with us in the struggle against communism" and "drive" the alleged dictatorial countries "into the arms of Soviet Russia." Zablocki, Wisconsin Democrat, asserted that the Dominican government had fought the Communists before the United States fully recognized the Soviet peril and declared that the "foreign policy of the United States should be a single-purpose one—to defend this nation, this hemisphere, and the world against communism." Multer, New York's very articulate Democratic representative of the Jewish faith, referred to his recent visit to the Dominican Republic, pointed out that Trujillo had bestowed his benevolence upon Jewish refugees, and accused the "gentleman from Oregon" of opposing anti-Communist dictators in Latin America and supporting Communist dictators in other parts of the world. Hillings, Republican friend of Vice-President Nixon, unwittingly contradicted Jackson's assertion regarding nondiscrimination among the Latin-American countries by dwelling at length on the progress achieved in Guatemala under the rule of Carlos Castillo Armas, who had been especially favored with gifts from the United States, aggregating $30 million during fiscal years 1956-57.

Fighting his lone battle in the House, Representative Porter stressed three salient points: (1) The declared objective of the Organization of the American States is the promotion of genuine democracy and maximum personal freedoms in the Western Hemisphere; (2) the United States government, in granting military, economic, and technical assistance to Latin-American governments, was already engaged in intervention, in many instances in support of dictatorships and against opposing groups who were seeking to establish more democratic regimes; and (3) by discriminating against tyrants and in favor of liberals the United States would be more likely to achieve its ultimate goals.

Determined to drive his Democratic colleague from Oregon into the depths of despair, Jackson addressed the House for an hour on August 1.[14] Among his main arguments were the pledges against intervention which the United States had assumed in ratifying various earlier pacts as well as the charter of the inter-American organization, and two other contentions set forth in the following passages:

"Not too many years ago this nation expressed its sympathy for the aspirations of revolutionaries by the imposition of sanctions, [by] nonrecognition of regimes which we did not, as a people, approve, by armed might, and by other devices designed to bring down the tyrants and replace oppression by our own concepts of justice and equity. We proceeded on the assumption, since proven fallacious, that the other side of the coin marked 'oppression' is democracy. The history of Latin America is replete with instances of revolutions against one-man rule which resulted, not in easing the plight of the people, but in the installation of another strong man and an equally repugnant dictatorship under another name.

"What is equally important is the historical fact that in our obsession with what we believed to be right and just, we made enemies instead of friends. Even those who ascended to power as the result of our intervention, political, economic, and military, were among the first to cry, 'Yanks, go home,' and to reinvoke the specter of Yankee imperialism from the Straits of Magellan to the Rio Grande."

Excepting the assertion that the United States government had favored revolutionaries, the speaker's historical facts were essentially accurate. One of the mistakes of our early period of intervention was that of frowning upon revolutions without fully realizing that the peoples of Latin America were frequently deprived of the use of the democratic device of free elections, the only other means of determining policies and selecting personnel. With respect to the inter-American charter's dedication to democracy, freedom, and justice Congressman Jackson felt obliged to make this concession: "It is true that the implementation of these principles has, in a few instances, comprised only lip service." He contended, however, that "even that slight recognition implies that those who govern by strong-arm methods realize full well the tremendous reservoir of moral opinion in the Western Hemisphere represented by those lands and peoples who do practice what the charter lays upon each as a solemn obligation."

Jackson's contention that successful revolt against "one-man rule" is apt to be followed in Latin America by the "installation of another strong man and an equally repugnant dictatorship under another name" is not refuted by the history of the majority of the Latin-American nations. The historian who surveys these countries from the viewpoint of the welfare of the common people can hardly escape the conclusion that their leaders have not often governed in accord with the general welfare, but have rather been actuated by a trophy concept of administration, which in our own terminology corresponds with the maxim of "to the victor belongs the spoils." By ridding themselves of dictators the majority of these nations merely gain in the most fortunate circumstances the opportunity of working in favor of democracy. More likely than not the overthrow of tyrants will result in an anarchy which produces new tyrants.

Apparently not well versed in the history of the region, Porter scattered his ammunition over a front far too broad. If the agents of Trujillo could be proved guilty of two murders within the United States, that would be quite another matter, and some retaliation might be appropriate in the national interest. But the adoption of a general policy of promoting democracy in Latin America by employing sanctions against governments judged to be dictatorships or denouncing them would involve almost endless trouble and expense. For democracy seems to require tireless cultivation from generation to generation, with deep faith akin to that of the magnanimous Jefferson in the potentialities of human nature.

In reply to Jackson's speech Porter merely reiterated his main thesis:[15]

"Our present policies are based on the plainly false premise that the despotisms must be wooed because the United States needs them to help defend the hemisphere against overt attack by international communism. The best answer to communist subversion in Latin America is democracy and more democracy, freedom and more freedom, and enthusiastic encouragement by the greatest nation in the world, greatest in power, in wealth, in government, and in solicitude for individual rights."

Regarding the best answer to "communist subversion" the Oregon Congressman may be theoretically sound. But the application of the theory, judged by the futility of the drastic interventions of an earlier epoch, would be likely to result in more harm than good. Although the Washington authorities may sometimes have been too "chummy" with despots, it may be fairly assumed that neither Eisenhower nor any of his predecessors have dealt harmoniously with such rulers because they approved this type of government but rather because they actually felt that they had no better alternative. Removal of obstacles to the growth of democracy is a slow process, demanding an abundance of patience and tact. Important among these obstacles —to repeat what has been said on numerous occasions by many thoughtful students of the problem—are: poverty, which fastens attention upon immediate practical considerations rather than democracy; illiteracy, which accompanies as well as perpetuates poverty; social immobility, which frustrates the more ambitious young intellectuals; and political behavior characterized by intolerance, repugnance to innovation, selfishness, extreme nationalism, and demagoguery. Such obstacles can be removed only by careful persuasion on the part of well-endowed diplomats, favored by time, good fortune, and other assets, some of them hard to identify.

But Congressman Porter at least focused attention upon the dilemma which confronts public officials of this country in their efforts to promote democracy, liberty, security, and prosperity in a manner calculated to contribute to the political influence and welfare of the masses in the underdeveloped world and requiring an administrative staff almost global in its ramifications. The "outs" may shout against the programs of foreign aid and gladly accept them when they at length become the "ins," but their clamor seems likely to plant in the popular mind the seeds of hostility toward the United States; and even before the "outs" get possession of the reins of power they may compel the governments which they oppose to adopt the device of devious caution in respect to the foreign policy of the United States.[16] Progress in the direction of democracy and improvement of the welfare of the common people, in Latin America and elsewhere as well, may prove to be such a long and slow process that it will exhaust either the patience or the wealth of the people of the United States.

2.

The heavy costs and formidable difficulties of "reform" in Latin America are illustrated by Bolivia,[17] another Latin country which received some attention—though not enough—in the United States during the course of 1957. It will be recalled that for more than a decade the United States government had been trying to foster the economic and political progress of this small nation, a country inhabited by some three and a half million Caucasians, Indians, and mestizos. Accumulated costs in grants and cheap loans had amounted to between $115 and $225 million (depending upon the exclusion or inclusion of sums paid out for unneeded metals purchased for stockpiling); and still Bolivia was probably in a worse state in 1957 than in 1942 or 1945.

Nazi influence in Bolivia during World War II had caused uneasiness in Washington and led to grants and Exim Bank loans amounting to approximately $35 million. An alleged Nazi plot against the Bolivian government had provoked the declaration of a state of siege in July, 1941, that lasted for several months and caused the arrest of numerous conspirators, including Víctor Paz Estenssoro, the leader of a new political faction called the *Movimiento Nacional Revolucionario* (MNR). Released from prison after a few days, Paz Estenssoro resumed his efforts to seize the Bolivian government. Collecting funds and arms from the German Nazis and their sympathizers in Argentina, he and the members of the MNR, aided by a secret organization of young army officers, finally deposed the Enrique Peñaranda government of Bolivia on December 20, 1943, and hoisted Major Gualberto Villarroel into the Presidential Palace; whereupon the government of the United States, in full agreement with all the Latin-American governments save the somewhat pro-Nazi dictatorship in Buenos Aires, refused to extend recognition to the MNR administration until it complied with certain demands, among which was the dismissal of its pro-Nazi members. However, shortly after recognition was granted to the Villarroel regime by the foreign offices of the Pan American nations, the alleged pro-Nazis returned to their posts—Paz Estenssoro even advancing to the office of Minister of Foreign Affairs, a position which he continued to occupy until the Villarroel government was driven from power on July 21, 1946.

The revolt which put an end to the rule of Villarroel (and hung his bullet-riddled body on a lamppost with an army boot stuck under his arm) seems to have been a popular uprising, a violent protest of a hungry people against the deprivation and oppression inflicted upon them by the MNR and the army officers associated with that faction. Hunger and tyranny were nothing new in Bolivia, but the tyranny of 1944-46 was one of the worst that Bolivians had experienced since independence. Paz Estenssoro managed, however, to escape from the anger of the La Paz populace and flee to Argentina, where he remained—except for brief intervals in Uruguay—in close association with Dictator Juan D. Perón until the MNR, in combination with Communists and other Marxist groups, deposed the Bolivian military government headed by General Hugo Ballivián on April 9, 1952.

Worried in the 1940's by the pro-Nazi elements associated with Villarroel, United States officials now became uneasy about the activities of extremists of a different type in the administration of Paz Estenssoro. But just as the State Department under Franklin D. Roosevelt had gambled that Villarroel could be held in line by Lend-Lease and other aid, so the State Department under Dwight D. Eisenhower, advised by the President's brother and a member of the diplomatic service,[18] accepted the "calculated risk" of supporting the Víctor Paz Estenssoro administration in the hope of preventing Communist and Marxist subversion.[19] The United States thus engaged in a Bolivia gamble twice within a decade.

But the second gamble not only proved far more expensive than the first by the end of 1957; it seemed destined to prove still more expensive to the taxpayers of the United States in years to come. In fact, it was not yet certain at the close of 1957 that the United States would win the stakes in its second bet, no matter how great the ultimate cost, unless the Washington government should decide to risk still more drastic intervention in Bolivian internal affairs.

Hundreds of Bolivians forced into exile were protesting against the Bolivian policy of the Eisenhower administration.[20] Both the politics and the economy of Bolivia were completely upset by the expropriation of the major mining properties, by the arming of the industrial workers and the peasants, and by the seizure of the estates of the Bolivian landlords; and it appeared that economic collapse and grave political disorder could be prevented only by the continuation of economic and technical assistance by the United States for a period of decades and by the most astute sort of propaganda on the part of its Information Agency. Marxists of both the Stalinist and the Trotskyite variety were numerous, persistent, and influential. Much of the financial aid would probably have to be expended on the suppression of revolts and conspiracies or would be wasted in graft,[21] inefficiency, and imprudence. Moreover, if the debts owed by the bankrupt La Paz government to foreign bondholders and the dispossessed owners of Bolivian mines and agricultural lands were ever to be paid off, citizens of the United States would most likely have to foot the bills. The redemption of this single small country in accord with the "reform" program of even the most moderate leaders of the MNR promised to become both a very expensive and a very risky operation, involving a form of intervention apt to cause resentment on the part of many Bolivians and other Latin Americans as well, some of whom were already describing Bolivia as a "captive" country "at the mercy of Yankee business enterprises."[22]

How many more operations of this sort, scattered over Latin America from Argentina and Colombia to Guatemala and Haiti and over Eastern Europe, Africa, and Asia from Yugoslavia and Greece to Turkey, Iran, Libya, Pakistan, India, Thailand, Laos, and Cambodia, could the United States undertake without serious economic injury to itself and severe damage to its reputation and influence? Surely the time would soon arrive for a more careful forecast of the costs and political liabilities of this global program, for a more prudent calculation in the national interest of its numerous "calculated risks."

CHAPTER 14 MYOPIC DRIFTING?

LATIN AMERICA fared somewhat better in respect to aid from the United States in fiscal years 1956 and 1957 than in most previous postwar years, despite the fact that the Eisenhower Administration encountered difficulties in obtaining from Congress the appropriations desired for "mutual assistance." Latin America's average for these two fiscal years (excluding indirect aid through the United Nations and its affiliated agencies) was approximately $260,357,000; the annual average during the decade of 1946-1955 had been only some $178,501,000. The United States Congress was more generous than the United States Executive Branch in dealing with these neighbors of the Western Hemisphere. By June 30, 1957, direct aid extended by the United States government to the people of this part of the world since July 1, 1945, aggregated slightly more than $2,336,018,000: grants, $848,250,000; low-interest credits utilized, $1,487,768,000.[1]

Congress had acquired the habit of earmarking special funds for both specific countries and for Latin America as a whole. The major proponents of increased assistance to these hemispheric neighbors were several Senators, especially those from such border states as Florida and New Mexico. The attitude of the Executive Branch with reference to aid to the Latin-American countries was clearly revealed in the course of its pleas for "mutual assistance" for fiscal year 1958. Statements illustrating the sentiments of the Eisenhower Administration follow:

The International Cooperation Administration's *Summary Presentation, June 1957* (page 131):

"Massive grant aid programs are not called for in Latin America. Because of its geographical location there is no immediate threat of large-scale external Communist aggression.... Latin

MYOPIC DRIFTING?

America has had and probably will have more and larger opportunities than other geographic areas to obtain—through trade, through private and public enterprise, through private investment both local and foreign, and through loans from public institutions such as the Export-Import Bank and the International Bank for Reconstruction and Development—the external resources required for economic development."

Leonard J. Saccio, ICA's general counsel (May 28, 1957):[2]

"The relatively small size of this program, as well as its specific purposes and general composition, reflect the fact that the problems to be dealt with in Latin America differ . . . from the problems which confront the United States elsewhere in the free world. In the first place, because of its geographical location, there is no immediate threat of massive external Communist aggression, such as exists around the perimeter of the Soviet bloc . . . and hence no pressing requirement for the creation and maintenance of large modern military forces. . . . In the second place, again because of its geographical location, Latin America does not at the moment, in terms of present strategic concepts, have the same significance to the defense of the United States as certain other overseas areas which provide essential base sites intermediate between the United States and the Soviet Union. . . . In the third place, . . . Latin America has had, and has the prospect of continuing to have, more and larger opportunities than these other areas to obtain, by trade, through private investment, and by recourse to the public lending institutions, the external resources required for such development."

Secretary John Foster Dulles (June 18, 1957):[3]

"In the case of the Americas, . . . they are now in the main able to meet their increased demands through private loans and Export-Import Bank loans and World Bank loans."

Secretary Dulles, opposing the setting aside of specific funds for Latin America (August 19, 1957):[4]

227

"If you . . . get into the practice of legislating in terms of special countries, that is going to lead increasingly to the development by every country beneficiary of this plan of . . . a lobby designed to promote aid to it. There is going to be pulling and hauling and I don't think it is a dignified or proper procedure. . . . You are going to destroy your flexibility entirely."

The second statement made by Secretary Dulles had reference to a special fund of $20 or $25 million for Latin America. On the initiative of Senator George Smathers of Florida an extra sum of $15 million had been earmarked exclusively for the region for fiscal 1957 and had been expended as follows: A grant of $1.5 million to the Pan American Sanitary Organization for the eradication of malaria; a grant of $500,000 to the Inter-American Institute of Agricultural Sciences; loans ranging from $850,000 to $3,000,000 to Chile, Costa Rica, Ecuador, Honduras, Panama, Paraguay, and Peru, amounting to an aggregate of $12,850,000, at around 3 per cent interest and running from 20 to 30 years.[5] Having obtained a special $15 million for fiscal 1957, Senator Smathers attempted to "wangle" $25 million extra for Latin America for fiscal 1958. But it is not absolutely certain that the region will receive an additional $20 million, if even that much.

Action on this extra money for the other Americas was rather complicated. An authorization of an additional $25 million specifically for Latin America passed both the Senate and the House only to be eliminated because the Deputy Assistant Secretary of State for Inter-American Affairs had made this statement before the House Committee on Appropriations: "Our position in the State Department has been that we did not consider this necessary."[6] But Senator Smathers and his Florida colleague, Spessard Holland, then exerted themselves and succeeded in having $20 million extra included in the Senate appropriation bill. In one of his appeals Senator Holland disclosed that he and Senator Smathers were fishing for the votes of naturalized citizens from Latin America living in their state: "Senator Smathers and myself happen to be real close to Latin America geographically and . . . have a great many people of the various Latin-American races who have become our good citizens."[7] The same motive probably accounts for the favorable attitude of Senator Dennis Chavez of New Mexico. Senator Leverett Saltonstall of Massachusetts appears to have supported this special favor for Latin America because the region had become a profitable field of investment for Boston banks. The practice deprecated by Secretary Dulles was well under way.

The Senate's special fund of $20 million failed to gain the approval of the House conferees, but the Senate-House conference agreed in recommending that "not less than" $20 million should be set aside for Latin America, 90 per cent of the total to be bestowed in the form of cheap loans. The final words on the subject, so far as Congress was concerned, were these:[8]

"Mr. Smathers. Was it the feeling of the conferees that the $20 million . . . would be taken from the special assistance fund . . . ?

"Mr. Hayden [chairman of the Senate Committee on Appropriations]. Thereby even more than $20 million would be available, whereas originally not more than $20 million would be available.

"Mr. Smathers. In view of the action of the conferees, is it the belief of the conferees and the Senator that the $20 million can be used in the same fashion as originally contemplated . . . ?

"Mr. Hayden. Yes."

If the Executive Branch should respond to this pressure, Latin America's share in the foreign-aid appropriation for fiscal year 1958 (excluding gifts and cheap sales of agricultural products and many millions channeled through the United Nations and other international agencies) might amount to $114.5 million, even though the global appropriation was almost a billion dollars less for that year than for fiscal 1957.[9]

John B. Hollister, director of ICA, had made his position clear on the benevolent phase of foreign aid as early as April 2, 1957, when he said: "I personally feel it is not the duty of the Government to spend substantial amounts of the taxpayers' money for the general welfare of the rest of the world unless there is security tied to it." In short, he opposed heavy expenditures for purely benevolent purposes. He also referred to other motivations and to two sources of pressure when he remarked: "Enthusiastic ambassadors and people in our organization feel . . . that the country they work in is the most important in the world," and when he complained: "I have great pressures brought on me by American manufacturers and members of Congress . . . to give preference to American producers."[10] He might have mentioned other sources of influence, particularly the pressure exerted by certain racial blocs, such as the naturalized Polish citizens, or the Zionists, or perhaps the Negroes in the northern cities whose votes might be won by enlarging aid to the peoples of Africa.

For these and various other reasons, besides the sane and sensible desire to safeguard the national security, foreign assistance had become almost global. The following statement by Congressman Charles H. Brown of Missouri in July, 1957, does not seem absurd:[11]

"By attempting too much in too many places . . . [we] are actually doing so little in each place that we neither have a theory that we can live up to nor a program that we can live with. . . . What we have evolved . . . is a poor man's Marshall Plan . . . applied wholesale to practically every . . . nation of the world."

The practical objectives of these programs need to be defined more rigidly. The programs should be restricted to countries of supreme importance to national security, which should be their prime, if not their sole, motivation.

From July 1, 1945, through June 30, 1957, the United States government had distributed over $68.5 billions in foreign aid to 66 independent countries and 13 dependent territories. Latin America's share of this bounty, as already indicated, was in excess of $2.3 billion. Latin America's share in fiscal years 1956 and 1957 was distributed as indicated in Table 29.[12]

TABLE 29

GRANTS AND CREDITS BY THE U. S. GOVERNMENT TO LATIN AMERICA
FISCAL YEARS 1956-1957

(In Thousands of Dollars)

Country	Grants	Credits Utilized	Total
Argentina	$ 84	$	$ 84
Bolivia	41,235	4,901	46,136
Brazil	23,012	115,291	138,303
Chile	4,788	4,903	9,691
Colombia	6,684	1,447	8,131
Costa Rica	6,983	6,181	13,164
Cuba	989	8,851	9,840
Dominican Republic	747	.....	747
Ecuador	3,927	10,348	14,275
El Salvador	2,713	58	2,771
Guatemala	35,416	2,046	37,462
Haiti	10,456	9,414	19,870
Honduras	3,496	14	3,510
Mexico	2,739	23,915	26,654
Nicaragua	4,555	74	4,629
Panama	7,321	.....	7,321
Paraguay	3,883	3,541	7,424
Peru	15,589	43,174	58,763
Uruguay	556	.....	556
Venezuela	271	4,442	4,713
Organ. of Am. States	2,693	.....	2,693
Pan Am. San. Organ.	1,500	.....	1,500
Unspecified	101,689*	789	102,478
Total	$281,326	$239,389	$520,715

* The major part of this sum, namely, $99,750,000, was in the form of military aid to twelve of the twenty countries: Brazil, Uruguay, Chile, Peru, Ecuador, Colombia, Nicaragua, Honduras, Guatemala, Cuba, Haiti and the Dominican Republic.

Too much or too little, the assistance extended to Latin America was small in comparison with that bestowed upon Indochina, Taiwan, Korea, the Philippine Republic, Israel, and Turkey. These six countries received from the United States government during fiscal years 1946-57 a grand total of approximately $7.5 billion, well over $6.6 billion in outright grants. For fiscal years 1956 and 1957 their aggregate was more than $1.8 billion, nearly all of this also in grants. In all cases, possibly excepting those of the Philippines and Israel, however, the paramount objective was that of safeguarding the security of the United States by the prevention of military aggression by the Communists. It would be more appropriate to compare the assistance received by Latin America with the aid extended to the twenty underdeveloped countries listed in Table 30.[13] The total for these

TABLE 30

Grants and Credits by the U. S. Government to 20 Underdeveloped Countries in Asia and Africa, Fiscal Years 1956-1957
(In Thousands of Dollars)

Country	Grants	Credits Utilized	Total
Near East			
Iran	$ 79,000	$ 25,584	$104,584
Iraq	5,681	155	5,836
Jordan	14,412	.....	14,412
Lebanon	8,470	.....	8,470
Saudi Arabia	66	.....	66
Syria	131	102	233
Total	$107,760	$ 25,841	$133,601
Other Orient			
Afghanistan	$ 5,482	$ 14,800	$ 20,282
Burma	744	.....	744
Ceylon	5,942	1	5,943
India	134,780	−5,164	129,616
Indonesia	16,792	13,082	29,874
Nepal	2,904	.....	2,904
Pakistan	153,998	52,166	206,164
Thailand	59,876	10,211	70,087
Total	$380,518	$ 85,096	$465,614
Africa			
Egypt	$ 36,079	$ 3,815	$ 39,894
Ethiopia	6,850	2,400	9,250
Liberia	3,107	3,550	6,657
Libya	34,811	.....	34,811
Morocco	2,197	.....	2,197
Tunisia	6,648	.....	6,648
Total	$ 89,692	$ 9,765	$ 99,457
Grand Total	$577,970	$120,702	$698,672

twenty nations of the Orient and Africa, some of them with far larger populations than even the largest countries of Latin America and most of them much more exposed to the Communist peril, was only $1,965,201,000 during fiscal years 1946-1957— or some $370 million less than the twenty Latin-American nations received. Their aggregate of nearly $698.7 million for fiscal years 1956-1957, however, exceeded the total for Latin America by some $178 million.

Recall now that the aggregate direct assistance extended to Latin America during these two fiscal years was $520,715,000, excluding most of the Smathers special fund amounting to $15 million. Remember also that the population of these 20 countries of Asia and Africa was approximately three times as large as the population of Latin America. Recall likewise that most of the African and Oriental countries are much closer to the Sino-Soviet bloc. The conclusion that the hemispheric neighbors received in fiscal years 1956-57 was about as much as they deserved in the circumstances appears to be justified.

2.

The fostering of private economic enterprise both at home and abroad is the policy constantly proclaimed by the dominant political and economic leaders of the United States. While most of them would admit that the private-enterprise system has its defects, all contend that these can be remedied by sensible restraint on the part of management, labor, merchants and government, and that, in any case, the defects are far less dangerous than Communism or any other form of State Socialism. Putting the problem bluntly, the only alternative to private economic enterprise in the long run is *statism*, which means a monopoly of power in the hands of an omnipotent bureaucracy miscalled public servants. So long as political and economic power can be kept separate, neither will hold absolute sway and the liberty of the individual will be shielded by an equilibration of the two. The peril of State Socialism, whatever the brand, is ultimate tyranny imposed by those who possess a monopoly of power—a tyranny of public authorities who absolutely control the production and distribution of goods along with all opportunity for individual economic achievement and cultural development. A mixture of public and private enterprise is often discussed and sometimes approved by those who give the latter preference, but the nature of the mixed system is never described with precision. The basic principle for the determination of the mixture is often stated thus: "Let the state undertake whatever it can do more efficiently than private enterprise can." But who will be the judge? Is not policy more apt to be decided by the influence of pressure groups than by the wisdom of genuine statesmen?

A third of the earth's inhabitants are now subjected to the tyranny of despots who exercise a monopoly of political and economic power, and the United States, if we are to believe the salesmen of these programs of "mutual assistance," is resolutely attempting to prevent the spread of this oppressive system. But are not the dominant leaders of this nation concerned almost exclusively with the imperial advances of the Sino-Soviet bloc, the stimulation of exports, the search for more abundant raw materials, and the fulfillment of presumed moral obligations? The first of these objectives is supremely important. But are any or all of the other three combined more important than the objective of preventing the spread of State Socialism?

How can the results of this effort—or alleged effort—to promote the growth of private economic enterprise in the retarded countries be measured? Can it be done without the collection and analysis of statistics? Yet, if adequate statistics have been assembled by any agency of the United States government, they must have been concealed from the public under the label "top secret"—and the same is true of the private Foundations. Some of these aid programs have been in operation for more than a decade and none of them for less than half that time. Did their enthusiastic proponents employ any statisticians from the outset to ascertain the extent to which the various public authorities all around the world were engaged in economic activities or exercising control over private economic enterprise? In all probability they did not.

It is unlikely that those employed to distribute this largess would voluntarily have undertaken this statistical task; but was it not the duty of the President and Congress to demand such data at the very beginning? If this subject had been given first priority, taxpayers and businessmen might now be able to measure economic trends in that two-thirds of the world not yet subjected to Communism. Have the dominant political and economic groups in this country been so alarmed by the threat of Sino-Soviet imperialism, so absorbed in global benevolence, and so afraid of another economic depression that they have forgotten to concern themselves seriously with the ultimate effects of the spread of socialization of property and business enterprise?

Which of the two major antagonists in this global conflict is the more likely to reap the advantage from a drift toward State Socialism? It may not be altogether absurd to suggest that the Communist dictators expect the economic and technical phases of these "mutual-assistance" programs to work out in their favor, since it is not easy to imagine what else these tyrants could have done to initiate and perpetuate these programs. They have promoted crisis after crisis, and the response of the United States government has been always the same—more grants and cheap loans in every instance. Having no clear concept of the extent of socialization at the time when the programs were started, officials of the United States have had no reliable means of ascertaining the direction in which the recipients of this largess have been moving. Surely it is not too early—in fact, it may be rather late—for those who by no means favor State Socialism to consult the stars and the compasses and try to determine the destination toward which the inhabitants of this planet are traveling.

A beginning of the solution of the statistical problem has recently been made by an agency which might have been least expected to deal with the advance of socialization. The International Labour Office, because it has been assigned the task, among others, of looking after the world's working people, published early in 1956 some data on government employment. The data are far from complete, especially those relating to the retarded countries; but the specialists of the ILO have given considerable attention to the "public sector" of the national economies in all of the seventy member countries.[14] Starting with these statistics, the chief supporter of these programs of technical and economic assistance, with the possible aid of some of the minor contributors, should set up at once an agency for continuous collection of data and constant observation, *if* the political and economic leaders of the United States expect the taxpayers and consumers of this country to accept at par value their reiterated professions of deep devotion to private economic enterprise.

Although aware of the inadequacy of their information, the experts of the ILO ventured to offer a significant conclusion (I, 26):

"The outstanding ... difference between the present structure of industry throughout the world and that of 35 years ago is the very great enlargement of the public sector—an enlargement which in many cases is not inspired by any particular political or economic philosophy but has come about empirically and due to the pressure of circumstances."

In effect, these experts, using the word *industry* to cover all economic activities, are saying that two-thirds of the people of this planet—those who have not yet been compelled to submit to Communism—have been drifting more or less absent-mindedly into a species of State Socialism. The ILO committee did not specify the currents of circumstance that had floated these people along, but they doubtless had in mind the two recent

World Wars, the global economic depression of the 1930's, the cold war, and the struggles for political and economic independence on the part of various groups that have been ruled by the colonial powers. And to these pressures should be added, among others, those of benevolent though shortsighted relief agencies and clergymen and of bureaucrats eager to expand and multiply.

Those who would not knowingly approve the probable drift of events have unwittingly floated on the currents, have found themselves helpless, or have neglected to act with sufficient energy. Perhaps more important still, they have been too quick to ask the government for help in times of trouble and have failed to define, and keep to the fore, the proper limits of government regulation and government activities in the economic sphere. The time has come for all who wish to travel toward a different destination to effect a drastic reorientation. Already, according to the incomplete data assembled by the ILO committee, from 10 to 33 per cent of the world's labor forces this side of the despotic curtains are employed by public officials, perhaps no less than a third of these in government economic enterprises. Agriculture, manufacturing, and merchandizing are about the only economic activities in which the state is not dominant in most of the so-called "free world," and the state has begun to invade these in many countries. Moreover, this movement has probably been fostered by these programs of economic and technical aid, for they have been characterized by official gifts and cheap loans to governments ready and eager both to control and to participate in economic activities. This result seems all the more likely in the case of supplementary aid in the form of food and fiber taken from the surpluses stored by the Commodity Credit Corporation and doled out to foreign governments without asking whether the 150,000,000 consumers dwelling in the urban centers of the United States are being exploited by farm programs which seem so little concerned with the welfare of these millions of consumers.

This writer does not propose at the moment to enter into minute and perhaps tedious detail. He is in no mood for that. His purpose here is to urge careful examination of this significant report of the ILO committee, to point to what seems to be a global tendency, and to warn those who dislike this tendency that the hour has arrived to demand a scientific investigation and greater alertness in inspection in order to determine what ought to be done and what can be done to halt the advance of socialization. Those who are really dedicated to the protection and promotion of private economic enterprise and the preservation of the freedoms traditional in the Western World—and they may still constitute a majority—cannot afford to be indifferent any longer. Such of them as reside in the United States—and they are almost certainly in the majority here—should make their sentiments known to the hucksters engaged in selling the foreign-aid programs to Congress. Surely this cannot be an unreasonable recommendation in behalf of millions of businessmen, taxpayers, and consumers who are compelled to pay the bills without receiving any of the economic benefits in return for the heavy burdens imposed upon them.

Only such expenditures as are strictly involved in safeguarding the security of the United States can truly be described as outlays serving the national interest. All other expenditures on these extravagant aid programs serve mainly the material interests of exporters, importers, financiers, shippers, and those producing for export, at the expense of consumers, taxpayers, businessmen and workers supplying the domestic market, retired citizens depending upon pensions and annuities, and all who are engaged in cultural pursuits except the propagandists.

It may be true that 75-80 per cent of the dollars spent on these aid programs are spent in this country and that all of the dollars sent abroad eventually return home; but the trouble is that almost none of them ever return to those from whom they are taken by the government, for these dollars are shifted from the pockets of the many to the purses of the few. In short, some 90 per cent of the people of the United States suffer deprivation for the economic benefit of the other 10 per cent. Moreover, in the long run not even all the exporters will continue to profit, for while total exports may expand with the economic development of the retarded countries, a shift will gradually take place in the types of goods exported, so that many who are now engaged in production for export, especially farmers and manufacturers of consumer goods, will eventually suffer injury because of increase in agricultural output and the spread of manufacturing in these many underdeveloped countries. This is no way to cure or prevent economic recessions.

Nor should the blunders and waste, admitted even by the high officials of the United States, be forgotten. They have occurred in some of these programs in almost every recipient country. But they probably have been less prevalent in Latin America than elsewhere, despite the imprudent extravagance involved in the building of the Inter-American Highway across Central America and the Rama Road across Nicaragua, and in spite of the expensive futility of the rubber-plantation projects and the heavy subsidies granted to the "reformers" in Bolivia.

Panama and Nicaragua have managed to exact heavy compensation for the control and use of the Canal Zones across the American Isthmus. But these outlays are small when compared with the costs of strategic bases in Europe, Asia, and Africa, where a score of countries have been provided with crowbars to pry open the United States Treasury. From now on it might be cheaper to concentrate on rockets and inter-continental ballistic missiles, making use of appropriate launching bases from Alaska and northwestern Canada southward—cheaper and probably more reliable and effective. Maybe the defense of Europe can soon be left largely to the most efficient and dependable European nations with their intermediate-range missiles. Then the United States could gradually resume its traditional policy of emphasis on the Western Hemisphere and the dreams and ideals of those great statesmen who founded our nation and guided it safely through the critical decades of the first century of its existence.

Fully as alarming as the waste, extravagance, and "squeeze"—not to use the word *blackmail*—that have accompanied these "mutual-assistance" programs have been the multiplication of lobbies and pressure groups in this country for the purpose of obtaining appropriations, and the enormous expansion of the area over which the contents of the "pork-barrel" are being spread. The area is no longer limited to certain parts of the United States, such as river valleys and seaports; it embraces most of the world. Representatives of our racial blocs akin to peoples in foreign nations, representatives of our religious organizations with interests and affiliations abroad, representatives of professional social workers organized under the deceptive label of "voluntary relief agencies"—these and many more have joined the lobbyists. Political success in the United States is coming more and more to depend upon the purchase of votes rather than appeals to national security and the general welfare. If the transformation is not promptly halted and reversed, the government of our country will shortly be called upon to subsidize everybody except American taxpayers and consumers. Will historians of the year 2000, when they survey the history of the twentieth century, describe it as the epoch in which the inhabitants of this planet drifted into State Socialism? This may turn out to be the case unless the political and economic leaders of this generation and the next, especially the political and economic leaders of the United States, engage at once in a mighty effort to discover and direct the present trend of events.

Notes

Notes

CHAPTER 1

1. Arthur P. Whitaker, *The Western Hemisphere Idea: Its Rise and Decline* (Ithaca, N. Y., 1954), pp. 131, 154-76.
2. From the Farewell Address, of course.
3. Both passages are quoted in Whitaker, *op. cit.*, pp. 28-29.
4. *The Works of Henry Clay*, V (Calvin Colton ed., New York, 1857), 242-43.
5. From his famous message of December 2, 1823.
6. International American Conference, *Reports of Committees*, I (Washington, D. C., 1890), 42-43.
7. *Documents on Inter-American Cooperation*, I (Robert N. Burr and Roland D. Hussey ed., Philadelphia, 1955), 22-23.
8. *Ibid.*, I, 27 and 37.
9. *Ibid.*, I, 25-26.
10. *Ibid.*, I, 30-31. The Latins of America have not always included the United States in their projects of integration. Sometimes they used the term "American States" to embrace only themselves, just as the people of the United States have employed the adjective "American" in an exclusive manner. Canada was usually ignored until shortly before 1900, but Canada has been at liberty to occupy its vacant seat in the Pan-American organization at almost any moment it desired since that time.
11. Letter of Jan. 5, 1818, as quoted by Samuel F. Bemis in his *John Quincy Adams and the Foundations of American Foreign Policy* (New York, 1949), pp. 242-43.
12. *Memoirs*, V (Philadelphia, 1875), 324-25. I have changed the entry to direct discourse without modifying its meaning.
13. *The Works of Henry Clay*, V (Calvin Colton ed., New York, 1857), 145-47.
14. Letter of Nov. 30, 1813, in *The Writings of Thomas Jefferson*, IX (P. L. Ford ed., New York, 1898), 345.
15. Letter dated Dec. 6, 1813, *ibid.*, IX, 430-31.
16. Letter of May 17, 1818, *ibid.*, X (1899), 108-9.
17. Letter dated Aug. 1, 1816, in *The Works of John Adams*, X (C. F. Adams ed., Boston, 1856), 223.
18. J. D. Richardson ed., *Messages and Papers of the Presidents*, II (n.p., 1903), 329f.
19. William R. Manning, *Diplomatic Correspondence of the United States: Inter-American Affairs*, V (Washington, D. C., 1932), 3.
20. P. 20.
21. Jefferson to John Adams, May 17, 1818, cited in note 16 above.
22. Colton, *op. cit.*, V, 242-43.
23. *We of the Americas* (Chicago, 1949), pp. 23, 253.

24. *Ibid.*, pp. 10, 42.
25. *Ibid.*, pp. 24, 54.
26. *Ibid.*, pp. 34, 243-44.
27. *Free Men in America* (New York, 1943), p. 131.
28. See *Foreign Affairs*, Jan. 1954, pp. 277-78, and 272-74, for this and the following quotations from Padilla.
29. *Ibid.*, p. 276.
30. *Free Men in America*, pp. 134-36.
31. Luis Quintanilla, *A Latin American Speaks* (New York, 1943), pp. 85-86.
32. *Senate Document* No. 224, 73 Cong., 2 Sess. (1934): "Proposed Inter-American Highway," pp. 9-10.
33. Eduardo Villaseñor, "Inter-American Trade and Financial Problems," in *Inter-American Solidarity* (Chicago, Harris Institute, 1941), p. 94.
34. Robert J. Donovan, *Eisenhower: The Inside Story* (New York, 1956), pp. 138-39.
35. House Committee on Appropriations, 83 Cong., 1 Sess., *Hearings:* "Mutual Security Appropriations for 1954," pp. 434-35.
36. House Committee on Foreign Affairs, 83 Cong., 2 Sess., *Hearings:* "Mutual Security Act of 1954," p. 372.
37. *Id.*, 84 Cong., 2 Sess., p. 290.
38. *An Economic Program for the Americas*, p. 3.

CHAPTER 2

1. Writers of textbooks on United States history sometimes mention early investments in Cuba, but they seldom refer to those made in Canada, the Hawaiian Islands, Mexico, Central America, or the European countries. Cleona Lewis, in *America's Stake in International Investment* (Washington, D. C., 1938), p. 606, estimates the total private investments of United States citizens abroad at $684.5 million at the end of 1897, but evidently ignores the Hawaiian Islands, where some $40 or $50 million were invested.

2. I know of no estimates of United States capital in Latin America as a whole for any period before 1897. The best sources of information regarding the number and character of investments in the region before 1870 are the letters of United States consuls and the reports of claims commissions. (See John Basset Moore, *History and Digest of International Arbitrations* [6 vols.; Washington, 1896], especially Vols. II-IV.) I have dealt with the subject to some extent in my *Latin America and the Industrial Age* (New York, second ed., 1947). Prominent among the early shipping lines connecting the United States and Latin America were the Red "D" line (1838) and the lines of the Pacific Mail Steamship Company (1848). The Panama Railroad Company, founded in 1849, completed the railway across Panama early in 1855. Other lines of transportation connecting the eastern and western parts of the United States by way of the isthmian routes were ephemeral; the most important of them was Cornelius Vanderbilt's. Among the early trading firms were Samuel B. Hale and Company, in Buenos Aires, and a branch house of Heminway and Brown of

NOTES

Boston, in Valparaíso. Both were established in the 1830's and both were still in existence half a century later (Michael G. Mulhall, *The English in South America* [Buenos Aires, 1878], p. 612; *House Executive Documents*, No. 50, 49 Cong., 1 Sess., Serial 2392, pp. 323, 440). Two Delano brothers William and Paul, began their commercial life in Chile before 1830, and William Wheelwright started his business career there at about the same time (Mulhall, pp. 374, 382). Levi Woodbury's brother not only invested in Cuban sugar plantations but founded the port town of Cárdenas around 1828 (*Louisiana Planter* [New Orleans], XXXI [1898], p. 105). Doctor John Baldwin, during the 1820's, built sawmills on the Mexican Isthmus of Tehuantepec, established a mercantile house, and founded the town of Minatitlán (Moore, IV. 3235). The list of more than a thousand claims of United States citizens considered by the Mexican-American Claims Commission of 1869 discloses hundreds of investors, including thirteen mining companies and several other business organizations besides the numerous individuals owning farms, ranches, stores, and other properties (*Senate Executive Documents*, No. 31, 44 Cong., 2 Sess., Serial 1720).

3. I have dealt with some of the business activities of United States citizens in Latin America during this period in my *Latin America and the Industrial Age* (see especially pp. 51-95, 115-51, 177-87, 200). The commercial commission sent by the United States government to Latin America in 1884-1885 found their fellow citizens engaged in business of one kind or another in every country they investigated. I quote the following sentences from one of their reports: "As dentists and photographers, our countrymen easily lead in nearly every large town. In many cities American physicians enjoy lucrative practice.... In every Republic will be found American businessmen with wide circles of influence.... Moreover, resident merchants offer the best means to introduce and increase the use of our goods.... It has resulted favorably in almost every city of South and Central America we visited." (*House Ex. Docs.*, No. 50, 49 Cong., 1 Sess., Serial 2392, pp. 24-25.) Further information on the travels and proceedings of this commission will be found in *House Executive Documents*, No. 226, 48 Cong., 2 Sess., Serial 2304. A member of the consular service of the United States estimated American investments in Mexico at the end of the year 1887 as follows: railroads, $80 million; mines, $20 million; ranches and farms, $5 million; commerce, $1 million; total, $106 million (*Consular Reports*, No. 89, February 1888, pp. 339-40). A mining boom in Honduras in the 1880's resulted in a fairly large investment of United States capital in that country, perhaps $8 to $10 million (Council of the Corporation of Foreign Bondholders, *Fourteenth Annual Report* [London, 1887], p. 81; Cecil Charles, *Honduras* [Chicago, 1890], pp. 54-70).

4. In compiling Table 1, I have depended largely upon the volume by Cleona Lewis mentioned in n.1 (see pp. 575-606), but I have raised her estimates in some cases and lowered them in others in order to make them conform with seemingly reliable information drawn from other sources too numerous and scattered to be conveniently cited here. For example, I have reduced her estimate for the Central American countries because she included the capital of the Panama Railroad, which had long been controlled by Frenchmen and which should have been listed under Colombia in any case, since Panama was still a part of the Colombian national do-

main; I have reduced her total for South America by approximately $10 million because I felt unable to justify a larger figure on the basis of any available evidence; and I have slightly increased her estimates for Mexico and the Dominican Republic. Nathaniel Macon's figures for investments of United States citizens in Latin America at the beginning of 1899, published in *Yale Review,* IX (New Haven, 1900), 275-76, are too low for Mexico and Central America, but his figure for South America, $31.5 million, seems satisfactory.

5. Again, in compiling Table 2, I have relied heavily on Lewis, pp. 575-606, but I have supplemented her data and made some modifications in accordance with information obtained elsewhere.

6. Compiled mainly from data supplied by Lewis, pp. 575-606, 652-55; but I have presented my own estimates in some cases. My total for Cuba is probably a little higher than hers—she does not give separate estimates for Cuba, but includes that island with the other West Indies—yet I feel that my figure is not exaggerated. Max Winkler, in his *Investments of United States Capital in Latin America* (Boston, 1929), p. 275, gives estimates for the year 1913 which seem wide of the mark in some cases. John Ball Osborne's estimates for early 1912, published in *North American Review,* CXCV (1912), 687-700, supply valuable details for some of the minor countries thrown together by Lewis. His total for the investment in Cuba is $220 million. I have little doubt that an additional $45 million flowed into the island between the early months of 1912 and the end of 1914. I have accepted Miss Lewis's figure for Mexico. It is much smaller than the estimate sent by Consul Marion Letcher to the State Department in 1912 (*Daily Consular and Trade Reports,* No. 155, July 2, 1912, p. 316), but a destructive revolution had swept over Mexico since that estimate (for 1911) was made. The Letcher document placed the total, including properties of United States nationals—perhaps numbering between 50 and 60 thousand at this time, more American citizens than ever resided in any other Latin-American country and more than were then living in all of the other republics combined—domiciled in Mexico (excluded by Miss Lewis), at approximately $1,058 million. I have also accepted Miss Lewis's figure for Colombia, although it seems somewhat too high. Enthusiasm for the establishment of branch banks in Latin America was just getting under way in 1914, but five had been opened in Panama since 1904, one was founded in Mexico City in 1903, and one began operating in Colombia in 1913 (Clyde William Phelps, *The Foreign Expansion of American Banks* [New York, 1927], pp. 142-62, 211-12).

7. These are Miss Lewis's figures for the portfolio. She uses par values, which are much higher than market values, especially the figure for Mexico, $266.4 million, or around three-fourths of the total.

8. See the works cited in n. 6 above.

9. But see n. 7 above.

10. Firmer ground has now been reached. Intense interest in foreign investments developed in the United States after World War I. It would be pointless to list here all the works on the subject, but a few will be mentioned besides the volume by Miss Lewis already so frequently cited. Most useful in compiling Table 5 was *Trade Information Bulletin No.* 767, entitled "A New Estimate of American Investments Abroad," published by

NOTES

the United States Department of Commerce, Bureau of Foreign and Domestic Commerce (Washington, D. C., 1931). I have followed, in the main, the estimates for Latin America given in this monograph, but I have supplied some additional details derived from other sources and checked the data with those furnished by Lewis, pp. 575-606, 652-55, by Max Winkler, p. 278, and by Robert W. Dunn, *American Foreign Investments* (New York, 1926), pp. 61-135. Winkler's estimates for Cuba and Mexico are much too high, and some of his estimates for South American countries seem too low. The figures given in the Department of Commerce monograph, pp. 16-19, and the figures in my Table 5 represent market values for portfolio and a combination of market and book values for direct investments.

11. *Trade Information Bulletin No. 731* (Washington, D. C., Department of Commerce, Bureau of Foreign and Domestic Commerce, 1931), pp. 18-19. The title of this bulletin is "American Direct Investments in Foreign Countries."

12. *Ibid.* The total for banks and finance could not be ascertained, but American capital was dominating the banking field in the Dominican Republic, Haiti, and Cuba.

13. United States Treasury Department, *Census of American-owned Assets in Foreign Countries* (Washington, D. C., 1947), pp. 67-70 *et passim*. The Treasury Department figures represent market values for securities (portfolio) and book values for other assets, and unlike the Commerce Department estimates for 1929 and 1930 they include short-term investments and investments of United States citizens residing in Latin America, amounting to a combined total of around $200 million perhaps, although certain duplications may reduce the sum considerably. This difference in the items included should not be concealed, but I think it is not significant in view of the fact that returns given by owners who may have had a suspicion that the government had in mind some new plan for securing additional revenue would err on the side of moderation.

14. *Economic Series No. 20* (Washington, D. C., Department of Commerce, Bureau of Foreign and Domestic Commerce, 1942), p. 13.

15. It would be a most difficult task to determine the numbers involved on either side, especially the Latin-American side. Even a careful census—and no such census has ever been taken so far as I know—of the management, labor force, and patrons of these hundreds of business organizations would not disclose the full impact; the families of Latin-American officials, directors, workers, and patrons as well as the impact, direct and indirect, on entire national economies would be involved; and it would be necessary to include not only the organizations owned by citizens of the United States living at home but enterprises of citizens of the United States living in Latin America and owning property there. Statistics for all the corporate-controlled enterprises operating in the region, with the exception of those in Haiti and the Dominican Republic, indicate that around 2,400 officers and directors from the United States were associated as managers with somewhat more than that number of Latin-American officers and directors. In order to present an accurate picture of the relations of this United States managerial and technical group with Latin-American labor it would be necessary to investigate labor policies with the view of deter-

mining the extent to which the workers were dealt with by Latin-American management associates, and a similar investigation would be necessary in order to obtain a correct impression of the relationships of United States management and Latin-American purchasers of services and buyers and sellers of commodities. In other words, it would be necessary to ascertain whether, and to what extent, the relationships of each business organization were immediate and personal or remote and impersonal. The contacts between buyers and sellers, in the case of both services and goods, were probably the most numerous if not also the most intimate. Latin-American patrons of the public services owned by investors of the United States must have numbered two or three millions, without including the families of those who paid the telephone, electric, gas, and water bills; and the patronage of merchantile firms probably amounted to another million. Workers were less numerous than patrons, but Latin-Americans employed by these "Yankee" business organizations—office help, technicians, laborers on the plantations and in the manufacturing and extractive industries—probably numbered several hundred thousand. And finally, in arriving at a reasonably accurate estimate of the number of contacts involved, consideration must be given to the more than 1,500 property-owning citizens of the United States domiciled in Latin America in the early 1940's. The whole subject is as complicated as it is significant. Until an exhaustive census is made the investigator must depend upon Moody's *Manuals*, accessible company reports to stockholders, and such information as can be gleaned from government publications of the type suggested by the footnotes accompanying this chapter.

16. Consult *Stock Exchange Official Year-Book* (London), *Mining Year Book* (London), *Mines Handbook* (Suffern, N. Y.), and Moody's various manuals for the financial records of the companies dealt with in the following paragraphs.

17. Fritz Hoffmann, "Edward L. Doheny and the Beginnings of Petroleum Development in Mexico," *Mid-America*, XXIV (1942), 94-108, and *Moody's Manual: Industrials* (New York), index under the names of the companies mentioned.

18. Statistics presented in this and the following paragraphs have been compiled from two monographs published by the United States Department of Commerce: *International Transactions of the United States During the War* (Washington, D. C., 1948), pp. 70, 211, and *The Balance of International Payments of the United States, 1946-1948* (Washington, D. C., 1950), pp. 91-96, 258. Net earnings and income from other regions during the war years were of course much smaller than from Latin America, if the Near East and Africa are excepted. But the fact that the investment in these regions expanded more rapidly than the investment in Latin America during the "boom" period of 1919-1930 suggests that profits must have been higher during the 1920's, as they were during 1946-1955.

CHAPTER 3

1. These tables and the first section of this essay are based upon the following sources: U. S. Senate, Committee on Finance, *Hearings*, 72 Cong.

NOTES

1 Sess. (1931-32): "Sale of Foreign Bonds or Securities in the United States"; U. S. Senate, Committee on Banking and Currency, *Hearings*, 72 Cong. 2 Sess. (1933): "Stock Exchange Practice"; and *Senate Report*, No. 1455, 73 Cong., 2 Sess., Serial No. 9771.

2. Senate Committee on Banking and Currency, *op. cit.*, pp. 1011, 1128.
3. See note 5 below.
4. *Ibid.*, pp. 1892-1913, 1976-2014.
5. Senate Committee on Finance, *op. cit.*, pp. 1279-94, 1363-75, 1406, 1439, 1765, 2115.
6. Paul H. Douglas, "The American Occupation of Haiti," *Political Science Quarterly*, XLII (1927), 230, 383.
7. Senate Committee on Banking and Currency, *op. cit.*, pp. 2136-62.
8. Harold E. Peters, *The Foreign Debt of the Argentine Republic* (Baltimore, 1934), pp. 37, 41.
9. Edgar Turlington, *Mexico and Her Foreign Creditors* (New York, 1930), pp. 236, 243-44.
10. Russell H. Fitzgibbon, *Cuba and the United States* (Menasha, Wis., 1933), pp. 231-37.
11. But the par value of the investment of citizens of the United States in the dollar bonds of Western Europe at the end of 1930 had been in the neighborhood of $2,500 million—the market value at that time was $2,-328.4 million—and the par value of their capital in the dollar bonds of Eastern Europe, where tremendous losses were later suffered as the result of World War II and the spread of Communism, was probably not less than $250 million, since the market value at the end of 1930 was over $238 million.
12. Data presented in this and the preceding paragraph have been compiled from the following sources: *Survey of Current Business*, May 1954, pp. 12-13, Aug. 1955, p. 12, Aug. 1956, p. 18; *Balance of Payments of the United States, 1949-1951* (Washington, 1952), p. 164, and the same for 1946-1948, p. 216; Cleona Lewis, *America's Stake in International Investments* (Washington, D. C., 1938), p. 659.

Bolivia, the most persistent defaulter in Latin America, resumed interest payments on its government dollar issues at the end of 1956, so that the long period of Latin-American defaults was finally terminated; but Bolivia's funds for the service of these bonds were in effect a gift from the U. S. Treasury, which had been granting several millions annually to Bolivia since 1953! See Chapter 11 below.

CHAPTER 4

1. All rates have been calculated on the basis of book values at the beginning of each year. This results in more or less exaggeration of the rates, depending on the rapidity of the expansion of the capital; but utilization of year-end totals would have the opposite effect even in greater degree by virtue of the fact that a good part of the annual expansion of the investment was in the form of "reinvested" earnings. The rates have been computed from data supplied by the following sources, all published by the Department of Commerce: *Balance of Payments of*

the United States, 1946-1948, pp. 162-64, and *1949-1951*, pp. 162-63; *Survey of Current Business*, Nov. 1949, p. 21, Jan. 1954, pp. 6-7, Nov. 1954, pp. 11-12, Aug. 1956, pp. 18-23.

2. The U. S. Department of Commerce's Office of Business Economics lists six Latin-American countries—Bolivia, Ecuador, El Salvador, Haiti, Nicaragua, Paraguay—together under the caption of "other countries." The rates of profits for these were 13.4 per cent for net earnings and 9.9 per cent for income.

3. As it turned out, very few of the some $95 million in gross profits taken by investment bankers of the United States in connection with the flotation of Latin-American government bonds during the 1920's were extracted from Latin America. The profits were derived from American investors who bought those "souvenirs of misplaced confidence."

CHAPTER 5

1. *Foreign Grants and Credits by the United States Government, June 1955 Quarter* (Washington, D. C., Oct., 1955), tables 3 and 6.

2. *Foreign Grants and Credits by the United States Government, December 1955 Quarter* (Washington, D. C., April, 1956), table 3.

3. Consult the references cited in footnotes 1 and 2 above. Table 3 has been compiled from data extracted from the National Planning Association's pamphlet entitled *Technical Cooperation in Latin America* (Washington, D. C., June, 1956), p. 185.

4. See House Committee on Appropriations, 84 Cong., 2 Sess., *Hearings* (Jan.-Feb., 1956): "Department of State Appropriations for 1957," pp. 615-18. The data for Table 23 have been drawn from this document.

5. National Planning Board, *op. cit.*, p. 187; International Bank for Reconstruction and Development, *Tenth Annual Report* (Washington, D. C., 1955), p. 42.

6. This table has been laboriously compiled and computed from the following sources: UN Children's Fund, *Report of the Board of Auditors* (New York, 1956), p. 21; UN Technical Assistance Board, *Eighth Report* (New York, 1956), p. 93; House Committee on Appropriations, 84 Cong., 1 Sess., *Hearings* (1955): "Mutual Security Appropriations for 1956," pp. 556-57. Although the totals are correct, they may not correspond with the rounded figures in the columns.

7. The information included in this paragraph has been drawn mainly from the *Hearings* of the House Committee on Appropriations during the years 1949-1956. Table 25 is the result of many careful computations from data printed in the *Hearings* of the House Committee on Appropriations, 84 Cong., 2 Sess., dealing with appropriations for the State Department for fiscal year 1957, especially pp. 608-15.

8. *House Miscellaneous Doc.* No. 10, Serial 11689, pp. 18-21.

9. Grants to both the "American-sponsored schools" and the Gorgas Memorial Laboratory were a part of the appropriations made to the State Department for many years. Beginning with fiscal year 1955, however, the laboratory appropriation was shifted to the Department of Health, Education, and Welfare.

10. Population statistics are for the early 1950's and have been assembled from UN publications, especially the *Seventh Report* of the UN Technical Assistance Board (New York, 1955), pp. 77-134, 150-211.

11. Table 26 has been compiled and computed from the data published by the Office of Business Economics in the document cited in note 1 above. The grants listed do not include donations for the relief of Arab refugees from Israel, apparently aggregating $121,450,000.

12. Table 27 is based upon the documents cited in note 6 above. It seems unnecessary to give page references here since the pages for these countries are near those for the nations of Latin America. The figures in the two columns of this table are rounded and therefore may not add up to the totals given, but the totals are correct.

13. International Bank for Reconstruction and Development, *op. cit.*, pp. 27-28.

14. This table has been derived from references cited in note 7.

15. See below, Chapter 14. Under the International Wheat Agreements the nations of Latin America, along with many others, have long been able to purchase wheat at lower prices than were available to consumers in the United States; and beginning with fiscal year 1955 they started to receive foods and fiber as grants or on easy credit according to the terms of the Agricultural Trade Development and Assistance Act of 1954, although competing countries such as Argentina, Uruguay, Brazil, Mexico, and Peru were not altogether pleased with this act. By the end of the year 1957, the Latin-American countries had received under authority of this law grants aggregating $40,463,000 and cheap loans exceeding this sum, while grants to underdeveloped African countries totaled $23,840,000 and grants to underdeveloped Asia amounted to $71,092,000. (*Congressional Record*, daily, March 18, 1958, p. 4118.) Christmas gifts distributed allegedly under authority of this Agricultural Trade Development and Assistance Act, 1955-57, reached a total of $16,688,000!

16. But no satisfactory appraisal is likely to be made by bureaucratic investigators or scholars with bureaucratic ambitions.

CHAPTER 6

1. At times, both the railroad and the highway were conceived as extending through Canada to Alaska. See, for instance, Hinton Rowan Helper's *Three Americas Railway* (New York, 1881) and Senate Special Committee Investigating the National Defense Program, 80 Cong., 1 Sess., *Hearings* (1947): "Inter-American Highway," index under "Alcan Highway." (Alcan is an abbreviation of Alaska-Canada.)

2. A report of the Bureau of Public Roads, published in 1934 as *Senate Document* No. 224, 73 Cong., 2 Sess., estimated the length of the highway at 3,265 miles (p. 143): Mexico's segment, 1,738 miles; from the southern boundary of Mexico to the Panama Canal, 1,527 miles. But later estimates raised the Central American stretch to 1,590 miles.

3. The suggestion of a Pan-American Highway first appeared in official documents in 1923. The *Report of the Delegates of the United States of America to the Fifth International Conferences of American States* (Wash-

ington, D. C., 1923), p. 14, indicates that a resolution supporting the project and calling for a Pan-American highway congress to consider means of implementing it was proposed by one or more of the following delegates: Frank B. Kellogg, William E. Fowler, and Williard Saulsbury. Saulsbury's wife was a DuPont, and the DuPonts had investments in General Motors. The names of many of the other promoters are mentioned in *Senate Document* No. 224, 73 Cong., 2 Sess., pp. 145-48. Among them were: H. H. Rice, Pyke Johnson, J. Walter Drake, and Roy D. Chapin, representing the automobile industry; Harvey S. Firestone and W. O. Rutherford from the rubber industry; Williard Saulsbury, Fred I. Kent, and Guillermo Sherwell, representing the bankers; Lt. Col. Henry C. Jewett, Army Engineers; Frank Page and Frank T. Sheets, State highway departments; F. L. Bishop, Dean of the M. I. T. Engineering School and Dean A. N. Johnson, University of Maryland, representing the Society for the Promotion of Engineering Education; F. A. Reimer, American Road Builders' Association; B. B. Bachman, Society of Automotive Engineers; Thomas H. MacDonald and Edwin W. James, U. S. Bureau of Public Roads.

4. These various activities are described in *Senate Document* 224, pp. 145-48, and by Senator Tasker L. Oddie (Republican, Nevada) in *Congressional Record*, 71 Cong., 1 Sess., Oct. 8, 1929, pp. 4342-66, and 71 Cong., 2 Sess., March 12, 1930, pp. 5039-46. The most prominent of the newspapermen who championed the highway project was Karl Miller of the staff of the *Detroit News* whose reports on Latin-American highways were reprinted in pamphlet form (Detroit, 1925) under the title of *South America: Continent of Opportunities*. His main contention was that good roads were a prerequisite to good automobile markets. Among his striking subtitles were: "Peru Cuts Road Through Inca Burial Ground"; "Touring in Argentina Looks to Good Roads"; "Brazil Needs Sales Talk on Motoring Joys"; "Chile Is Trying to Pull Out of the Mud." Miller was sent as a "technical adviser" to some of the highway congresses.

5. Among the Michigan congressmen who supported the highway scheme were: Clarence J. McLeod (Detroit), Louis C. Crampton, Robert H. Clancy, and Henry W. Temple. Supporters from Ohio were Congressmen James T. Begg, and Frank B. Willis, who put Warren G. Harding's name before the Republican Convention at Chicago in 1920 as candidate for the presidency. In addition to Senator Oddie, already mentioned, other supporters of the highway were: Representative Cyrenus Cole from Iowa, a friend of Thomas H. MacDonald, head of the Bureau of Public Roads, who began his career in Iowa; Congressman William E. Hull of Illinois; Congressman John C. Linthicum of Maryland; Congressman John J. O'Conner of New York; and Senator Lawrence C. Phipps of Colorado. Congressional delegations from the Far Western States were highway enthusiasts; their States were large and their populations were small. Oddie, Hull, and Cole served as delegates to some of the highway congresses.

6. J. Walter Drake, Herbert Hoover's assistant secretary of commerce, was an official of the Hupp Motor Company.

7. Two members of Congress opposed the first $15,000 appropriation. Representative Thomas L. Blanton of Texas declared: "This is nothing in the world but a proposal in behalf of the automobile industry and the road-building machinery industry to take $15,000 out of the public treasury

to advertise their business in the South American countries." Representative Crampton of Michigan replied that while the great industries mentioned might be "directly benefited, all would share" the profits of the expanded trade that would result from this small expenditure. Representative Linthicum seemed to be little concerned with possible wider benefits. "If there is one thing we ought to do," he remarked, "it is to assist South America in building highways. We will sell more automobiles, ... parts that go with them, and a multiplicity of things for the comfort and convenience of motor travel." *(Record,* 68 Cong., 2 Sess., Feb. 18, 1925, pp. 4843-45, and March 3, 1925, pp. 5380-81.) The sole opposition in the Senate was expressed by Senator W. H. King of Utah. Coming from a Far Western Republican, his statement must have been a surprise. He declared that he could not "conceive of any particular benefit coming from a meeting in Buenos Aires to determine about highways." *(Ibid.,* Feb. 27, 1925, p. 4843.) There was no opposition to the expenditure of the second $15,000. The Senate passed the second appropriation for the survey without debate and without a record vote. The House first balked and then consented after the Senate acted. *(Ibid.,* 71 Cong., 2 Sess., Feb. 20, 1930, p. 4017, March 17, 1930, p. 5376, and March 19, 1930, p. 5634.) Assurance that none of the taxpayer's money would be spent for the construction of highways in Latin America was given by Congressman Cole during the discussion of the authorization bill. In this connection, Cole said: "The roads to be built through the republics to the south will be paid for by the countries affected. American capital may be called upon to help finance some of these projects, but that will be done outside the Government. ... It is not contemplated that this country will invest out of the United States Treasury a dollar in building a mile of road outside of this county." *(Ibid.,* 70 Cong., 2 Sess., Feb. 18, 1929, pp. 3685-86.)

8. The sources cited in note 4 above describe these activities.

9. See note 10 below.

10. Here are some of the quotations: "I look forward hopefully to the time when ... the two continents ... will be united in physical fact through modern highways, as they are today united through bonds of friendship and good will." (Calvin Coolidge.) "For many years ... the engineers have carried a dream in their minds that they might some day have a railway from Canada to Tierra del Fuego. That dream is more likely of realization ... through the development of the great new form of transportation by automobile." (Herbert Hoover.) These statements and others were read into the *Record* (71 Cong., 2 Sess., March 12, 1930, pp. 5041-43) by Senator Oddie.

11. Members of Congress frequently referred to Blaine's great foresight in advocating the Pan-American Railway. See, for instance, the following short documents: *House Report* No. 1179, Serial 8388; *Senate Report* No. 1372, Serial 8391; *Senate Document* No. 189, Serial 8413; and *House Report* No. 1124, Serial 8837. Both Linthicum and McLeod dwelt upon the great road-building achievements of ancient Rome. Linthicum: "The Roman Empire was consolidated by its splendid road system. The Appian Way has gone down in history as the greatest highway in the world. Let us cooperate with our Central and South American friends in the building of roads. ... It will help social conditions, accentuate trade,

253

and better consolidate us as one people. . . ." (*Record*, 70 Cong., 1 Sess., March 28, 1928, p. 5530.) McLeod: "Just as we now measure the power of the Roman Empire by her military roads, so the people of the world 1,000 or 5,000 years hence will judge our civilization by the roads we leave. . . . The highway will commemorate a different kind of civilization. . . . It will stand, not for the engineering achievement of a military emperor, but for the more advanced genius of mutual cooperation between friendly republics." (*Ibid.*, March 30, 1928, pp. 5697-98.)

12. These quotations are from pp. 3, 8, and 9. There were no references to Roman roads, James G. Blaine, or military needs.

13. Subcommittee of the House Committee on Appropriations, 73 Cong., 1 Sess., *Hearings* (1934): "Additional Appropriations for Emergency Purposes," pp. 256-58. Harold Ickes declared that the appropriation would promote international friendship and increase employment in the United States. Edwin C. Wilson of the State Department said: "The money has to be spent in this country for materials and machinery." For further information, consult *Foreign Relations for the United States*, 1934, IV, 467-94; 1935, IV, 241-65; 1936, V, 151-73; 1937, V, 175-97.

14. House Committee on Foreign Affairs, 77 Cong., 1 Sess., *Hearings* (1941): "Inter-American Highway," p. 28. The appropriations and authorizations are detailed in a letter by Thomas H. MacDonald to Sol Bloom.

15. *Hearings* cited in note 14 above. This authorization had passed the Senate on May 26, 1941, several months before the Pearl Harbor catastrophe, but action was delayed in the House. Secretary Hull's main arguments in support of expenditures for the highway were that most of the money would be spent in the United States; that trade and tourist traffic would be expanded; that the development of the material resources of Central America would be stimulated; that the governments of the region would be stabilized so that they could deal more effectively with "any attempted subversive activities." (*Ibid.*, pp. 2-4: letter dated April 28, 1941, addressed to President Roosevelt.) But proponents of the authorization in the House of Representatives stressed national defense and the military advantages of the highway, quoting an alleged statement of the Chief of Staff, George C. Marshall, to the effect that it "would be of great military benefit, that it would insure . . . land communications, no matter what the situation should be at sea." (*Record*, 77 Cong., 1 Sess., Dec. 16, 1941, pp. 9869-79.)

16. Senate Subcommittee of the Committee on Appropriations, 78 Cong., 1 Sess., *Hearings* (1943): "Second Deficiency Appropriation Bill for 1943," p. 67. The statement quoted was made by Edwin W. James of the Public Roads Administration, who indicated that this further appropriation would complete the highway, perhaps by July 1944!

17. Department of Commerce, Office of Business Economics, *Supplement to Foreign Transactions of the U. S. Government: Major Legislation, July 1, 1940 through December 31, 1948* (Washington, May 1949), p. 16.

18. The fiasco of the Army Engineers is fully, if not fairly, set forth in *Senate Report* No. 440, 80 Cong., 1 Sess., Serial 11116 (1947): "The Inter-American Highway," and by the Senate Special Committee Investigating

the National Defense Program, in its *Hearings*, 80 Cong., 1 Sess. (1947): "Inter-American Highway." Dwight Eisenhower, in a memorandum of June 4, 1942, expressed the view that the "utility of the proposed road to the . . . war effort" was "problematical," but was willing to recommend its "future construction in the interest of continental solidarity and for its possible long-range military value" rather than "on the ground of present military necessity." (*Hearings*, p. 21621.) Lucius D. Clay, deputy chief of staff for Requirements and Resources, in a memorandum of June 17, 1942, recommended that the project be "deferred for at least a year." (*Senate Report* No. 440, p. 63.) In a letter to Representative Bloom, dated July 16, 1941, Chief of Staff Marshall said he was unwilling to support the highway "purely on the basis of its military importance. . . ." (*Hearings*, p. 21732.) Later, however, as observed in note 15 above, he seems to have changed his mind. Secretary Henry L. Stimson wrote to Secretary Hull on July 23, 1942, as follows: "After detailed study it has been concluded that the completion of an all-weather pioneer road by May 1943 is an urgent military necessity, and . . . the Chief of Engineers has been directed to initiate construction thereof immediately. . . ." (*Ibid.*, p. 21774.)

19. An abundance of information on the highway for the postwar years is published in the following documents: Senate Subcommittee of the Committee on Public Works, *Hearings* (1950) and *Hearings* (1952), 81 Cong., 2 Sess., and 82 Cong., 2 Sess.: "Federal Aid to Highway Act of 1950" and "Federal Aid to Highway Act of 1952" (consult the indexes under "Inter-American Highway"); and Senate Subcommittee of the Committee on Appropriations, 83 Cong., 2 Sess., *Hearings*, "Department of Commerce Appropriations for 1955," pp. 666-85. The main arguments used by the promoters were these: (1) The highway will prevent the spread of Communism by contributing to the economic prosperity of the Central Americans and (2) refusal to continue financing the highway, or even delay in supplying funds, might disappoint the people of the region and result in the loss of their friendship.

The governments of the six Central American countries had also spent considerable sums on this highway, but they had borrowed most of the money they had spent from the Export-Import Bank. Moreover, the pretense of 1941 that they would pay a third of the costs on a "matching" basis was abandoned within a few months. The United States was supplying far more than two-thirds of the expenditures.

20. Senate Subcommittee of the Committee on Appropriations, 83 Cong., 2 Sess., *Hearings* (1954): "Department of Commerce Appropriation for 1955," p. 668.

21. Edward G. Miller, assistant secretary of state for Inter-American Affairs, made this statement regarding the importance of the highway in 1952: "I think it is the most constructive project we have anywhere in the world. I think it is directly related to the whole theory of the Point IV program." (*Hearings:* "Federal Aid Highway Act of 1952," p. 364.)

22. The automobile at inflated postwar prices is a luxury far beyond the reach of the vast majority of the eight million inhabitants of Central America, who would obtain greater benefits from modest cart roads from farm to market. Peasants who drive their calves and pigs to market do not like hard-surfaced roads because automobiles frighten and imperil their

animals and because the hard surface makes them lame. Men who make their living by transporting goods in ox-carts or on the backs of animals will be injured and aggrieved by the competition of trucks. The motorization of Central America will not confer immediate benefits upon the major part of its people and probably will fail for a considerable period to win the friendship of the masses. Senator Ferguson observed the complaints of the pig-drivers. Thomas H. MacDonald spoke of substituting motor transportation for the more expensive transportation by ox-cart without noting that cartmen would be gravely injured by the competition of the new means of shipping. (Senate Subcommittee of the Committee on Appropriations, 82 Cong., 1 Sess., *Hearings* (1951): "Department of Commerce Appropriations for 1952," pp. 721-22.)

23. *Cong. Record* (daily), April 1, 1955, p. 3506.
24. *Ibid.*, April 13, 1955, pp. 3698-3700.
25. *Ibid.*, April 14, 1955, pp. 3801-6. The appropriation eventually voted for the Rama Road was $2 million for fiscal year 1956.
26. *Ibid.*, May 17, 1955, pp. 5484-87, May 24, pp. 5844-72, June 8, pp. 6713-25, June 16, p. 7266, and June 29, pp. 8069-71; Sen. Committee on Foreign Relations, 84 Cong., 2 Sess., *Hearings*: "Mutual Security Act of 1956," pp. 279-80.
27. The U. S. Congress voted an additional $10 million for this highway in 1958.

CHAPTER 7

1. *Hispanic American Report*, August, 1956, p. 378. While in Panama in July, 1956, at a meeting of the presidents of the American Republics President Eisenhower signed a treaty providing for the construction at the assumed cost of $10 million of a high bridge across the canal.
2. *Congressional Record* (daily), July 29, 1955, pp. 10468-89.
3. *Congressional Record* (daily), 82 Cong., 2 Sess., June 3, 1952, p. 6432. For the full record of this investigation, see Senate Special Committee Investigating the National Defense Program, 80 Cong., 1 Sess., *Hearings* (1946-47): "Inter-American Highway," which will be cited hereinafter as *Hearings*: "Inter-American Highway." Estimates of the length of the projected road have varied from 180 to 158 miles, suggesting that construction was started hastily before a careful survey had been made. Its exact length probably will not be known until its construction is completed. Apparently no detailed description of the terrain over which it is to run has ever been published.
4. *Hearings*: "Inter-American Highway," pp. 21212-15.
5. *Ibid.*, pp. 21363-64.
6. Cabot said that a joint communiqué was issued, and the *New York Times*, May 4, 7, 23, and 26, 1939, seems to corroborate his assertion.
7. *Hearings*: "Inter-American Highway," pp. 21418-19, 21424-29.
8. *Ibid.*, p. 21775.
9. *Ibid.*, p. 21776.
10. "Practically every political disturbance ... in recent years has originated on the eastern coast, which has been out of touch with the rest of

NOTES

the country. For purposes of internal policing this road will have considerable value."

11. For the condition of the road in 1948-1954, see the sources cited in notes 12, 15, and 20 below.

12. Senate Subcommittee of the Committee on Public Works, 81 Cong., 2 Sess., *Hearings* (1950): "Federal Aid Highway Act of 1950," p. 451.

13. *Congressional Record* (daily), 81 Cong., 2 Sess., August 22, 1950, p. 1298. "This is the way money is being spent . . . on boondoggling," declared Ferguson, "and this amount should not be expended, not one dollar of it."

Ferguson had observed in the course of his earlier investigation that gravel "piled up . . . to surface the road . . . was disappearing." Paid for by the United States, "it was being taken by the Nicaraguan Government for another project." "Suppose they pad their pay rolls, which we understand they continually try to do?" "Suppose inflation increases all the costs, are we going to pay that?" (*Hearings:* "Inter-American Highway," pp. 21431-32.)

14. Senate Subcommittee of the Committee on Public Works, *Hearings* as cited in note 12 above, p. 282.

15. These letters were published in the *Hearings* (1952), p. 371, of the Senate Subcommittee of the Committee on Public Works. The *Hearings* are entitled "Federal Aid Highway Act of 1952" (82 Cong., 2 Sess.). The Somoza letter is admittedly incomplete, and this may also be true of the Roosevelt letter.

16. The word "highway" in the first sentence of this letter is a bit confusing. Did Roosevelt have in mind a highway westward from Lake Nicaragua where it would connect with the projected barge canal or did he have in mind a highway as a substitute for the canal? C. P. Gross, who had charge of the canalization survey, does not say that he surveyed the Rama Road, but he does assert, as already noted, that he recommended the Rama Road.

Roosevelt refers to the possible defense value of the waterway, but the waterway was not constructed. Welles refers to the defense value of the Rama Road, *if it were in existence;* but plans were not made to bring it into existence in less than four years.

17. The entire memorandum, undated but transmitted to Senator Chavez by the State Department on March 15, 1951, is printed at pp. 370-74 of the *Hearings* cited in note 14 above. Argument number 6 is omitted because it is long and because it would introduce misunderstanding regarding what was done about the extra loop in the Inter-American Highway that was made to accommodate Somoza's plantation. This highway will not follow the loop, but Somoza has his road none the less, and the cost was $1.4 million! Waynick, a road enthusiast, was once the head of the highway organization of the State of North Carolina, and was probably responsible for having Charles M. Upham, a famous highway engineer with Carolina experience, join in the effort to influence Congress.

18. Neither Meader nor Ferguson was opposed to the financing by the United States of the much larger and far more expensive project known as the Inter-American Highway, although both were shocked by the extravagance and waste of the Army Engineers and others.

257

19. *Cong. Record* (daily), 82 Cong., 2 Sess., June 3, 1952, pp. 6431-35. On the interpretation of this canal treaty, the Bryan-Chamorro Treaty, I agree with Ferguson and Meader. The Nicaraguan negotiators of the period must have known very well that the United States was more interested in controlling a rival canal route than in constructing another expensive canal and that a further motive was the desire to supply Nicaragua with much needed revenues. See my *Caribbean Danger Zone* (New York, 1940), pp. 180-81 and the sources cited. But consult also Thomas A. Bailey, "Interest in a Nicaraguan Canal, 1903-1931," in *Hispanic American Historical Review*, XVI (Feb., 1936), 2-28. Interest in the construction of a second canal developed in the United States to some extent during the decade following 1929, and Anastasio Somoza, who seized the government of Nicaragua in 1936, eagerly turned the course of events to his advantage, exerting pressure at a period of great crisis.

20. Senate Subcommittee of the Committee on Appropriations, 83 Cong., 2 Sess., *Hearings* (1954): "Commerce Department Appropriations, 1955," pp. 670, 683-85. Appropriations for fiscal years 1956 and 1957 were increased to two millions annually. Construction progressed slowly during 1956 and 1957, mainly because of the torrential rains, and heavy rainfall would create serious problems of maintenance.

CHAPTER 8

1. For a fuller account of this early episode, see J. Fred Rippy, *Latin America and the Industrial Age* (New York, 1947), pp. 166-76, 271-72.
2. *The Memoirs of Herbert Hoover: The Cabinet and the Presidency, 1921-1933* (New York, 1952), pp. 81-83. Charles R. Whittlesey, in his *Government Control of Crude Rubber* (Princeton, 1931), discusses the subject at length. Sir James Stevenson was chairman of the committee which formulated the program, and it became known as the Stevenson Plan.
3. U. S. Department of Commerce, *Trade Promotion Series*, No. 23: "Rubber Production in the Amazon Valley," pp. vii-viii.
4. *Ibid.*, No. 40: "Possibilities for Para Rubber Production in Northern Tropical America," pp. xi-xii.
5. House Committee on Interstate and Foreign Commerce, 69 Cong., 1 Sess., *Hearings* (Jan., 1926): "Crude Rubber, Coffee, Etc.," pp. 348-49, 354, 357.
6. *Ibid.*, p. 256.
7. *Ibid.*, pp. 372-73, *passim.*
8. *Trade Promotion Series*, No. 23, as cited in note 3 above, pp. 41-50 and 98-100; *ibid.*, No. 40, as cited in note 4 above, pp. 37-39, 40-44, *passim.* The Amazon survey party's report seems slightly less optimistic than the statements by Klein and Whitford; the survey team which investigated northern tropical America was apparently more hopeful than its superiors.
9. Jesse H. Jones, *Fifty Billion Dollars* (New York, 1951), p. 397.
10. *Ibid.*, pp. 397-401; R. D. Rands and Loren G. Polhamus, *Progress Report on the Cooperative Hevea Rubber Development Program in Latin*

NOTES

America (U. S. Department of Agriculture, Circular No. 976, Washington, 1955), p. 1.

11. Jones, *op. cit.*, pp. 396-433.
12. *Ibid.*, p. 420.
13. *House Report*, 78 Cong., 2 Sess., No. 2098, Serial 10848, pp. 2 and 19.
14. House Committee on Agriculture, 77 Cong., 2 Sess., *Hearings* (Jan., 1942): "Guayule Rubber," p. 24.
15. *Ibid.*, p. 30.
16. *Ibid.*, p. 6, and Senate Committee on Military Affairs, 77 Cong., 1 Sess., *Hearings* (Dec., 1941): "Guayule," p. 3.
17. House Committee on Agriculture, as cited in note 14 above, p. 92. See also pp. 40, 77, and 113 for statements of approval.
18. *Ibid.*, pp. 26, 98-99, *passim*.
19. House Committee on Appropriations, 80 Cong., 2 Sess., *Hearings:* "Department of State Appropriation Bill for 1949," pp. 376-78. The *House Report* cited in note 13 above, pp. 10, 18, 20-22, reckoned the cost at $37.7 to $56.7 million; and yet Congressman Poage recommended that the farmers take charge under a government guaranty of price support at a minimum of 28 cents per pound for *guayule* rubber.
20. House Committee on Agriculture, 77 Cong., 2 Sess., *Hearings* (Jan., 1942): "Guayule Rubber," p. 29.
21. House Committee on Appropriations, 78 Cong., 2 Sess., *Hearings* (1944): "State Department Appropriation Bill, 1945," pp. 195-97.
22. House Committee on Appropriations, 79 Cong., 1 Sess., *Hearings* (1945): "State Department Appropriation Bill, 1946," pp. 233-40.
23. *Ibid.*, 80 Cong., 2 Sess., *Hearings:* "State Department Appropriation Bill, 1947," pp. 237-38.
24. *Ibid.*, 80 Cong., 2 Sess., *Hearings:* "State Department Appropriation Bill, 1948," pp. 1048-49.
25. *Ibid.*, 80 Cong., 2 Sess., *Hearings:* "State Department Appropriation, 1949," p. 378.
26. For Bennett's masterful appeals for funds, see House Committee on Foreign Affairs, 82 Cong., 1 Sess., *Hearings* (June-July): "The Mutual Security Program," pp. 1444, 1461; Sen. Committee on Foreign Relations, 82 Cong., 1 Sess., *Hearings* (July-Aug., 1951): "Mutual Security Act of 1951," p. 426; House Committee on Appropriations, 82 Cong., 1 Sess., *Hearings* (Oct., 1951): "Mutual Security . . . Appropriations for 1952," pp. 702, 705.
27. An International Operations Subcommittee of the House Committee on Government Operations, some of whose members made a brief tour of inspection in four of the rubber countries—Bolivia, Peru, Colombia, and Mexico—in October, 1955, made no mention of the program and revealed no awareness of its existence. The subcommittee's report, *House Report* No. 1985, 84 Cong., 2 Sess., is entitled "United States Technical Assistance in Latin America." The inspection also included Chile, Argentina, and Uruguay.
28. Rands and Polhamus, *op. cit.*, p. 28. See note 10 above for the full title of this monograph.
29. *Ibid*, pp. 69-73.

30. Senate Committee on Interior and Insular Affairs, 83 Cong., 2 Sess., *Hearings* (1954), Part 9, pp. 457-59.

CHAPTER 9

1. U. S. Senate Committee on Finance, 84 Cong., 2 Sess., *Hearings* (Jan., 1956): "Sugar Act Extension," p. 40; *Senate Report*, No. 1461, 84 Cong., 2 Sess., pp. 8-9.
2. U. S. Senate Committee on Finance, document cited in note 1, pp. 181, 185.
3. U. S. House Committee on Agriculture, 73 Cong., 2 Sess., *Hearings* (Feb., 1934): "To Include Sugar Beets and Sugarcane as Basic Agricultural Commodities," p. 206. This statement by Jefferson was quoted by the National City Bank. International sugar agreements have operated intermittently for nearly a century, the latest of them signed in 1937 and 1953, and all of them designed to restrict production and imports.
4. U. S. Senate Committee on Finance, 73 Cong., 2 Sess., *Hearings* (Feb., 1934): "To Include Sugar Beets and Sugarcane as Basic Agricultural Commodities . . . ," pp. 7-8, 32.
5. U. S. House Committee on Agriculture, 73 Cong., 2 Sess., *Hearings* (Feb., 1934): same subject, pp. 27, 40, 45.
6. Samuel I. Rosenman ed., *The Public Papers and Addresses of Franklin D. Roosevelt*, III (New York, 1938), 86-87.
7. These acts are conveniently printed in Earl B. Wilson's *Sugar and Its Wartime Controls*, I (New York, 1950), 172ff.
8. U. S. House Committee on Agriculture, 82 Cong., 1 Sess., *Hearings* (June-July, 1951): "Extension of the Sugar Act of 1948," p. 147, and 84 Cong., 1 Sess., *Hearings* (June-July, 1955): "Amendments to the Sugar Act of 1948," p. 489. My figures are estimates based upon incomplete data printed in these documents.
9. U. S. House Committee on Agriculture, 84 Cong., 2 Sess., *Hearings* (June-July, 1955): "Amendments to the Sugar Act of 1948," p. 2.
10. *Congressional Record* (daily), July 30, 1955, p. 10632.
11. U. S. House Committee on Agriculture, 84 Cong., 1 Sess., *Hearings* (June-July, 1955): "Amendments to the Sugar Act of 1948," p. 54. Observing that the program permitted no producer referendum on allotments of acreage, Mr. Poage had remarked in June, 1947: "This legislation . . . differs from all our other crop legislation in that there is no pretense of democracy about it." *Ibid.*, 80 Cong., 1 Sess., *Hearings:* "Sugar Act of 1948," p. 25.
12. *Ibid.*, 84 Cong., 1 Sess., *Hearings* (June-July, 1955): "Amendments to the Sugar Act of 1948," p. 689.
13. U. S. Senate Committee on Finance, 73 Cong., 2 Sess., *Hearings* (Feb., 1934): "To Include Sugar Beets and Sugarcane as Basic Agricultural Commodities," p. 15.
14. Reclamation interests participated in the hearings of 1951, 1955, and 1956 and advocated the expansion of beet farming.
15. So it was repeatedly alleged.
16. Rosenman, *op. cit.*, VI (New York, 1941), 263.

NOTES

17. *Ibid.*, VI, 321-22, 347-48.
18. *Ibid.*, VIII (New York, 1941), 229.
19. *Ibid.*, IX, 137.
20. *Congressional Record* (daily), July 30, 1955, p. 10651.
21. U. S. House Committee on Agriculture, 84 Cong., 1 Sess., *Hearings* (June-July, 1955): "Amendments to the Sugar Act of 1948." See pp. 240, 312, and 403 for the quotations.
22. *Congressional Record* (daily), Feb. 7 and 8, 1956, pp. 1869-72, 1874-1909, and 1998-2025 for the Senate discussion. The statistics which follow have been compiled from a table on p. 1871 and from the documents cited in note 1 above.
23. The act as finally passed and signed by the President terminated in 1960 instead of 1962; otherwise it was practically identical with the Senate bill. It is likely that production of both cane and beet sugar in continental United States has become more efficient since the 1930's, and that it would not be easy for these sugar-producing states to transfer their capital and effort to other economic enterprises that would return equal profits.
24. Professor Seymour Harris of Harvard pointed out these advantages without much exaggeration early in 1955 when he stated: "In my opinion, the export interests have gotten away with murder in the last 40 years. They have been subsidized to the extent of $120 billion through Government . . . [policies and programs] of all kinds, inclusive of taking a great deal of goods that we do not need, and the net result therefore is that exports are in a very highly inflated position. It is interesting to note that the businessmen who have suddenly become free traders are almost invariably exporters." U. S. House Committee on Ways and Means, 84 Cong., 1 Sess., *Hearings* (Jan.-Feb., 1955) "Trade Agreements Extension," p. 1691. For data on tariffs, excise taxes, and quotas, consult Howard S. Piquet, *Aid, Trade, and the Tariff* (New York, 1953) pp. 61-65, 80f. Don D. Humphrey's *American Imports* (New York, 1955) is another illuminating volume on the subject.
25. U. S. House Committee on Ways and Means, 84 Cong., 1 Sess., *op. cit.*, p. 1364.
26. Pan American Union, *Latin American Foreign Trade in 1929* (Washington, D. C., 1931), p. 3, and *Latin American Foreign Trade, 1940* (Washington, D. C., 1942), pp. 4-5; International Development Board, *An Economic Program for the Americas* (Washington, D. C., 1954), p. 23.
27. International Development Board, *op. cit.*, pp. vii, 3, 15.
28. *The National System of Political Economy* (New York, 1904), p. 295. This summary of the attitude of Latin-American leaders is based upon a careful reading of the reports of United States delegations to various inter-American conferences from the one at Chapultepec (1945) to the Tenth Inter-American Conference which met at Caracas in 1954. See especially the report of the delegation to this Caracas assembly (published by the State Department in 1955), pp. 15-24, 132-41. Here the *Latinos* suggested that all the resolutions of postwar conferences be compiled—probably for ready reference to remind the United States of its numerous benevolent promises!
29. The statistics in this paragraph have been laboriously compiled from

Balance of Payments of the United States, 1949-1951, pp. 118-27, and *Survey of Current Business*, June 1949, pp. 4-5, March 1953, pp. 8-9, March 1954, pp. 22-23, March 1955, pp. 10-11, and March 1956, pp. 6-7.

CHAPTER 10

1. The *New York Times* has occasionally mentioned the subject. The newspapers of California have naturally given it more space. *Hispanic American Report*, published by Stanford University, has followed the controversy rather consistently since early 1951. The appropriations committees of the House and Senate have wrestled with the problem for five years. But no public agitation has occurred in this country except on the Pacific Coast.
2. Senate Committee on Appropriations, 82 Cong., 2 Sess., *Hearings* (February-March, 1952): "State Department Appropriation for 1953," pp. 340-41.
3. *Ibid.*, p. 342.
4. *Ibid.*, p. 1181.
5. Senate Committee on Appropriations, 83 Cong., 1 Sess., *Hearings* (March-May, 1953): "State Department Appropriation for 1954," p. 1637.
6. The U. S. Department of Commerce's publication entitled *Foreign Grants and Credits by the United States Government* (Washington, April, 1955) lists grants for the eleven Pacific-Coast countries amounting to $157,947,000 and loans and other credits totaling $354,609,000 for the period indicated. But the Department of Commerce's figures for grants are incomplete. They do not include the contributions of the United States to the Inter-American Highway and to the Inter-American Institute of Agricultural Sciences, or to the United Nations' Children's Fund and the technical-aid programs of this world organization and the Organization of the American States, all of which are shared by these countries.
7. United Nations International Law Commission, *Regime of the Territorial Sea: Comments by Governments* (A/CN. 4/90, 29 March, 1955), p. 9.
8. Senate Committee on Appropriations, 83 Cong., 2 Sess., *Hearings* (March-April, 1954): "State Department Appropriation for 1955," pp. 1261-62.
9. These five vessels were flying the Panama flag and belonged to a Greek named Aristotle Onassis, who may or may not have been a naturalized citizen of the United States. The fine, imposed by Peru, amounted to $2.8 million and was paid late in November, 1954. *Hispanic American Report* for September and November, 1954, pp. 26 and 28 respectively, gives an account of the episode.
10. House Committee on Appropriations, 84 Cong., 1 Sess., *Hearings* (February, 1955): "State Department Appropriation for 1956," p. 435.
11. *Department of State Bulletin*, XXXII (June 25, 1955), 939.
12. *Ibid.*, XXXII, 698.
13. Senate Committee on Appropriations, 82 Cong., 1 Sess., *Hearings* (May-July, 1951): "State Department Appropriation for 1952," p. 1544.
14. *Ibid.*, p. 2061.

15. *Ibid.,* 82 Cong., 2 Sess., *Hearings* (Feb.-March, 1952): "State Department Appropriation for 1953," p. 342.
16. *Ibid.,* p. 345.
17. *Ibid.,* p. 1180.
18. *Ibid.,* 83 Cong., 1 Sess., *Hearings* (March-May, 1953): "State Department Appropriation for 1954," p. 1637.
19. *Ibid.,* 82 Cong., 1 Sess., *Hearings* (May-July, 1951): "State Department Appropriation for 1952," p. 1544.
20. *Hispanic American Report,* August, 1952, p. 27, and October, 1954, p. 28.
21. Special inter-American conferences in Mexico City and Ciudad Trujillo early in 1956 eased the tension but failed to solve the problem. (*Ibid.,* March 1956, pp. 149-52.) Mexico's claims and activities in the Gulf of Mexico have interfered with fishermen from the southern part of the United States.

CHAPTER 11

1. September 1956, pp. 440-41.
2. These figures have been compiled from data published by the Department of Commerce, Office of Business Economics. See its *Foreign Grants and Credits,* a quarterly, 1953-1956.
3. The information summarized in this long paragraph has been gleaned from sources too numerous to cite here. But consult especially the hearings of Congressional committees dealing with mutual aid and the following works: Olin E. Leonard, *Bolivia: Land, People, and Institutions* (Washington, D. C., 1952); Harold Osborne, *Bolivia, A Land Divided* (London, 1955); and Carlos Victor Aramayo, *Memorandum sobre los problemas de la industria minera de Bolivia* (n.p. 1956). First published in 1947, Aramayo's *Memorandum* dwelt on the enormously difficult problems of the mining industry in Bolivia and the mistakes of recent governments, and forecast the distressing events of the decade that followed. See *American Metal Market,* November 3, 1956, for a summary of a report by the firm of Ford, Bacon and Davis on the inefficiency of government mining operations in Bolivia.
4. House Committee on Government Operations, 84 Cong., 1 Sess., *Hearings* (October 1955): "Technical Assistance and Related Activities in Latin America," pp. 384-88.
5. Angel del Río ed., *Responsible Freedom in the Americas* (New York, 1955), pp. 45, 48, 54, 98. The last reference is to the excitement aroused by this Bolivian's assertions, which were condemned as both erroneous and lacking in gratitude.
6. These platforms are all quoted by Germán Arciniegas in his *State of Latin America* (New York, 1952), pp. 129-38. He does not include dates for some of them, but they were adopted during the years 1946-1951.
7. Senate Committee on Foreign Relations, 84 Cong., 1 Sess., *Hearings* (May 1955): "Mutual Security Act of 1955," pp. 300-1. Antenor Patiño, Simón Patiño's son, published a letter of protest addressed to Acting Secretary Sparks and sent me a copy along with a short sketch of the career

of his remarkable father, who died in 1947; the letter was published in Mexico City in 1956 and the sketch in New York in 1950. The long residence of the Patiño family abroad was probably motivated in part by business activities in connection with tin refineries and marketing agreements with British investors in Malayan and African tin mines.

8. *New Leader,* October 15, 1956, p. 9.
9. *National Review,* October 6, 1956, pp. 12, 13.
10. *Op. et loc. cit.,* pp. 9-10.
11. *Op. et loc. cit.,* p. 13.

CHAPTER 12

1. *An America to Serve the World* (Puerto Rico, 1956), pp. 3f. It is evident that the author wants America to serve itself first. He says almost nothing about global service.
2. John M. Cabot, *Toward Our Common Destiny* (Boston, 1955), p. 14. Cabot was Assistant Secretary of State for Inter-American Affairs in 1953-1954, at the time he made this statement. This volume contains some of his addresses and interviews while he occupied his position. The destiny he had in mind seems to have been global rather than hemispheric.
3. Cabot, *op. cit.,* pp. 15-16.
4. Quoted in *Some Aspects of Postwar Inter-American Relations* (Austin, Texas, 1946), p. 70.
5. *Revista de América,* April 1945, pp. 14-15.
6. Cabot, *op. cit.,* p. 18.
7. Quoted in Galo Plaza, *Problems of Democracy in Latin America* (Chapel Hill, N. C., 1955), pp. 49-50.
8. Quoted in *ibid.,* p. 64.
9. *Ibid.,* p. 83.
10. Luis Muñoz Marín, *The Commonwealth of Puerto Rico* (Puerto Rico, 1956), pp. 13-14.
11. *An America to Serve the World,* p. 12.
12. *Ibid.,* p. 8.
13. The U. S. Overseas Information Program (Washington, D. C., 1955?), p. 2.

CHAPTER 13

1. P. 7348.
2. See *Congressional Record* (daily), February 28, 1957, pp. 2491-97, for the entire speech.
3. *Ibid.,* July 15, 1957, pp. 10116-19.
4. *Ibid.,* July 19, 1957, pp. 11037-45, and July 22, 1957, pp. 11212-15.
5. For this and the three quotations that follow, see *Ibid.,* Feb. 28, 1957, pp. 2497-2503, and April 1, 1957, pp. 4415-16.
6. Appendix, p. 2476.
7. Pp. 5322-26 for Long's entire address.
8. Appendix, p. 3496.

NOTES

9. Appendix, pp. 4065-68.
10. *Congressional Record*, pp. 7834-35.
11. *Ibid.*, pp. 10409-10. Meantime Porter had visited Costa Rica, Colombia, and Panama as well as Puerto Rico and had published a collaborative article on the subject of dictators in the June issue of *Coronet*.
12. Appendix, pp. 5762-65.
13. Consult *Congressional Record* (daily), pp. 11037-45 for this debate.
14. *Ibid.*, pp. 12037-42.
15. *Ibid.*, p. 12047.
16. Latin Americans in control of the various governments in this region are usually, though sometimes not frankly, willing to accept aid in almost any form from the United States; but they pose as ardent champions of nonintervention, and while assuming that posture rarely hesitate in their campaigns against "colonialism" to demand intervention in the affairs of the colonial powers, without regard for the economic and political viability of the new nations which they seek to create or the costs which their support may entail. John A. Houston gives a satisfactory factual account of the attitude of Latin-American leaders on the issue of colonialism in his *Latin America in the United Nations* (New York, 1956). For a broader and more detailed account, see *The Idea of Colonialism*, edited by Robert Strausz-Hupé and Harry W. Hazard (New York, 1958).

For evidence that the granting of assistance by the United States to the dictators of Latin America is resented in that region, consult the daily *Congressional Record*, July 15, 1957, pp. 10617-18, July 19, 1957, pp. 11037-45, and August 1, 1957, pp. 12047-52. This resentment is not confined to the oppositions in the despotic nations; it includes some individuals both in power and out of power in the more democratic countries. Recall also the unpleasant experiences of Vice-President Nixon and his wife during their "goodwill tour" of May, 1958, which occurred after this volume had been written.

17. This summary of the recent history of Bolivia and its relations with the United States is based mainly upon the hearings of congressional committees on the "Mutual-Aid" programs and upon the following non-official sources: annual surveys, 1941-1944, edited by Arthur P. Whitaker under the title of *Inter-American Affairs* (New York, 1942-1945); *The Inter-American*, 1942-1946, a monthly magazine published in Washington, D. C., and New York; and *Hispanic American Report*, a monthly survey edited by Ronald Hilton and distributed from the campus of Stanford University.

The belief that Paz Estenssoro and the army clique that supported him in the 1940's were pro-Nazi was almost universal.

18. Dr. Milton Eisenhower, who was sent by his brother as a special ambassador to Latin America in June-July, 1953, is said to have recommended that special aid be granted to the Paz Estenssoro government. Dr. Eisenhower was honored in April, 1956, by the cross of the National Order of the Andes, conferred upon him by Víctor Andrade, Bolivian Ambassador in the United States, for whom Dr. Eisenhower seems to have arranged speaking engagements in this country. Further evidence of their mutual cordiality appeared in an interview with Andrade published by the editors of *Visión* in that magazine, September 27, 1957. Assistance to the

Paz Estenssoro regime was also urged by Edward J. Sparks, ambassador of the United States in La Paz, who seems to have been deeply impressed by the program of the MNR.

19. In July, 1954, Assistant Secretary of State Henry Holland said: "The Bolivian government now in power accepted Communist collaboration when it seized power in April 1952." (Senate Committee on Appropriations, 83 Cong., 2 Sess., *Hearings:* "Mutual Security Appropriations for 1955," p. 248.) In June, 1957, the International Cooperation Administration submitted the following statement to the House Committee on Foreign Affairs: "There was a basic social, political, and economic Bolivian upheaval in 1952. . . . A new revolutionary coalition came to power in a country which had been badly disorganized by that upheaval. The coalition consisted of both moderate and extremist forces, the former . . . initially in the ascendant. . . . Communists and fellow travelers were in evidence both in and out of the government. . . . If the moderate forces had not been able to prevent economic deterioration, they would have lasted about as long as the Kerensky regime in Russia in 1917. United States aid helped . . . the moderates to stay at the head of the government. . . ." (House Committee on Foreign Affairs, 85 Cong., 1 Sess., *Hearings:* "Mutual Security Act of 1957," p. 612.)

20. One of my briefcases is filled with copies of these protests, all of which declare in effect that this Marxist government would long since have been driven from power if the United States had not supported it.

21. The Paz Estenssoro government confronted at least six revolts and twice as many conspiracies during its first two years in power; the Hernán Siles Zuazo administration, which succeeded Paz Estenssoro's in August, 1956, has enjoyed only a little more tranquillity. Much of the food sent as a gift to the Bolivian people through the Paz Estenssoro government found its way into the hands of speculators who smuggled it out of the country at handsome profits for themselves. (Senators Mike Mansfield and Bourke Hickenlooper, "Report on the Technical Cooperation Programs in Peru, Bolivia, and Ecuador," pp. 8-9. This report was printed in March, 1957.)

22. See *Hanson's Latin American Letter,* No. 656, Oct. 12, 1957. Bolivia's "reform" administrations have agreed to resume services on Bolivia's dollar bonds long in default and have granted to corporations of the United States important mining and petroleum concessions. Senator Theodore F. Green has already begun to exert pressure in favor of adequate and more prompt compensation to the large mining companies whose properties were "nationalized." They should be compensated, of course, but taxpayers of the United States are likely to pay the costs indirectly through grants to Bolivia. The original and fundamental mistake was the seizure of these mining properties at a time when the Bolivian government lacked the will and the capacity to operate them efficiently and profitably. The bonds issued to the landlords in return for the lands that have been seized are apt to remain worthless unless the people of the United States spend millions in the effort to improve the farming methods of the former tenants who have now become landowners. Henry Holland, attorney for oil companies and Assistant Secretary of State for Inter-American Affairs during 1953-1956, is under suspicion in some quarters and may be subject to investigation by a Senate committee in the near future in order to deter-

NOTES

mine whether he has made improper use of his official influence in Bolivia. To deny the possibility of improprieties and abuses of this sort in connection with the Foreign-Aid Programs would require immense confidence in the integrity of *homo sapiens*.

CHAPTER 14

1. Department of Commerce, Office of Business Economics, *Foreign Grants and Credits by the United States Government, June 1957 Quarter*, Tables 3 and 6.
2. Senate Committee on Foreign Relations, 85 Cong., 1 Sess., *Hearings*: "Mutual Security Act of 1957," pp. 294-95.
3. House Committee on Appropriations, 85 Cong., 1 Sess., *Hearings*: "Mutual Security Appropriations for 1958," p. 132.
4. Senate Committee on Appropriations, 85 Cong., 1 Sess., *Hearings*: "Mutual Security Appropriations for 1958," pp. 606-7.
5. Apparently most of these credits were not utilized before the end of fiscal year 1957 and therefore were excluded by the Office of Business Economics in reporting the credits utilized for that year.
6. House Committee on Appropriations, 85 Cong., 1 Sess., *Hearings*: "Mutual Security Appropriations for 1958," p. 668.
7. Senate Committee on Appropriations, 85 Cong., 1 Sess., *Hearings*: "Mutual Security Appropriations for 1958," p. 152.
8. *Congressional Record* (daily), Aug. 29, 1957, p. 15048.
9. The Executive Branch had asked for only $94.5 million for Latin America for fiscal year 1958. On August 19, 1957, John B. Hollister, the director of ICA had said with reference to the additional $20 million: "If Congress sees fit . . . it would be very useful in Latin America, but it is not one of the points we are emphasizing." The Administration had been disappointed because Congress had not displayed much enthusiasm for a big development fund to be used at the discretion of the Executive Branch. See the Senate *Hearings* cited in note 7, p. 597. The global appropriation for mutual security for fiscal 1958 was $2,768,760,000; for fiscal 1957 it was $3,766,570,000.
10. House Committee on Appropriations, 85 Cong., 1 Sess., *Hearings*: "Mutual Security Appropriations for 1958," pp. 14, 43, 46.
11. *Congressional Record* (daily), July 16, 1957, p. 10736. There are elements of absurdity in the economic arguments for the programs. By stimulating exports they are benefiting some people to the detriment of many others who pay for them doubly because of both higher prices and heavier taxes. If the programs make more foreign raw materials available, they also tend to exhaust domestic raw materials by expanding exports of manufactured products. It is likely that little harm would be done if some of the peoples in Latin America, Europe, and elsewhere were dropped from the list of recipients.
12. This table has been compiled from the document cited in note 1.
13. See the source cited in note 1. It will be observed that the major recipients in 1956 and 1957 were Iran, Afghanistan, India, Indonesia, Pakistan, Thailand, Egypt, and Libya. These eight countries had been receiving

the lion's share of assistance since the initiation of these programs. By June 30, 1957, their totals, mostly grants, were as follows (in thousands of dollars): Iran, $327,928; India, $499,787; Pakistan, $343,796; Egypt, $87,425—total, $1,258,936. Afghanistan, $46,709; Indonesia, $286,114; Thailand, $104,027; Libya, $49,969—total, $486,819. The total for these eight nations was $1,745,755,000. This left only $219,446,000 for the other twelve countries specified in Table 30.

14. *Report of the Committee on Freedom of Employers' and Workers' Organizations.* Geneva, March 6-10, 1956. Mimeographed; 4 volumes. The members of this committee were: Arnold McNair, a British lawyer; Pedro de Alba, a Mexican diplomat with experience in labor negotiations; and Justice A. R. Cornelius of Pakistan. They carefully refrained from expressing any preference for either private or public enterprise.

Index

Adams, John: on Spanish America, 8
Adams, John Quincy: on Spanish America, 8; on maritime and commercial principles, 12
Afghanistan: direct and indirect aid from U. S. government, 91-93, 222-23
Agricultural Trade Development and Assistance Act: aid to Bolivia under, 176; aid to other Latin-American countries under, 229, 251(n15)
Aid to underdeveloped countries from U. S. government: fiscal years 1946-55, 81-95; fiscal years 1956-57, 226-33
Aiken, George: on "exploitation" of Bolivians, 183
Alexander, Robert J.: on Bolivian crisis, 184, 186-87
Allen, Edward W.: on fishery dispute with Latin America, 169, 173
Alvarado, Felipe J.: fee from U. S. bankers, 59
American Community: bases of, 2-3, 7; agencies of, 20
Amparo Mining Company: profits of, 49, 50
Anfuso, Victor L.: on Trujillo dictatorship, 213
Argentina: investments of U. S. citizens in, 33, 36, 38, 39, 41, 43, 45, 54, 62, 64, 66, 68, 69; aid from U. S. government, 84, 87, 231
Argüedas, Alcides: book on Bolivia's maladies, 180

Bailey, C. M.: advocates tariffs and import quotas, 161
Ballivián, General Hugo: deposed, 224
Bankers, U. S. investment: practices and profits of, 53-61; list of those floating Latin-American bonds, 56

Bennett, Henry G.: on rubber development in Western Hemisphere, 143-44
Benson, Ezra Taft, 154, 155
B. F. Goodrich Company, 107
Blaine, James G.: advocates Western-Hemisphere concept, 5
Bolívar, Simón: advocates Western-Hemisphere concept, 5-6
Bolivia: investments of U. S. citizens in, 36, 38, 39, 41, 43, 45, 54, 62, 64, 66, 68, 69, 249(n12), 250(n2); aid from U. S. government, 84, 87, 176-77, 222-23, 231; troubles in, 175-78, 222-25
Bolster and Company: fee from U. S. bankers, 59
Borda, Antonio: fee from U. S. bankers, 59
Brandes, Elmer W.: advocates plantation-rubber program in Western Hemisphere, 136, 137-38, 140-42
Brazil: investments of U. S. citizens in, 34, 36, 38, 39, 41, 43, 45, 54, 62, 64, 66, 68, 69; aid from U. S. government, 84, 87, 231
Bridges, Styles, 169
Brown, Charles H.: on "mutual-aid" program, 230
Burma: direct and indirect aid from U. S. government, 91-93, 232-33

Cabot, John M.: on Latin America, 114-15, 190, 191-92, 193-94
Canada: investments of U. S. citizens in, 30, 36, 40, 53, 70, 71, 72, 73, 74, 75, 79
Cárdenas, General Lázaro, 177
Carnegie, Andrew: enthusiast for a Pan-American Railway, 96
Castillas (Castilloas), 126, 129, 133
Castillo Armas, General Carlos: as Guatemalan chief executive, 218
Ceylon: aid from U. S. government, 232-33

269

INDEX

Charter of the Organization of American States: contradictory provisions of, 203-5, 219, 220
Chavez, Dennis: advocates assistance for Latin America, 104, 106-7, 118, 124-25, 229
Chile: investments of U. S. citizens in, 30, 32, 33, 36, 38, 39, 41, 43, 45, 54, 62, 64, 66, 68, 69; aid from U. S. government, 84, 87, 231
Chile Copper Company: profits of, 48, 50
Churchill, Winston: supported British rubber restrictions, 130, 134
Clay, Henry: advocates Western-Hemisphere concept, 4-5, 18; on prospects for democracy in Spanish America, 8-9
Coffee, H. B.: urges *guayule* rubber program, 137
Colombia: investments of U. S. citizens in 31, 32, 33, 34, 36, 38, 39, 41, 43, 45, 54, 62, 64, 66, 68, 69; aid from U. S. government, 84, 87, 231
Commodity Credit Corporation: wartime rubber program of, 134-35
Communists: in Bolivia, 180-83, 224-25, 266(n19); threat in Latin America, 212-22
Compulsory charity: U. S. taxpayers subjected to, 94-95, 164
Cooley, Harold D.: favors *guayule* program, 137; on sugar legislation, 154-55, 157
Corporations (of the U. S.): significant role in Latin America, 46-47
Costa Rica: investments of U. S. citizens in, 33, 36, 38, 39, 41, 43, 45, 54, 62, 64, 66, 68, 69; aid from U. S. government, 84, 87, 231
Crawford, Fred: urges tax expenditures for Latin-American highways, 124
Creole Petroleum Corporation: profits of, 50
Cuba: investments of U. S. citizens in, 30, 31, 32, 33, 36, 38, 39, 41, 43, 45, 54, 62, 64, 66, 68, 69; aid from U. S. government, 84, 87, 231

Cuban American Sugar Company: profits of, 47, 50
Cummings, Fred L.: as beet sugar advocate, 151

Dávila, Carlos: advocates Western-Hemisphere concept, 21-22
Davis, Norman: unearned fee, 56
Democracy: obstacles to development of in Latin America, 14, 16, 221-22
Dictatorship: problems of in Latin America and elsewhere, 13-16, 205-25
Díez de Medina, Fernando: shocking statement by, quoted, 181-82
Direct investments: of U. S. citizens abroad, early, 30-47; profits from, 47-53, 73-77; a postwar decade of, 71-80. *See also* Investments, foreign, of U. S. citizens
Doheny, Edward L.: profits from Mexican petroleum, 49-50
Dominican Republic: investments of U. S. citizens in, 31, 32, 33, 36, 38, 39, 41, 43, 45, 54, 62, 64, 66, 68, 69; aid from U. S. government, 84, 87, 231. *See also* Trujillo, Rafael, and Dictatorship
Douglas, Paul: on sugar policy, 149
Dulles, John Foster: on aid to Latin America, 227-28

Ecuador: U. S. private investments in, 31, 33, 34, 36, 38, 39, 41, 43, 45, 54, 62, 64, 66, 68, 69; aid from U. S. government, 84, 87, 231
Eder, Phanor J.: fee from U. S. investment bankers, 59
Egaña, Juan: advocates Western-Hemisphere concept, 5
Egypt: direct and indirect aid from U. S. government, 91-93, 232-33. *See also* Investments, foreign, of U. S. citizens.
Eisenhower, Dwight D.: Latin-American policy of, 26, 221, 226-27; supports Inter-American Highway, 106, 254-55(n18), 256(n1)

270

INDEX

Eisenhower, Milton: urges aid for Bolivia, 224; friendship with Bolivian ambassador, 265 (n18)

El Potosi Mining Company: profits of, 48

El Salvador: investments of U. S. citizens in, 33, 36, 38, 39, 41, 43, 45, 54, 62, 64, 66, 68, 69; aid from U.S. government, 84, 87, 231

Ethiopia: direct and indirect aid from U. S. government, 91-93, 232-33

Europe: investments of U. S. citizens in, 30, 36, 40, 53, 70, 71, 72, 73, 75, 76, 79, 249 (n11)

Ferguson, Homer: investigates expenditures on the Rama Road, 111-14; opposes appropriations for Rama Road, 118, 123, 124

Firestone, Harvey S.: refuses to invest in Western-Hemisphere rubber plantations, 132; plantations in Liberia, 135, 139

Fishery interests of the U. S. West Coast: list of, 167; troubles of with Latin America, 166-74

Flood, Daniel J.: on Dominican Republic, 213

Ford Motor Company: rubber fiasco in Brazil, 130, 139, 140, 141, 142

Foreign Bondholders Protective Council: negotiations regarding Latin-American defaulted bonds, 63

Foreign investments of the United States. *See* Investments, foreign, of U. S. citizens

Fresnillo Company, The: profits of, 48, 50

Fulbright, William: opposed sugar bill of 1956, 159

Galíndez, Jesús de: mysterious disappearance of, 208-9

General Tire and Rubber Company, 136

Good Neighbor Policy, 156, 191, 197, 207, 213

Goodyear Tire and Rubber Company, 137, 142, 146

Gorgas Memorial Laboratory (Panama): support by U. S. government, 89-90

Great Britain: buttressed Monroe Doctrine, 10; opposed maritime and commercial policies of the U. S., 11-12

Gross, C. P.: on barge-canal survey and Rama Road, 113-14

Guatemala: investments of U. S. citizens in, 33, 36, 38, 39, 41, 43, 45, 54, 62, 64, 66, 68, 69; aid from U. S. government, 84, 87, 218, 231

Guayule (rubber): wartime production program, 135, 136-37; failure of, 137-38

Haiti: U. S. private investments in, 36, 38, 39, 41, 43, 45, 54, 62, 64, 66, 68, 69; aid from U. S. government, 84, 87, 231

Hardesty, M. N.: on aid to Latin America, 27

Harding, Warren G.: Latin-American policy of, 207-8

Hardy, Porter: in Bolivia, 181

Harris, Seymour: on export subsidies, 261 (n24)

Harrison, William Henry: recalled because of intervention in Colombian political affairs, 15

Hayden, Carl, 229

Hays, Brooks: supported Inter-American Highway, 107

Helfert, G. A.: fee from U. S. bankers, 59

Helper, Hinton Rowan: interest in Pan-American Railway, 96

Heveas, 126, 129, 133, 144

Hispanic American Report: on Bolivian disorders, 175

Holland, Henry F.: on Latin America, 27; on Bolivia, 266 (n19); influence in Bolivia, 266 (n22)

Holland, Spessard: favors Rama Road, 125; urges extra assistance for Latin America, 228-29

Hollister, John B.: on foreign aid, 230

Honduras: U. S. private investments in, 33, 36, 38, 39, 41, 43, 45,

271

Honduras—*Contd.*
54, 62, 64, 66, 68, 69; aid from U. S. government, 84, 87, 231
Hoover, Herbert: rubber policy of, 130-31; Latin-American policy of, 207
Hopkins, Harry: supports construction of Inter-American Highway, 104
Howe Sound Company: profits of, 48, 50
Hull, Cordell, 99, 254(n15)
Humboldt, Alexander von: Jefferson's letter to, 9
Humphrey, Hubert: on "exploitation" of Bolivia, 184

Ickes, Harold: requests funds for Inter-American Highway, 104, 254(n13)
India: direct and indirect aid from U. S. government, 91-93, 232-33. *See also* Investments, foreign, of U. S. citizens
Indochina (Cambodia, Laos, Vietnam): aid from U. S. government, 231-32
Indonesia: direct and indirect aid from U. S. government, 91-93, 232-33. *See also* Investments, foreign, of U. S. citizens
Inter-American Highway: construction of, 25, 96-108, 251-56; waste in construction of, 102-3; cost of, 104, 107; length of, 105, 112, 116, 256(n3)
Inter-American Institute of Agricultural Sciences (Costa Rica): financial support by U. S. government, 85-86
Inter-American Tropical Tuna Commission, 171-72
International Cooperation Administration, 144, 226, 266(n19)
International Development Board: on importance of Latin America, 27, 162
Intervention by the U. S. in Latin America: history of, 15-16, 206-7;

Intervention by the U. S.—*Contd.*
"mutual assistance" and the problem of, 203-25
Investments, foreign, of U. S. citizens: early, 30-52; imprudent investment in bonds of foreign governments, 53-70; a postwar decade of, 71-80; income from, 47-52, 67-68, 73-77. *See also* individual countries
Iran: direct and indirect aid from U. S. government, 91-93, 232-33
Iraq: direct and indirect aid from U. S. government, 91-93, 232-33
Israel: direct and indirect aid from U. S. government, 91-93, 231-32

Jackson, Donald L.: on nonintervention in Latin America, 217, 219-20
James, Edwin W., 251-52(n3), 254(n16); on Rama Road, 111-13
Jefferson, Thomas: advocates Western-Hemisphere concept, 4; on political development in Spanish America, 9-10; on free trade, 149
Jones, Jesse H.: wartime efforts to procure rubber, 134-35
Jones-Costigan Act (May 9, 1934): inaugurates system of sugar quotas, 152
Jordan: direct and indirect aid from U. S. government, 91-93, 232-33

Kearney, "Pat": on conditions in the Dominican Republic, 214
Keith, Minor C.: fee from U. S. bankers, 57
Kendall, Willmoore: on Bolivia, 184-86, 187-88
Kennedy, Leonard: profits in Bolivia and Brazil, 58
Klein, Julius: advocates rubber plantations in Western Hemisphere, 131
Korea: magnitude of aid from U. S. government, 231-32

Lafayette, Marquis de: Jefferson's letter to, 9

INDEX

Latin America: dictatorships in, 14, 16, 205, 219-20; investments of U. S. citizens in, 30-80; aid from U. S. government, 81-90, 226-31; worries about foreign investments, 77-80, 180-83, 193-95. *See also* individual countries and Democracy
Lebanon: direct and indirect aid from U. S. government, 91-93, 232-33
Lechín, Juan, 176, 183, 188
Leguía, Juan: bribe from U. S. bankers, 57, 59
Liberia: direct and indirect aid from U. S. government, 91-93, 232-33. *See also* Investments, foreign, of U. S. citizens
Libya: direct and indirect aid from U. S. government, 91-93, 232-33
Lincoln, Abraham: tries to encourage democracy in Latin America, 13
Lipton, Sir Thomas: use of his name by rubber propagandists, 127
List, Friedrich: statement regarding advocates of free trade, 163-64
Lleras Restrepo, Carlos: on tariff policy, 192-93
Loker, Donald B.: on fishery troubles, 169, 172, 173
Lombardo Toledano, Vicente, 177
Long, George: defends Trujillo regime, 213-14, 215, 216-17
Lucky-Tiger Combination Mining Company: profits of, 48

McCarran, Pat: letters to on fishery troubles, 169, 172
McCormack, John: defends Trujillo government, 214, 215
MacDonald, Thomas H.: as head of the Bureau of Roads, 99-101, 251-52(n3 and 5), 253(n5), 255-56(n22)
Machado, Gerardo: loans from U. S. bankers, 56, 60
Maginnis, Samuel A.: fee from U. S. bankers, 59
Malone, George: approves financing of Latin-American highways by U. S. government, 106, 107
Márquez, Javier: on Latin-American tariff sentiment, 192
Marsh, Richard O.: urged rubber plantations in Panama, 132-33
Marshall, General George: statements on Inter-American Highway, 254-55(n15 and 18)
Marshall Plan, 118, 230
Marxism: influence in Bolivia, 180-88, 224-25
Meader, George: opposed appropriations for Rama Road, 123, 124
Mexican banker-bureaucrat (Villaseñor): declares U. S. cannot prosper without foreign investments, 25-26
Mexican Telegraph Company: profits of, 47
Mexico: investments of U. S. citizens in, 30, 31, 32, 33, 36, 38, 39, 41, 43, 45, 54, 62, 64, 66, 68, 69; aid from U. S. government, 84, 87, 231. *See also* Rubber-plantation failures in the Western Hemisphere
Miller, Joaquin: use of his name by rubber propagandists, 127
Mining companies, Bolivian: Aramayo, Hochschild, and Patiño, 177, 183, 184, 188, 224, 225. *See also* Investments, foreign, of U. S. citizens
Monroe, James: advocates Western-Hemisphere concept, 5
Monroe Doctrine: promulgation and enforcement of, 10, 17, 29, 201
Moore, Ross: urged appropriations for rubber experiments, 141-42
Morocco: aid from U. S. government, 232-33
Moya, Manuel de: offensive address of, 211, 216-17
Multer, Abraham: defends Trujillo regime, 218
Muñoz Marín, Luis: on inter-American collaboration, 189, 193, 196

273

INDEX

Muñoz Tebar, Antonio: advocates Western-Hemisphere concept, 6
Murphy, Gerald Lester: mysterious disappearance of, 208-9

National Revolutionary Movement (MNR): seizure of Bolivian government by, 176, 223; policies of, 177, 186
Nepal: aid from U. S. government, 232-33
New York and Honduras Rosario Company: profits of, 48, 50
New York Times: editorials against dictatorships, 208
Nicaragua: investments of U. S. citizens in, 36, 38, 39, 41, 43, 45, 54, 62, 64, 66, 68, 69; aid from U. S. government, 84, 87, 231; uses leverage of canal-zone concession, 111-25. See also Somoza, Anastasio
Nixon, Richard M., 106, 218, 265 (n16)

Office of Business Economics: keeps account of foreign aid by U. S. government, 81, 83, 90
Office of Cultural Relations: activities of, 198
O'Hara, Barratt, 217-18
O'Neal, Edward, 137
Organization of the American States: technical program of, 83-85; provisions of charter, 203-5

Padilla, Ezequiel: advocates Western-Hemisphere concept, 22-24
Pakistan: direct and indirect aid from U. S. government, 91-93, 232-33
Panama: investments of U. S. citizens in, 31, 34, 36, 38, 39, 41, 43, 45, 54, 62, 64, 66, 68, 69; aid from U. S. government, 84, 87, 231; use of canal-zone leverage, 109-11; Treaty of 1955 with the U. S., 110-11. See also Rubber-plantation failures
Pan-Americanism: See Western-Hemisphere concept

Pan-American Highway: movement to construct at U. S. expense, 96, 106, 108
Pan-American Railway: failure of movement to build, 96
Pan-American Sanitary Organization: support by U. S. government, 85, 86
Pan-American Union: support by U. S. government, 85, 86
Paraguay: investments of U. S. citizens in, 36, 38, 39, 41, 43, 45, 54, 62, 64, 66, 68, 69; aid from U. S. government, 84, 87, 231
Patiño, Simón, 183-84, 263-64(n7)
Paz Estenssoro, Víctor: seizes Bolivian government, 176, 223; policies of, 177, 186, 223-25, 266(n21)
Peñaranda, General Enrique: as Bolivian chief executive, 223
Pérez Jiménez, Marcos, 216
Perkins, Milo: on curing economic depressions, 24
Perón, Juan D., 224
Peru: investments of U. S. citizens in, 32, 34, 36, 38, 39, 41, 43, 45, 54, 62, 64, 66, 68, 69; aid from U. S. government, 84, 87, 231
Philippine Republic: investments of U. S. citizens in, 76, 80; direct and indirect aid from U. S. government, 91-93, 231-32
Phleger, Herman: on freedom of the seas, 171
Poage, Congressman W. R.: statement on rubber program, 135-36; on sugar program, 154-55
Poinsett, Joel Roberts: recalled from Mexico for interference in Mexico's domestic politics, 15
Polhamus, Loren: advocates rubber cultivation in Western Hemisphere, 136; co-author of monograph on the subject, 258(n10), 259(n28)
Porter, Charles O.: attacks Rafael Trujillo and other dictators, 208-12; opposition in House of Representatives, 212-22

INDEX

Pressure groups: insist on foreign aid by U. S. government, 95, 228-29, 240; urge construction of highways in Latin America, 96-97, 108; advocate *guayule* rubber program, 136-37; urge tariffs, excise taxes, and import quotas, 150-51, 160-61; favor sugar program, 150, 155-58, 164

Rabaut, Louis C., 140
Rama Road (Nicaragua): construction of at expense of U. S. taxpayers, 111-25, 256-58
Rands, Robert D.: advocates Western-Hemisphere rubber program, 139-40; co-author of monograph on the subject, 258(n10), 259(n28)
Reece, Carroll: defends Trujillo regime, 215-16
Robsion, John M., Jr.: on Trujillo regime, 213
Roosevelt, Franklin D.: Latin-American policy of, 17, 156, 197, 207, 213; agrees to finance transportation in Nicaragua, 121-22; sugar policy of, 151-53, 156
Roosevelt, Theodore: begins policy of intervention in Latin America, 105, 206
Rubber-planting failures in Western Hemisphere: early, 126-30; from 1920 to 1955, 130-47

Saccio, Leonard J.: on aid to Latin America, 227
Salt, T. V.: fee from U. S. bankers, 59
Saudi Arabia: direct and indirect aid from U. S. government, 91-93, 232-33
Shaw, G. Howland: on Rama Road, 115-16
Siles Zuazo, Hernán: as Bolivian reformer, 175, 176, 188; troubles of, 266(n21)
Simpson, Richard M.: advocates tariffs, excises, and import quotas, 161-62

Smathers, George: advocates more assistance to Latin America, 228-29
Smith, Harold D.: memorandum of on Rama Road, 115-16
Somoza, Anastasio: uses canal-zone leverage to obtain financial aid from U. S. government, 109-10, 112, 113, 114, 116, 119, 121
South American Gold and Platinum Company: profits of, 48, 50
Sparks, Edward J.: on conditions in Bolivia, 183-84; urges aid for Bolivia, 265(n18)
State Department: *See* U. S. State Department
State Socialism: tendency toward in Latin America, 190, 194-96; apparent global drift toward, 233-40
Stefan, Karl, 142
Stevenson Plan (for control of production and sale of rubber), 133, 258(n2)
Sugar Acts: various, 152-53, 157-60
Syria: direct and indirect aid from U. S. government, 91-93, 232-33

Taiwan (Formosa): magnitude of aid from U. S. government, 231-32
Tenth International American Conference: hears Latin-American claims to jurisdiction over the high seas and their resources, 170
Thailand (Siam): direct and indirect aid from U. S. government, 91-93, 232-33
Trujillo, Generalissimo Rafael Leónidas: Congressional debate on his regime in the Dominican Republic, 214-22
Truman, Harry S., 118, 217
Tugwell, Rexford: on sugar program, 151
Tunisia: aid from U. S. government, 231-32
Turkey: magnitude of aid from U. S. government, 231-32
United Fruit Company: profits of, 47-48, 50

UN Children's Fund: assistance to Latin America, 87; to other retarded nations, 92
UN International Law Commission: considers fishery dispute, 166, 170
UN Technical Assistance Board: aid to Latin America, 87; to other retarded countries, 92
United States and Latin America: early interest in, 1-16. *See also* Inter-American Highway, Rama Road, etc., and Latin America and various nations thereof
U. S. Army Engineers: waste of efforts in Central America, 102-3
U. S. Bureau of Public Roads: activities in Central America, 97, 99-100, 101, 102, 103, 104, 105, 111-13, 115, 117
U. S. commercial policy, 10-13, 148-65
U. S. Congress: aid to Latin America, 27, 226, 228-29; appropriations for Central-American highways, 97-98, 101, 103, 104, 105-07, 118-19, 120-21, 123-25
U. S. Department of Agriculture: rubber program in Western Hemisphere, 130-46; sugar program, 150-60
U. S. Information Agency (USIA): facilities, purposes, and activities of, 198-200
U. S. private investments abroad: *See* Investments, foreign, of U. S. citizens
U. S. State Department: policy regarding defaults on Latin-American government bonds, 63; urges financing of Latin-American highways, 96-125; Bolivian policy of, 175-88, 223-25; "mutual-assistance" policy of, 226-30; position on the fishery problem, 171-73
Uruguay: investments of U. S. citizens in, 36, 38, 39, 41, 43, 45, 54, 62, 64, 66, 68, 69; aid from U. S. government, 84, 87, 231

Valle, José Cecilio de: advocates Western-Hemisphere concept, 6

Venezuela: investments of U. S. citizens in, 31, 33, 34, 36, 38, 39, 41, 43, 45, 54, 62, 64, 66, 68, 69; aid from U. S. government, 84, 87, 231
Villarroel, Major Gualberto: tyranny and death of, 223
"Voice of America": *See* U. S. Information Agency (USIA)
"Voluntary" agencies: participation in foreign-aid program, 94-95, 237, 240

Wallace, Henry: on Inter-American Highway, 25, 99-101; blamed for *cryptostegia* rubber fiasco, 135; on sugar policy, 150-51, 155
Washington, George: advocates Western-Hemisphere concept, 4
Waynick, Capus M.: plea for Rama Road appropriation, 122-23, 257 (n17)
Weaver, A. J. S.: opposed expansion of beet-sugar cultivation, 151
Welles, Sumner: on Rama Road, 119-20
Western-Hemisphere concept: conflict with United-World aspirations, 1, 3, 28-29, 201-2; definition of, 1-7; support of by Latin Americans, 2, 5-6, 20-26, 189-92, 195-96, 200; abandonment predicted, 2-3; may survive, 3-4, 26-28
White, William Allen: use of his name by rubber propagandists, 127
Whitford, H. M.: on rubber planting in Western Hemisphere, 131-32
Wilber, Edward B.: on tuna-fishing problem, 168
Wilson, Woodrow: Latin-American policy of, 15, 17, 206
World Bank: loans to retarded nations, 85-86, 93
W. R. Grace and Company: Latin-American interests of, 32, 46

Zablocki, Clement, 217; on Communism, 218